THE AMERICAN COWBOY

Exhibition and Catalog made possible by a grant from United Technologies Corporation

T HE

American Folklife Center

Lonn Taylor and Ingrid Maar

AMERICAN COWBOY

Library of Congress, Washington, 1983

An Exhibition at the Library of Congress
Washington, D.C.
March 26, 1983–October 2, 1983

The exhibition will travel to:

The University of Texas
Institute of Texan Cultures San Antonio
December 1, 1983–January 31, 1984

The Denver Museum of Art
Denver, Colorado
March 7, 1984–April 29, 1984

Glenbow Museum
Calgary, Alberta, Canada
June 4, 1984–July 27, 1984

San Jose Museum of Art
San Jose, California
September 3, 1984–October 26, 1984

This book was designed and produced by Derek Birdsall,
typeset by Balding + Mansell Limited, and printed by
Garamond/Pridemark Press in Baltimore, Maryland.
Printed in the United States of America.
Copyright © Library of Congress 1983

Studies in American Folklife, no. 2

Library of Congress Cataloging in Publication Data
Main entry under title:
The American cowboy.
   (Studies in American Folklife; no. 2)
"The exhibition will travel to: Institute of Texan
Cultures, the University of Texas, San Antonio,
Texas, December 1983–January 1984 [and others]"
   Bibliography: p.
   Includes index.
   Supt. of Docs. no.: LC 39.2: Am 3/2
   1. Cowboys—West (U.S.)—Exhibitions.
2. Cowboys—West (U.S.)—Folklore—Exhibitions.
3. West (U.S.)—Social life and customs—Exhibitions.
I. Taylor, Lonn, 1940–   . II. Maar, Ingrid.
III. Library of Congress. IV. American Folklife
Center. V. University of Texas Institute of Texan
Cultures at San Antonio. VI. Series.
F596.A46 1983   978'.02'07453   82–600291
ISBN 0-8444-0409-8 (pbk.)

Cover illustration:
from *The Log of a Cowboy*
by Andy Adams (see page 118)

CONTENTS

FOREWORD

The American Cowboy is one of the few national legends to have
become a myth while he was still a fact and to remain a fact of
American life despite all our romanticizing. This book depicts the
real and the imaginary lives of our American Cowboy, and, in
more ways than meet the eye, suggests his wonderful
Americanness. He lives on, not only in song and story and from
the artist's pen and brush but in the most modern American
media—in comic strip and movies, on radio and television. Our
cowboy has become more traditional with every retelling in every
new form. Of course he is a symbol and a parable of American
virtues—the optimism, the good-humored friendliness, the joy in
hard work, the nicknaming that gives every man and woman a
chance to start over, the testing of people by their direct
encounter with nature. All these qualities were more vivid here
than in the settled lands of the Old World. At the same time our
versatile, unpredictable American technology has proven its
ability to keep the cowboy alive in everybody's living room. The
exhibition from which this book arises, a celebration unexcelled in
variety and in quality, takes place in another uniquely American
institution, the Library of Congress, where the national foresight
of our Congress over two centuries has kept our past alive to
illuminate our present and inspire our future. To record that
exhibition and the insights it embodies, the Library of Congress is
publishing this book, taking this examination of the myth and
reality of the American Cowboy out to the nation that created
him.

Daniel J. Boorstin
The Librarian of Congress

Over the past several years, United Technologies has sponsored a variety of exhibitions devoted to aspects of the American culture.

We have supported a show of paintings of the American West; an exhibition of this nation's folk art; and a major show of paintings by America's nineteenth-century masters.

None of those seems so thoroughly "American," though, as the exhibition on the cowboy for which this book is the catalog. We are especially proud to join with the Library of Congress in presenting the cowboy's story.

Harry J. Gray
Chairman and Chief Executive Officer
United Technologies Corporation

Acknowledgments

"The American Cowboy" is the most comprehensive study of a folk hero ever assembled by a public institution. Together the exhibition and catalog offer a scholarly review of the changing image of the cowboy as depicted in paintings, sculpture, photographs, books, manuscripts, music, maps, prints, collectibles, and memorabilia. Through them the American Folklife Center takes a serious look at the cowboy as an American folk hero, examines his origins, and investigates some questions. Where did the cowboy come from? What happened to him as time passed? Has the image of the cowboy been commercialized? Does the cowboy still exist today? The cowboy iconography presented here has allowed us while addressing these questions to show off the varied treasures of the Library of Congress, one of the world's largest libraries.

Both the exhibition and catalog required the coordinated efforts of many individuals—curators, exhibition and book designers, researchers, editors, conservators, exhibition technicians, and many others throughout the Library of Congress—who responded to specific needs at opportune times. We wish to thank each and every one of them.

Great appreciation goes to Librarian of Congress Daniel J. Boorstin and his colleagues in the Office of the Librarian for their constant support and encouragement. Although activities associated with this exhibition have touched almost every department and division of the Library, the core team which guided the project from initiation to completion was the American Folklife Center, the Exhibits Office, the Publishing Office, the Information Office, and Special Events staff under the guidance of Carol Nemeyer, Associate Librarian for National Programs.

It is a long road from concept to grand opening. The task of coordinating the many aspects of this exhibition has been made a great deal easier because of the excellent support Alan Jabbour, director of the American Folklife Center, the Center's Board of Trustees, and my colleagues on the center's staff have provided.

Our greatest debt of gratitude goes to the guest curator, Lonn Taylor, a western historian and writer who accepted an idea with enthusiasm and embarked on an extended period of intensive research at the Library of Congress and in other major collections of western art and history. Lonn's extraordinary knowledge of the subject shapes the exhibition, and his patience and cooperation throughout the research, development, and installation phases are most appreciated. The Library's curator of exhibitions, Ingrid Maar, has overseen with enthusiasm the many details connected with the curatorial realization of a project of this size. We are grateful for her contribution.

William F. Miner, the Library's present exhibits officer,

directed the design implementation and installation of "The American Cowboy." J. Michael Carrigan, exhibits officer at the Library of Congress when this project was initiated, was very helpful and supportive in the early stages of planning and funding.

The design and installation of the exhibition were developed by the firm of Staples & Charles Ltd. Barbara Charles, Bob Staples, and their staff have elaborated an imaginative concept which is appropriate to the space and the requirements of the Library as well as to those of the hosts of the traveling exhibition. The staff of the Library's Exhibits Office is to be thanked for the fine workmanship associated with the installation of the exhibit.

The exhibition catalog stands alone as a tribute to the American cowboy and it also complements the exhibition. Derek Birdsall devised the graphic design for the catalog. He worked closely with the Library's director of publishing, Dana J. Pratt, and editor Evelyn Sinclair. These three took an idea, photographs, illustrations, and manuscript copy and created a handsome addition to the Library's long list of publication credits. We thank the contributors to the catalog—Royal Hassrick, who has known cowboy life firsthand and has written from his experiences in the introduction; Byron Price, who takes a look at the modern cowboy's life on the Texas plains; and Dave Hickey, who presents an urban view of the cowboy in the 1980s.

The support provided by the Library's information officer Nancy Bush and James McClung were of inestimable value in bringing public attention to the exhibition and to the Library as an exhibiting institution in the nation's capital. Kendall Taylor provided valuable assistance in developing corporate support for this project and has been an astute manager of its traveling phase.

Lonn Taylor would especially like to thank the following people for their continuing interest, valuable suggestions, and personal kindnesses during the development of this exhibit: Ron Tyler, Joe B. Frantz, W. Eugene Hollon, Howard W. Marshall, Archie Green, Susan Conrad, John Williams, Louis Bradford, Kristin Brown, Mary Payer, and Patrick Butler. His early research at the Library was made easier by the great cooperation received from many individuals caring for the Library collections from which a major portion of the exhibition comes. Special thanks go to Ann Hallstein, Dennis Everett, and Kevin Maricle, Copyright Office; Barbara Humphrys and Emily Sieger, Motion Picture, Broadcasting, and Recorded Sound Division; Marita Stamey and David Doyle, Photoduplication Service; Bernard Reilly, Elena Millie, and Leroy Bellamy, Prints and Photographs Division; Joseph C. Hickerson and Gerald E. Parsons, Jr., Archive of Folk Culture; Oliver H. Orr, Jr., Manuscript Division, and Clark Evans, Rare Book and Special Collections Division.

Carl Fleischhauer deserves credit for the creation of the video disc program included in the exhibition, which is part of his cooperative work with other Library divisions to develop ways of using video disc capabilities in the Library's ongoing storage and retrieval operations.

A number of interns and short-term employees carried out many of the unglamorous tasks that are necessary to bring a project of this magnitude to fruition. Specifically, we would like to thank Kevin Farley, for his early assistance to the guest curator in researching the collections of the Library, and Victoria Westover, who aided the curator of exhibitions in the curatorial preparation of materials for this volume.

The generosity of the lenders to "The American Cowboy" is worthy of special note. Their loans add an exciting dimension to the display and enhance the overall presentation of the cowboy myth.

Most importantly, we wish to acknowledge the generous financial support provided by United Technologies Corporation in the development of the exhibition and the production of this volume. The generosity of United Technologies has made it possible to present to the American public a broad exhibition of scholarly significance. The guidance and support provided by Gordon Bowman, that corporation's director of creative programs, was of special importance.

The nameless cowboy is one American image that is universally recognized. We thank all of you for making it possible to pay tribute to a humble folk hero who touches our daily lives and figures large in our cultural consciousness.

Ray Dockstader
Coordinator
American Folklife Center

LENDERS TO THE EXHIBITION

Acme Boot Company, Incorporated, Clarksville, Tennessee

Blue Bell, Incorporated, Greensboro, North Carolina

Buffalo Bill Historical Center, Cody, Wyoming

Mr. D. Harold Byrd, Jr., Dallas, Texas

Amon Carter Museum, Fort Worth, Texas

Oleg Cassini, Incorporated, New York, New York

Chicago Historical Society, Chicago, Illinois

Colorado Historical Society, Denver, Colorado

Colorado Springs Fine Arts Center, Colorado Springs, Colorado

Adolph Coors Company, Golden, Colorado

Mr. James Cotter, Vail, Colorado

Dallas Historical Society, Dallas, Texas

Mr. Charles Dalton, Copperas Cove, Texas

Delaware Art Museum, Wilmington, Delaware

Detroit Public Library, Detroit, Michigan

Mr. David G. Drum, Polson, Montana

Mr. Jeff Dykes, College Park, Maryland

Mrs. Charles B. Fahs, Oxford, Ohio

Mr. Carl Fleischhauer, Washington, District of Columbia

Mr. Skeeter Hagler, Dallas, Texas

The Nita Stewart Haley Memorial Library, Midland, Texas

Hake's Americana & Collectibles, York, Pennsylvania

Elaine Horwitch Gallery, Scottsdale, Arizona

Mr. Luis Jimenez, El Paso, Texas

Kohler Company, Kohler, Wisconsin

Ms. Linda Lavender, Denton, Texas

McCreedy & Schreiber, Incorporated, New York, New York

Ms. Julie McNair, Mississippi State, Mississippi

The Howard Wight Marshall Family, Columbia, Missouri

The Minneapolis Institute of Arts, Minneapolis, Minnesota

Claude Montana, Société Anonyme, Paris, France

Montana Historical Society, Helena, Montana

Montana Stockgrowers Association, Incorporated, Helena, Montana

Philip Morris USA, New York, New York

Mr. William Morris, Yuma, Arizona

Museum of New Mexico, Santa Fe, New Mexico

Museum of the City of New York, New York, New York

Museum of the Plains Indian, Browning, Montana
United States Department of the Interior

National Cowboy Hall of Fame and Western Heritage Center
Oklahoma City, Oklahoma

National Museum of American History, Smithsonian Institution
Washington, District of Columbia

Neiman-Marcus, Washington, District of Columbia

Nocona Boot Company, Incorporated, Nocona, Texas

The R. W. Norton Art Gallery, Shreveport, Louisiana

The University of Oklahoma Libraries, Norman, Oklahoma

The Panhandle-Plains Historical Museum, Canyon, Texas

Petersen Galleries, Beverly Hills, California

Polo/Ralph Lauren, Incorporated, New York, New York

Poster Plus, Chicago, Illinois

Mr. B. Byron Price, Canyon, Texas

Bill Price's Western Shop, Lubbock, Texas

Remington Art Museum, Ogdensburg, New York

Will Rogers Memorial, Claremore, Oklahoma

Rough Riders Memorial and City Museum, Las Vegas, New Mexico

Mr. Stephen Sally, New York, New York

Ms. Susan Porter Schreiber, Takoma Park, Maryland

Mr. Robert Shay, Columbus, Ohio

Mr. Jim Shoulders, Henryetta, Oklahoma

Staples & Charles, Limited, Washington, District of Columbia

Mr. Lonn W. Taylor, Pojoaque, New Mexico

University Gallery, University of Delaware, Newark, Delaware

The University of Texas at Austin, Austin, Texas

Volkswagen of America, Incorporated, Englewood Cliffs, New Jersey

Warner Cosmetics, Incorporated, New York, New York

Wendy Watriss and Fred Baldwin, Houston, Texas

Victoria Westover, Baltimore, Maryland

William Wilhelmi-Kaffie Gallery, Corpus Christi, Texas

Mrs. Petra Williams, Jeffersontown, Kentucky

Wyoming State Archives, Cheyenne, Wyoming

INTRODUCTION

The cowboy—partly because his work is oriented to the wide and open spaces, partly because much of his time is spent on horseback, and partly because his job is hard and sometimes dangerous—has earned the reputation of being a courageous, resourceful man. Characterized as independent, daring, taciturn, or boyish, he has become the personification of the "rugged individualist." His work and his life contain both romance and excitement. Through fact and fiction, real and imagined, he has become the culture hero of America.

What is the cowboy really like? Having been in the cattle business for many years and having been a cowboy myself once, I have discovered that the cowboy actually possesses most of the commendable qualities attributed to him. What my friends and colleagues, my fellow cattlemen and cowpunchers, go through to bring good, quality beef to the households of America is a lot of rigorous, discouraging, hard work. As such, the cattle business tends to make both cattlemen and cowboys a little tougher, a little bit more independent, and a little bit more appreciative of the vagaries of economics and the wonders of nature than the average American.

There is a distinction between cattlemen and cowboys. Cowboys are really no more than hired hands working for a cattleman. As such, they enjoy meager pay for hard work and such other fringe benefits as a sporting occupation in the open air, pleasurable horseback riding, and ample exercise from pitching hay bales or slinging dung from a box stall. Then, too, there is the exhilarating excitement of being gored by an angry cow or kicked in the shin by a cantankerous horse. Sometimes they can enjoy beautiful western views while oiling a windmill sixty feet above a stock tank. From there, if they have time to contemplate, they can look farther and see less than from anyplace else in the nation.

A cattleman, on the other hand, the man who offers all these marvelous, romantic, recreational opportunities to the lucky cowboy, has every chance of becoming fabulously wealthy. Only a few simple problems stand in his way. Merely by weathering droughts and blizzards, surmounting sickness and disease among his livestock, thwarting rustlers, and outsmarting economic recessions involving overproduction, high interest rates, and bankers with no money to lend, the cattleman is on the road to easy street.

The cattleman can accomplish his goal in many ways. To balance his budget, he can save a bit of money by skimping on what he pays his cowboys. Hank Smith expected his cowhands to drive their cars to town to pick up parts for his tractor, his hay baler, his mowing machine. But he never paid them for gasoline. He expected his cowhands to help paint his house and fix his car on Sundays, which should have been their time off. He paid his men by the hour, but only when they were working. They were expected to report at

7:00 A.M. when they were making hay, but they got no pay when they were riding the hayrack to the field, nor did they get paid when returning on the rack to the barns to stack hay. He kept a stopwatch, so that everything was accurate and fair. But he never kept his hands more than a month and no man ever worked for him a second season. Hank Smith was a cheapskate.

A successful cattleman is a businessman in high-heeled boots and blue jeans. His work requires calculations, acumen, and scientific know-how. A smart cowman may dress down in worn-out Levis and a shoddy hat when buying cattle to give the impression that he can't afford to spend much money. On the other hand, he may sport the latest in shiny boots and an expensive Stetson to give a sense of quality when selling, hoping to cast a glow of superiority over the cattle he plans to market. My friend Newt kept two separate outfits for that very purpose.

A clever cattleman will fault a bunch of cows he hopes to buy in order to give himself bargaining power. As Ed Walters pointed out, "I look for the bad points just as much as the good, because I'm paying for it." Invariably he offers at least 25 percent less than he's willing to pay. The seller, aware of this ploy, usually asks more than he expects to receive. It's part of the game to dicker for cows, and when buyer and seller agree on a price a handshake is usually sufficient to seal the deal.

Determining the precise time of year to market a calf crop demands a knowledge of the market, what weight calves are selling best, and the supply and price of feed on hand and involves a calculated risk. Few men have much leeway. Calves born in the spring are ripe for market in the fall. Ranchers in the western range country rarely have enough surplus feed to carry their calves over the winter. Buying hay and grain is expensive and usually not profitable. So each autumn the market is glutted with young steers and heifers. Some men plan to sell early while the market is up; others try to hold out until the glut has passed. It's easier, more fun, and far less work to lose money gambling in Las Vegas.

Necessary scientific know-how includes not only knowledge of agronomy, crop rotation, pasture grasses, and fertilization, but knowledge of current practices of animal husbandry, pregnancy testing, artificial insemination, and animal diseases as well. The hired hand, the cowboy, may not be familiar with the intricacies of the germinating propensities of alfalfa, but he learns to plow a straight row. He may know little about nitrogen content in the soil, but he can "spread joy" by running the manure spreader against the wind. A cowboy may be ignorant of the principles of ovulation or the causes of "scours," but he's adept at pulling a calf and skillful at innoculating a sick "dogie."

As in any business, effective marketing is essential. The stockman accomplishes this in a variety of ways. He may place an ad in a local newspaper or a stockman's journal. He may exhibit his animals at a county fair or a national stock-show. Preparing livestock for a cattle show demands weeks, sometimes months of training and grooming. Cattle are shown either as single animals, in groups of so-called "pens," or in "carload lots." They are judged upon their conformation, physical condition, and overall appearance. Winners are those animals which excel in all these qualities, thus representing the highest standards of their breed. Today, even the carcass may be subject to examination and the choicest of the choice wins the blue ribbon.

A stockman enters his cattle in a sale-show for two reasons: one, to get a good price, and two, to bring his herd to the attention of the buying public. The day of judging is a tense one. The cattle have been washed, dried, and combed to conform to the latest modes of coiffure. The hair on the back may be carefully parted, the tail brushed out, the head clipped in the current style. Even the hoofs may be polished. Ladies' hair spray is excellent for grooming; commercial shoe polish is just right for feet. And sometimes a bottle of beer administered internally is great for adding "bloom" to the conformation. The judges are most often professors of animal husbandry. Sometimes, wearing business suits, galoshes, and tiny-brimmed fedora hats, they look silly. But they often know their business. That means they have chosen for the first prize the very animal or animals that you yourself have chosen as best.

I remember a carload of twenty prize yearlings all polished and combed and looking perfect. It was just after the judging and two things were important. We had won a green ribbon that stood for fifth place and the temperature was about twenty below. The weather had cooled down a bit that day! It was then that the yard man yelled "Okay, men, move 'em out," and the calves began to mill around the pen. One critter had the audacity to jump into the frozen stock tank. "Hey," yelled Clint, "get that dummy out of there or he'll be a block of ice." Well, I grabbed a gunny sack and began trying to wipe the frost and ice off the poor little devil.

It was about a hundred yards down the alleys in the stockyard to the sales barn, a hundred yards of frozen crud and gates. So pushing the cattle along, closing gates and wiping, brushing, currying, closing another gate, pushing, and punching, and catching up to that wet calf to make him look proper and profitable, and closing still another gate was one miserable job. But by the time we reached the sales barn, I had the calf looking quite presentable. Sure, I was as stiff as a hot dog lost in the bottom of a deep freezer, but the gates swung open, the calves rushed into the steamy sales barn, and I climbed the little ladder to the seats overlooking the sales ring.

Well we got forty-one cents a pound for those calves, two cents above the top price, and that included one damn wet calf. I was too frozen to cheer, but I did treat Clint to a double shot of cheap bourbon. It's the price that counts, not the color of the ribbon.

To a cattleman, his cows would seem most important. His grass, his barns and corrals, and his equipment are solid signs of his achievement. Combined, the number and quality of his cattle, the size of his ranch, the efficiency of his machinery, and the upkeep of his buildings are status symbols. But beyond all these things is the cattleman's horse.

It's the cow pony who does the real work on a cattle ranch. And a good horse knows just when to turn a cow, just how to cut a steer from the bunch. A good cow pony knows, as if by instinct, when to walk slowly through the brush, how to miss the gopher hole at a high canter. Many a cowboy owes his very life to his horse. The cowpoke and the cow pony become not just a team working in unison, they become as one. It was Newt who commented as he turned Old Paint into the night pasture, "Buck, I love that horse so much, I like him."

One cowboy summed up the cattle business pretty accurately when he wrote this bit of doggerel:

Pity not the lonesome cowboy,
His best friend is his horse.
He's got empty cows, dry grass,
And his banker, of course.

Cattlemen and cowboys seem to have certain characteristics in common and not all of them are praiseworthy. Some men are so determined in their approach as to be hard-headed if not stupid. And some cowboys are plain dumb. As one cattleman remarked about a cowboy set to the mundane task of plowing, after he had missed the turn and pulled up a hundred yards of barbed wire fence, "Oh God, he's so damn dim!"

And there was the neighboring cowman who walked into a hundred-acre treeless pasture to view his new bull. He was gored for five hours before his battered, bleeding body was discovered and hauled off. And the dummy had three good cowboys standing idle in a nearby night corral.

Cowboys can also be smart, but they sometimes outsmart themselves. It was cool, about ten degrees below zero, one day when we were planning to move some five hundred head of cattle to a pasture nearer the headquarters. All the horses were saddled and everyone was mounted, all except Walt. "Let's go, let's go," we yelled, but Walt couldn't seem to mount his horse. Strange, but he was surely walking stiff-legged. Finally, he led his gelding over to the corral fence, climbed up, and jumped on his horse like a buzzard landing on a dead jack rabbit. Walt had put on two pairs of chaps against the cold and couldn't bend his knees.

The cowboys I have known were pretty forthright. Given the

chance with a wallet full of greenbacks on payday, any man with a bit of wit will cut the dust with a small quart of bourbon. After trying to roll your own on a skittish horse, a pack or two of ready-mades is sheer heaven. When things went wrong all day and the job to be done couldn't be accomplished, my friend Dallas summed it up succinctly by saying, "Well, by God, we'll give her hell tomorrow." When Clint's favorite horse tramped on his foot, he failed to say, "Please, Old Paint, get off my boot, you're spoiling the polish and aggravating my corn." Rather, he hollered, "Get the hell off my foot, you dumb son of a bitch." And he punched the horse so hard in the head that to his astonishment, he killed it. He also broke his hand.

Cattlemen have been accused of being hard drinkers and heavy smokers and possessing a fabulous repertoire of swear words. This observation is correct. Moreover, they have an ingrained contempt for the dude who, all dressed up in western paraphernalia, can't sit his horse—the movie cowboy or celluloid hero who never punched a cow or pulled a calf.

But more importantly, cowboys have in common a love of animals and a respect for the land, an appreciation of the powers of nature. Drenching rain and freezing blizzards, scorching sun and searing drought and the marvels of a newborn calf are a very real part of their life. Cowboys have a gentle kind of camaraderie, for they are men who have shared the same rewards, survived the same ordeals. An eastern horsewoman, observing cattlemen at an annual livestock show, remarked what fine-looking, rugged men these people appeared to be. She was dead right on two counts. Fine looking to the eyes of a female beholder, rugged because only the toughest men survive cowpunching.

The American Cowboy offers an opportunity to become acquainted with a fascinating folk hero. Herein are shown the real and the fanciful aspects of a truly American phenomenon—the cowboy. This is a story of hardworking men whose way of life has thoroughly captured the imagination of the people. And as the cowboy took pride in his arduous occupation, a nation now takes pride in him.

Royal B. Hassrick

A Real Live Cowboy
T. W. Ingersoll (dates unknown)
Stereograph, Saint Paul, Minnesota
Copyright 1898
Documentary Photography Collection
Prints and Photographs Division
Library of Congress

THE OPEN-RANGE COWBOY OF THE NINETEENTH CENTURY

Lonn Taylor

The American open-range cowboy, the man from whom the myth was made, first came to the nation's attention in the years immediately following the Civil War. His occupation arose to meet the needs of the range cattle industry, and when that industry changed radically, after flourishing in its original form for thirty years, his job became obsolete and he passed on. By all rights, he should have joined the hunters of Kentucky, the whalers, the flatboatmen, the plainsmen, and all of the other American types who briefly caught the popular imagination, were popularized on the stage and in song, and were then forgotten.

But the open-range cowboy was never forgotten. He left behind him a legacy that has grown since the 1890s to the proportion of a national myth, a legacy that is presented to us daily in films, on television, and in magazines and affects the way we dress, walk, talk, and even think. The cowboy of the 1880s was, in the long run, simply a hired hand on horseback. The cowboy of the 1980s is a figure in a national morality play. His is an image of such force that Henry Kissinger once called it up to explain the success of his diplomacy by telling an interviewer that he had always acted alone like "the cowboy leading the caravan alone astride his horse, the cowboy entering a village or city alone on his horse. Without even a pistol, maybe, because he doesn't go in for shooting. He acts, that's all."[1] In this age, the cowboy has become a rider in the sky, bringing order from chaos and setting us all to rights.

Actually, the nineteenth-century cowboy left two separate legacies. One is the work done by flesh-and-blood men who manage cattle today all over the West and who consider themselves the cowboy's legitimate descendants. They dress as they think he dressed, with certain contemporary modifications. They talk as the films they see and the novels they read say he talked. And they do almost the same kind of work that he did, although they occasionally use helicopters and pickup trucks instead of horses. Sometimes, they are his actual descendants: the grandchildren and great-grandchildren of men who moved great herds of cattle a thousand miles on horseback, spending not days or even weeks but months in the saddle. They have a yearning to be like those ancestors. Even though they do their work a different way, they have the same pride in it that the open-range cowboy had. That is one of the legacies, and it is as real as the mud out of which a modern cowboy pulls a bogged cow.

The other legacy is a fantasy: the myth of the cowboy. The myth is exactly as old as the cowboy himself. It began along the transcontinental railroad, that nineteenth-century wonder that brought the East encapsulated in Pullman cars to the West. In the late 1860s, journalists began writing about the Texas cowboys who brought herds of cattle north to the Kansas railroad towns. Their articles attributed to the cowboy all of the characteristics of earlier

national heroes: skill, caring, individualism, love of the outdoors, and an innate sense of fairness, qualities hidden beneath a rough and noisy exterior. By the seventies the cowboy had appeared in dime novels and on the stage. In the eighties he was an indispensable part of the great American fantasy known as Buffalo Bill's Wild West show. In 1887, the year that marked the end of the range cattle industry, an English visitor to the West wrote that

the cowboy has at the present time become a personage; nay, more, he is rapidly becoming a mythical one. Distance is doing for him what lapse of time did for the heroes of antiquity. His admirers are investing him with all manner of romantic qualities; they descant upon his manifold virtues and his pardonable weaknesses as if he were a demi-god, and I have no doubt that before long there will be ample material for any philosophic inquirer who may wish to enlighten the world as to the cause and meaning of the cowboy myth. Meantime, the true character of the cowboy has been obscured, his genuine qualities are lost in fantastic tales of impossible daring and skill, of daring equitations and unexampled endurance.[2]

Thus there was a cowboy myth long before Owen Wister and Zane Grey, long before Frederic Remington and Charles Russell, long before Gary Cooper and John Wayne. These men built on the myth, but the cowboy's true character was indeed obscured many years before they began. Later, we will explore the myth; just now we are interested in the cowboy himself.

As Montana historian K. Ross Toole put it, the most puzzling thing about America's fascination with the cowboy is that there has been "such an enormous feast on so little food." The fact is that the cowboy who gave rise to the legend was part of a system of ranching that lasted only for about thirty years, or from 1865 to 1895. This system of open-range ranching involved raising cattle for the beef market by pasturing them on the vast, unfenced lands of the American public domain and then, when they were ready for market, driving them in herds to the nearest railhead. It developed after the Civil War because of a peculiar combination of economic factors, and it collapsed of its own weight in the late 1880s when overproduction drove beef prices down and the entire industry reorganized.

The open-range system had its origin in the new market for beef that was created in the eastern cities by methods of refrigeration and packing that made it possible to transport cuts of beef to retail markets and keep them in storage there. At the same time, the post-Civil War employment of the army to control the Plains Indians opened vast new areas of the West to grazing. The transcontinental railroad, completed in 1867, and the development of an integrated

1. Henry Kissinger, "An Interview with Oriana Fallaci," *New Republic* 167 (December 16, 1972):21.
2. "On a Western Cattle Ranch," *Fortnightly Review* 47 (1887):516.

rail system in the Northeast provided the means to move the beef from the plains to slaughterhouses in Chicago and Kansas City, and from the slaughterhouses to local markets. The beef itself, however, was on the hoof in South Texas, eight hundred miles from the nearest railroad. There, enormous herds of longhorn cattle, originally introduced by the Spanish and raised by them for hides and tallow, had increased during the four years of war. No one knows how many cattle there were in Texas. The 1870 census estimated 3.5 million, but there were no census-takers in the chapparal of South Texas, where most of the longhorns were. The problem was to get these cattle to ranges where they could be fattened and then move them to eastern markets. The system of open-range ranching and trailing that developed in the 1860s and flourished in the seventies and eighties was the solution: the cow found her own food, water, and shelter on the open range and provided her own transportation to a railhead, and the cowboy saw that she got there.

Open-range ranching took advantage of what seemed to be an unlimited natural resource: free public grass. Ranch owners permitted their cattle to graze at will on the open, unfenced prairies, rather than keeping a herdsman with them and bringing them in each evening to a pen or barn, as was the custom in the East. The word *range* had two meanings. It meant the entirety of the public domain, and it also meant that portion of it that was used by a particular rancher as his "customary range," which he usually controlled by securing title under the Homestead Act to the water sources on it.

In practice, cattle belonging to several ranchers might graze the same range or wander to other ranges, so that twice a year it was necessary to gather all of the cattle on a particular range, sort them out by brands, brand the calves, and return the strays to their own ranges. These roundups, which sometimes covered an area of a hundred square miles and lasted for a month, were one of the two distinctive characteristics of open-range ranching. The other was the trail drive, in which herds of from five hundred to fifteen hundred cattle were driven to a railhead by cowboys on horseback. Until the late 1880s the nearest rail connections between Texas and Chicago were in southern Kansas, at the cow towns of Abilene, Ellsworth, Newton, and Dodge City. Reaching these involved a drive of two or three months, during which the cowboys stayed with the herd, guiding it through the unfenced country west of the line of settlement, swimming it across rivers, and gathering it together after stampedes. It is estimated that, between 1867 and 1886, from six to nine million head of cattle were moved from Texas to Kansas this way. The high point of the whole range cattle industry may have been on a summer day in 1883 when Teddy Blue Abbott, looking for some strays from the herd he was moving, came over a

rise near the North Platte and saw seven trail herds grazing behind his cattle and eight more herds ahead of him, while across the river he could see the trail dust from thirteen other herds. It looked, he said, as if all of the cattle in the world were coming up from Texas.

The herds that Abbott saw were not going to Kansas railheads, but past them to stock new ranges that were being opened in the Northwest. The grasslands of eastern Colorado, northern Kansas, Nebraska, Wyoming, Dakota, and Montana first knew cattle in the 1850s, when Oregon travelers and goldseekers brought small herds onto them. By the seventies, they were the safety valve of the booming range cattle industry, providing a seemingly inexhaustible supply of grass. Texas cowboys trailed cattle for five or six months to reach these ranges and then frequently stayed at their destination to work for their purchaser. In this way, as the cattle boom grew, the techniques of cattle management developed in Texas spread across the Northern Plains and even into the Canadian provinces. By 1885, according to Joseph Nimmo, chief of the Bureau of Statistics of the Treasury Department, the range and ranch cattle area of the United States covered 1,365,000 square miles, or 44 percent of the nation's territory, excluding Alaska. Here, Nimmo said, range cattle, "from the time they are dropped until they are shipped to market, seek their own food, water, and shelter, as did the buffalo, the deer, and the elk before them."[3]

Like all booms, the cattle boom that generated open-range ranching eventually collapsed. In 1881 Texas range cattle sold for $7 a head; by the latter part of 1882 the price was up to $35 a head. In Chicago, Texas grass-fed steers sold for $6.80 per hundredweight in May of 1882, the highest price ever paid for beef up to that time. In the spring of 1883 the price dropped slightly to $6 and held steady there through 1884. In 1885 the market opened strong, but in December of that year the bottom fell out, and cattlemen saw the price of stock cattle drop from $35 to $8 or $10 and even $5 a hundredweight.

At the same time, Mother Nature attacked the cattlemen. The winter of 1884 was severe, and the range was becoming overstocked. The next summer there was a drought in Texas—there was no rain at all from June 5 to August 18. The winter of 1885–86 was terribly severe in Texas, New Mexico, and Kansas, and its effects were worsened by the fact that 200,000 cattle, ejected from the Cheyenne-Arapaho Reservation in Indian Territory by executive order of President Cleveland, were thrown onto an already overstocked range in those states. In the spring of 1886, vast numbers of cattle were driven from the depleted Texas and Oklahoma ranges to Wyoming, Montana, and Dakota. The Continental Cattle Company alone moved 32,000 steers north that year, and numerous others brought herds of 5,000 or 6,000. The winter of 1886 in those states was the worst in human memory. Deep snows and high winds were followed by temperatures in the minus thirties and forties for weeks at a time. Cattle drifted together for warmth and died, literally, by the hundreds of thousands. In Montana, the losses were 190,000 cattle; in Wyoming, 250,000. One ranchman recovered 100 head out of 5,500 Texas cattle turned onto the range in the fall. The range country was covered with carcasses from the Canadian border to the Rio Grande. Northwestern cattlemen tried to recoup their losses by shipping early in 1887, and in an ever-increasing volume. Prices, already low, fell drastically. By October, five to seven thousand range cattle were reaching Chicago every day. Northwestern range steers brought from $2.50 to $3.25 a hundredweight, while Texas steers went from $1.90 to $2.50.

The surviving cattlemen reorganized the industry. Herds were reduced, and, to control their movement and let the range recover, ranchers took advantage of the new barbed wire. Winter feed was planted and harvested and brought to cattle in fenced pastures. Selective breeding was introduced, and thoroughbred cattle were brought from the East and England. Wells and windmills began to appear.

There were other significant developments in the late 1880s. Homesteaders began to take up much of the open range, using barbed wire to fence off their claims and prevent the free movement of cattle. Central Texas acquired a direct rail link with Chicago, and the rail net began to spread over the Far West, eliminating the need for long trail drives. By 1900, cattle were still moved by men on horseback, but only from the pasture to the loading pen.

These developments brought about a profound change in the cowboy's work and in the cowboy himself. By the nineties, cowboys dug postholes, fixed fences, repaired windmills, and drove mowers and hay-balers. The two distinguishing characteristics of the ranching they had known, the roundup and the trail drive, were gone forever, and both cowboys and mythmakers mourned them with a very real sense that an era had passed. Frederic Remington saw it ending as early as 1881, on his first trip West. "I knew the railroad was coming," he wrote. "I saw the men already swarming into the land. I knew the derby hat, the smoking chimney, the cord-binder, and the thirty-day note were upon us in restless surge. I knew the wild riders and the vacant land were about to vanish forever."[4]

He was quite correct. A few years later, West Texas cowboy Don Biggers remembered wistfully that "by 1888 the open-range roundup virtually passed out of existence because the country had then become so completely fenced up that there was no open range to work; roundups were conducted within fenced pastures and were personal affairs." Richard Harding Davis summed the matter up in *The West from a Car-Window* (1892): "The coming of the barb-wire fence and the railroad killed the cowboy. . . . It suppressed him and

localized him and limited him to his own range. . . . The coming of the railroad also made this trailing of cattle to the markets superfluous, and almost destroyed one of the most remarkable features of the West."[5]

Not only did open-range ranching develop, flourish, and die within a very brief period, but relatively few people were involved in it. Although between six and nine million head of cattle were driven out of Texas, it took only ten men to move fifteen hundred cows George W. Saunders, founder of the Old Time Trail Drivers Association, estimated that about twenty-five to thirty thousand men went up the trail to Kansas; there were probably not more than fifty thousand cowboys in the United States during the cattle boom. For most of these men, cowboying was seasonal work. They signed up to work on a ranch's spring roundup in March or April. When that was over, they worked for a trail outfit through the summer, returning to Texas for fall roundup in September. If they were fortunate, they might be among the few cowboys who were kept on through the winter to do ranch work. If they were like most, they lived through the winter on their summer earnings or found a job washing dishes or tending bar. To the cowboy, his did not seem to be a particularly romantic existence, and some remained realistic about it even in their old age. G. O. Burrows of Del Rio, Texas, was a former cowboy and trail driver who was asked in the 1920s to "write his experiences" for the Old Time Trail Drivers Association. He responded:

Some of my experiences were going hungry, getting wet and cold, riding sorebacked horses, going to sleep on herd and loosing cattle, getting cussed by the boss, scouting for gray-backs [body lice], trying the sick racket now and then to get a night's sleep . . . but all of these things were forgotten when we delivered the herd and started back to grand old Texas. . . . I always had the "big time" when I arrived in San Antonio rigged out with a pair of high-heeled boots and striped pants and about $6.30 worth of other clothes. This "big time" would last but a few days, however, for I would soon be busted and have to borrow money to get out to the ranch, where I would put in the fall and winter telling about the big things I had seen up North. The next spring I would have the same old trip, the same old things would happen in the same old way, and with the same old wind-up. I put in eighteen or twenty years on the trail and all I had in the final outcome was the high-heeled boots, the striped pants, and about $4.80 worth of other clothes, so there you are.[6]

Burrows stayed in the saddle longer than most cowboys. Nearly all of them were young men, mostly in their twenties. Cowboying was not an old man's job, or even a middle-aged man's job, and ten years

3. Joseph Nimmo, *Report in Regard to the Range and Ranch Cattle Business of the United States* (New York: Arno Press, 1979), p.2.
4. Quoted in Peter H. Hassrick, *Frederic Remington: Paintings, Drawings, and Sculpture in the Amon Carter Museum and the Sid W. Richardson Foundation Collection* (New York: Harry N. Abrams, Inc., 1973), p.15.
5. Don Biggers, "History That Will Never Be Repeated," in Seymour V. Connor, ed., *A Biggers Chronicle* (Lubbock: Texas Technological College, Southwest Collection, 1961) p. 32. Richard Harding Davis, *The West from a Car-Window* (New York: Harper & Brothers, 1892), pp. 135–36.
6. J. Marvin Hunter, ed., *The Trail Drivers of Texas*, 2 vols. (San Antonio, Texas: Globe Printing Co., 1924), 1:120.

of hard riding was about all the human body could take. David Shirk, who drove longhorns from Texas to Idaho in 1871 and again in 1873, remembered that "it was an endless grind with worry and anxiety which only a strong physical frame could stand."[7] Shirk's brother had what would today be described as a nervous breakdown on a drive to Idaho and had to be sent home by railroad from Kansas.

Cowboying was almost exclusively the work of one generation: the children who were born just before the Civil War, grew to maturity in the Reconstruction South, and entered manhood in the 1870s and 1880s. Some men who worked cattle in the late 1860s and early 1870s were Civil War veterans, and a few at the end of the eighties were second-generation cowboys, but the bulk of the men who went up the trail and worked the great roundups had been children during the war, and thus were in their thirties and early forties when the cattle kingdom ended. Many of them lived on in small western towns until the 1930s and 1940s, known to their neighbors as "stove-up cowboys," remembering their youth through a golden haze. They played a significant part in the making of the myth.

In the myth, the cowboy is always white and frequently a southerner, a young man gone West to escape the aftermath of the war. He is permitted by his boss, a former cowboy himself, to brand a few head on his own, laying the foundation for a future cattle empire, to be claimed when he finally marries the schoolteacher and settles down. He wears spotless, elaborately decorated shirts and a big white hat, and he carries a pair of Colt .45 revolvers slung low on his hips. And in the myth, strangely enough, he seldom, if ever, works cattle, preferring to spend his time rescuing maidens and foiling bandits. On all these points, the myth diverges sharply from the reality.

The first point of divergence is on the very nature of the cowboy himself. In the myth, and in the movies, he is always a white Anglo-Saxon. In reality, he was often black or brown. Texas, the source of so many cowboys, was a slave state, and the coastal counties where cattle were raised in Texas before the Civil War had large slave populations, which in a few of them made up as much as 70 or 80 percent of the total population of the county. Slaves worked cattle, broke horses, and acquired all of the skills exhibited in the movies by white cowboys. After the war, they were joined by freedmen from all over the South who went West. Virtually all Texas trail outfits included black cowboys, and a few, like the one Jim Ellison took to Kansas in the spring of 1874, were all black.[8] In the 1920s George Saunders estimated that a third of all trail hands were either black or Mexican, and numerous cowboy memoirs and a few surviving photographs of trail outfits bear him out.

The Mexican vaquero was the direct ancestor, as well as the constant companion, of the Texas cowboy. It was the vaquero who brought the first herds of cattle into Texas in the eighteenth century, and it was the vaquero who first mastered the cowboy's distinctive tool, the braided rawhide rope called a *reata*, and then taught the Anglo-American to use it. The use of the reata was only one of several methods developed by the vaquero for controlling cattle. Others included the *coleado*, a manuever in which the animal is thrown to the ground by a rider who grabs and twists his tail, and the *luneta*, a small, sickle-shaped knife on the end of a pole, used to hamstring the animal. As cattle became valuable for their beef, rather than their hides, *la reata* emerged as the chosen tool for working them, and it quickly became the cowboy's lariat.

The close working relationship between Mexican and Anglo cowboys is evidenced by the fact that a great deal of the cowboy's working vocabulary is derived from Spanish. When he snubs his lariat around his saddle horn, he "dallies," from *dar la vuelta*, "to take a turn" (cowboys in the 1880s "dolly welted"). His leather chaps originally protected his legs from the *chaparro prieto*, the thorny, tangled brush that also gave the chaparral country of South Texas its name. The taps that protect his stirrups were once *tapaderos* ("covers"). His saddle is secured under his horse by a cinch, from *cincha*, "a girth." It is in turn fastened to a latigo, from *látigo*, "a lash." When he gets a horse from the *remuda* in the morning it may be a *bronco*, in which case he may ask the wrangler (*caballerango*, "horse herdsman") to give him a hand. In California and on the western slope of the Rockies, he may even take the vaquero's name and call himself a buckaroo.

This coalescence of Anglo and Mexican first took place in South Texas, where Mexican hands were plentiful and knowledgeable, and where many of the ranches along the north side of the Rio Grande were owned by old Spanish families. It was inevitable that Mexican hands should go up the trail to Kansas—indeed, a few drives may have been managed entirely by South Texas vaqueros. V. F. Carbajal, a member of an old Tejano family, recalled in the 1920s that in 1872 he was hired by a Karnes County rancher to take fifteen hundred steers from Texas to Nebraska. Carbajal went to his family home near Floresville, Texas, where he hired Miguel Cantu, Macedonio Gortari, Melchior Jimenez, Aurelio Carbajal, Juan Bueno, Anastacio Sanchez, Francisco Longoria, and a cook remembered only as el viejo Betancourt. Carbajal's employer gave him a compass and a map of Nebraska and told him to follow the compass north to Ellsworth, Kansas, and then use the map to get to the North Platte.[9]

Although Indian cowboys were nowhere near as numerous as blacks or Mexicans, there were a few, especially in Oklahoma and in the far Northwest. Samuel Dunn Houston recalled that the Dillon Ranch, on the Niobrara River along the Nebraska-Dakota border, had "half-breed" cowboys in 1879. One of them, in fact, showed him an Indian trail across the Laramie Plains. Of course, a number of ranches in Indian Territory were operated by Native American cowboys, both from the Five Civilized Nations and from the Plains tribes. The photographs that A. A. Forbes took in the Cherokee Outlet and the Oklahoma Panhandle in the eighties clearly show Indian cowboys, as well as blacks and Mexicans, posed side by side with Anglos.

The majority of white cowboys probably were southerners. Philip Ashton Rollins, a rancher and ex-cowboy who tried to analyze the cowboy myth in the 1920s and set the record straight, devoted considerable thought to the cowboy's ethnic and regional background and concluded that most cowboys were southerners and that, within that regional category, the largest subgroup was from Texas and western Missouri. Rollins offered a tongue-in-cheek explanation for the predominance of southerners: "The sticky clay of the South had prevented the building of good roads, and thus kept successive generations of Southern men out of wheeled vehicles and in the saddle, and so had developed the Southerner into an innate rider."[10] He also recognized, however, the presence of midwesterners and a conspicuous minority of Englishmen, many of them "delightfully companionable, mildly reprobate, and socially outcast members of the gentry and nobility."

Actually, the most typical trail outfit was probably mixed, like the one Bill Butler of Karnes County, Texas, took to Abilene in March 1868. It consisted of "Robert and Wash Butler, his brothers, L. C. Tobin, Buck and Jess Little, John Sullivan, Jim Berry Nelson, Boxie White, John Brady, M. Benevides, Juan Concholer, Juan Mendez, and Levi and William Perryman, the latter two negroes."[11]

Unlike the cowboy of the myth, the cowboy of the 1870s and 1880s seldom worked for a benign ranch owner. He was more likely to be employed by a corporation and supervised by a ranch manager, who was in turn responsible to a group of absentee owners. In Joseph Nimmo's 1885 report he commented on the corporate nature of ranching: "The very fact that the range cattle business is most profitably carried on in a large way, and that its successful prosecution involves organization and cooperative work, appears to have suggested at an early day the conduct of the business under corporate ownership and management. Accordingly this has been one of the marked features of the enterprise from the beginning. Incorporated companies are now extensively engaged in the cattle business from Southern Texas to the northern border line of the United States."[12] These corporations frequently involved eastern or European capital. Two of the best-known Texas ranches, the XIT and the Matador, were controlled by syndicates in Chicago and Scotland, respectively. The Matador not only owned half a million acres in Texas but also operated large ranches in South

Dakota and Montana. Of course some ranches, especially the older ones in Texas, were single proprietorships or limited partnerships.

Whether ranch owner or foreman, most employers took a dim view of cowboys running their own brands. Cowboys were paid to take care of their boss's cattle, not to cut into his herd by branding his calves with their own brands, and on most ranches it was a serious infraction of the rules to carry any branding irons except the owner's. Sometimes the penalties were irrevocable. Texas cattle baron Shanghai Pierce summarily hanged two of his hands, the Lunn brothers, who were his former boon companions, for "mavericking," that is, appropriating his cow's calves. When the nooses were around their necks someone asked if they had anything to say. "Yes," the youngest replied, pointing at Pierce, "I'd like ten minutes to tell that long-legged son of a bitch what I think of a man who hired us to steal for him and then after we learned his methods wants to hang us."[13]

The mythical cowboy dressed like a cross between Johnny Mack Brown and Buffalo Bill. The clothing of the real cowboy is clearly visible in nineteenth-century photographs taken on the range rather than in Dodge City photographers' studios. It was the ordinary working clothes of the 1880s, with a few important modifications: heavy-duty wool pants and a collarless flannel pullover shirt. The trousers were usually held up by a belt or sash, because suspenders were uncomfortable to a man on horseback. The coat was seldom worn because it bound the arms and interfered with roping, but the vest, which had pockets that could be easily reached by a man on horseback, was nearly always present. Trousers were usually tucked into boot-tops, both to prevent them from snagging on brush and from rubbing between the boots and the stirrup leather. A wide-brimmed hat was worn for protection from the sun and rain, and a bandanna, usually a printed cotton scarf of the kind manufactured in New England for the southern trade, was folded and tied around the neck so that it could be pulled over the face as a dust mask. In short, the cowboy's clothing was utilitarian, rather than decorative. This is not to say that it did not undergo stylistic change during the brief thirty years of the cattle kingdom. In a fascinating passage, Texas cowboy W. S. James recalled changing cowboy fashions:

During the war his clothing was made from home-spun cloth, he had no other, home-made shoes or boots, even his hat was home-made, the favorite hat material being straw. Rye straw was the best. Sometimes a fellow would get hold of a Mexican hat, and then he was sailing. . . . By 1872 most everything on the ranch had undergone a change. . . . But especially had style changed, the wool hat, the leather leggins, leather bridle, and the broad stirrup; the invention of an old fellow who lived on the Llano river had become

7. Martin F. Schmitt, ed., *The Cattle Drives of David Shirk from Texas to the Idaho Mines, 1871 and 1873* (Portland, Ore.: Champoeg Press, 1956), p. 93.
8. Hunter, *Trail Drivers*, 1:113.
9. Ibid., 2:549, 839.
10. Philip Ashton Rollins, *The Cowboy; His Characteristics, His Equipment, and His Part in the Development of the West* (New York: C. Scribner's Sons, 1922), pp. 22–23.
11. Hunter, *Trail Drivers*, 2:717.
12. Nimmo, *Range and Ranch Cattle Business*, p. 2.
13. J. Frank Dobie, *Cow People* (Boston: Little, Brown, 1964), p. 40.

so popular that one who was not provided with them was not in style. . . . The style changed again by '77. The John B. Stetson hat with a deeper crown and not so broad a rim, and the ten-ounce hat took the cake. Up to this date, the high-heeled boots were the rage, and when it was possible to have them, the heel was made to start under the foot, for what reason I never knew, unless it was the same motive that prompts the gals to wear the opera heel in order to make a small track, thus leaving the impression that a number ten was only a six. . . . By '77 or '78, the cow-man had in many places adopted the box-toed boot with sensible heels.[14]

In the myth, the cowboy wears a pistol and spends most of his time chasing outlaws and attractive women. In real life, the cowboy spent a lot of time with cattle and seldom carried a gun, although he usually owned one. Philip A. Rollins pointed out that a Colt .45 has an eight-inch barrel and weighs two and a half pounds. "When one recalls," he wrote, "that the average cowpuncher was not an incipient murderer, but was only an average man and correspondingly lazy, then one realizes to be true the statement that the average puncher was unwilling to encumber himself with more than one gun, and often failed to carry that."[15] Carrying a loaded pistol while working cattle on horseback could be dangerous. On trail drives, pistols were usually carried in the wagon and buckled on if a need was felt for them. Baylis Fletcher probably described the relationship between the cowboy and his pistol pretty accurately in his memoir of a trail drive across North Texas and Indian territory in 1879:

Leaving Fort Worth we followed the trail north . . . crossing parts of Wise, Denton, Cook, and Montague counties. Since Montague was a border county, we were told that we could wear side arms without fear of arrest, so every cowpuncher who had a six-shooter buckled it on just to enjoy the privilege of carrying a weapon. . . . in the Nation, where there was no pistol law and no one to enforce any law, our men continued to indulge in their penchant for toting six-shooters. All who had these weapons rubbed them bright and buckled them on. With two exceptions, we were novices on the trail and little knew how useless our guns would be in these parts. . . . we soon learned that all sorts of game fought shy of the Chisholm Trail. . . . After wasting much ammunition, we grew tired of such sport and returned our guns to the wagon.[16]

The daily reality of the cowboy was work. In the summertime, it was hot, dusty, bonebreaking work; in the wintertime, it was cold, wet, bonebreaking work, lasting always from ten to fourteen hours a day. Like all agricultural work, it was cyclical and seasonal and was basically divided into four phases. The spring roundup was followed by the summer trail drive, the fall roundup, and winter ranch work. An extended cowhunt, the spring roundup enabled ranchers to count their cattle, gather in strays that had wandered from their range, brand and castrate newborn calves, and collect the four and five year olds that were ready for market. All over the range country roundups were organized by regional and state cattlemen's associations, for the open-range system required close cooperation among its users. By 1880, most western states were divided into roundup districts, with each district covering a hundred square miles or so and under the supervision of a district superintendent, who set the day for beginning the spring roundup. In West Texas, the spring roundups usually began about May 20, and lasted thirty or thirty-five days; in South Texas they were earlier, and in the Northwest, later.

A roundup of the 1880s was an impressive sight. It was a chance for cowboys to socialize and renew friendships after a winter's separation, as well as a visual manifestation of the cooperative nature of ranching (a business usually pictured in the myth as one carried on with unbridled individualism). In the early 1900s, Don Biggers described the roundups he participated in near Colorado City, Texas, in the early 1880s:

On the appointed day big chuck wagons, drawn by four or six mules, would begin to arrive at the designated meeting place, and following the wagons would come droves of cowboys, driving herds of cow ponies; and from all directions would come one, two, three, and sometimes half a dozen men with their packs and little bunches of saddle ponies, these being the small ranchmen or men from other districts, come to join the work. On reaching the camp ground they would inquire for the particular outfit with which they wanted to work, and if it had not arrived they would throw in with any outfit and wait until the one they wanted did arrive. There would generally be a wait of three or four days, giving everybody time to get in before the work began. . . . At these meetings every phase and character of cowboy life asserted itself. It was everything from a singing convention to a theological argument . . . mumble-the-peg, poker, fuzzy-guzzy, chuck-a-luck, and other innocent amusements were the social events. As there were generally from ten to fifteen wagons and twenty-five to thirty men with each wagon, the number of men at one of these gatherings can easily be estimated at from two hundred and fifty to four hundred.[17]

Once everyone was together and the work started, there was no time for singing conventions. The district superintendent opened the roundup by announcing the order in which the ranges would be worked. The entire group worked one range at a time, with the foreman of the ranch whose range was being worked having charge of that range, under the general direction of the district superintendent. The task was to gather all the cattle on the range into one herd. In West Texas, it usually took three to eight days to work a range. In the Northwest, where a range might be the size of the state of Connecticut and yet only hold several thousand cattle, it could take a little longer.

Hiram Craig, who worked in a roundup on C. C. Slaughter's range in West Texas in 1882, described the way the cattle were gathered there:

> On the evening before the roundup Billy Stanefor, the roundup boss, went to all the wagons and called for two or three men from each wagon to go out from ten to fifteen miles and make what is called a dry camp. Each man was to stake his horse so that when daylight comes every man was ready to follow out instructions to bring all the cattle towards the grounds. The men so sent out, all going in different directions, formed a veritable spider's web with the roundup grounds in the center. There was little danger or chance of any cattle escaping, as when they would leave the path of one man they would drift into the path of the next man, and the nearer they came to the grounds, the more men would come in sight—finally forming one big herd.[18]

Although this technique sounds simple on paper, it was not so simple in broken country, or when a cow had to be pulled from a boggy place before she could move, or when she had to be persuaded to get her calf from its hiding place. Cowboys had to be careful not to "chouse" cattle, that is, to run them and cause them to lose precious weight. Cows and calves had to be moved slowly, gently, toward the gathering herd. It was a job that required patience and stamina.

Once the herd was gathered, the cutting began. Traditionally, the ranch whose range was being worked cut their cattle from the herd first, followed by other ranches in rotation. At the roundup that Craig worked in, the foreman called out "Number 1 cut and Number 2 hold," meaning that the men from wagon number one would cut their cattle from the herd while wagon number two held it. Then he called "Number 2 cut and Number 3 hold," and so on until every ranch present had a chance to cut. Cutting brought out the very best in cowboy skills and cooperation between man and horse. A cowboy would spot a cow and calf, the cow with his ranch's brand. He would ride into the herd without exciting it, turn his horse toward the desired animal, and deftly separate her and her calf from the other cattle, moving her over to another herd being held a short distance away. It took practice, skill, and a good horse.

When the herd was cut, branding started. Calves were roped, dragged to the fire, and held down while their mother's brand was burned on their flanks. At the same time that they were branded, they were castrated and dehorned—hot, noisy, bloody work. Finally the cows and calves were turned back to their range, the strays were gathered to be taken to their own ranges, and the roundup moved on to the next range to repeat the whole process again.

On a man-to-cow basis, the roundup at least provided a certain amount of excitement, and on a man-to-man basis it provided a few days of companionship and even sport. The trail drive, by contrast, meant months of grueling monotony and hardship interspersed with hours of very real danger.

Most trail drives were organized not by ranchers but by professional contractors, men who collected cattle in Texas and delivered them in Kansas. In some cases, the contractors purchased the cattle outright in Texas. Sometimes, they undertook to deliver them to buyers in Kansas for a set fee, usually a dollar to a dollar fifty per head. The profit to be made in trail contracting was considerable. Ike Pryor, who in 1884 alone moved forty-five thousand cattle from Texas to the northwestern ranges, estimated that it cost five hundred dollars a month in wages and provisions to move three thousand cattle five hundred miles. In less than two months a herd could be driven from Texas to a Kansas railhead for less than a thousand dollars, so a contractor charging a dollar a head for three thousand head stood to profit two thousand dollars on each herd—if nothing went wrong.[19]

The contractor's investment consisted of a wagon and a team of mules; groceries, usually coffee, sugar, bacon, dried apples, canned goods, and eggs; wages for a trail boss, a cook, a horse wrangler, and ten or twelve cowboys; and a herd of riding horses (which could be sold at the end of the drive). A trail boss earned around a hundred dollars a month; a cook, thirty-five; cowboys, thirty; and the wrangler, twenty-five or thirty. The cowboys furnished their own saddles and bedrolls, and usually horses. Their horses and the contractor's were thrown together into one remuda under the charge of the wrangler, who saw to their care and feeding on the trail.

There were specialized tasks on a trail drive. The trail boss, of course, was in charge of the whole operation and was responsible for seeing that the cattle got enough grass and water and, most important, did not lose weight during the drive. He designated bed grounds at night, watering spots during the day, and river crossings, and was responsible for keeping peace and order in the camp. He was responsible for making payments for supplies and keeping records, usually in the form of vouchers for money paid out; for choosing the precise path the herd was to follow within the confines of a given trail, taking care to see that it did not travel over ground that had already been overgrazed by other herds; and for

14. Quoted in William W. Savage, Jr., *Cowboy Life: Reconstructing an American Myth* (Norman: University of Oklahoma Press, 1975), pp. 113–14.
15. Rollins, *The Cowboy*, p. 41.
16. Baylis, John Fletcher, *Up the Trail in '79* (Norman: University of Oklahoma Press, 1968), pp. 27–32.
17. Biggers, "History That Will Never Be Repeated," pp. 32–33.
18. Hunter, *Trail Drivers*, 1:348.
19. Jimmy M. Skaggs, *The Cattle-Trailing Industry: Between Supply and Demand, 1866–1890* (Lawrence: University Press of Kansas, 1973), p. 3.

dealing with Indians trying to collect toll fees, irate Kansas farmers, and sheriffs trying to enforce local quarantine and cattle inspection statutes. The trail boss bore the tremendous responsibility of moving someone else's cattle on commission while being completely out of touch with both their owner and his own employer from the time he left Texas until he reached the end of the trail. He had to be cool and resolute, make decisions quickly, and get along with his men in such a way that they accepted his authority. Above all, he had to prove himself competent, and there were cases of cowboys "firing" an obviously incompetent boss and explaining themselves to their employer at the end of the trail.

The cook was responsible for setting up camp, feeding the men, and taking care of his wagon and mules. He was usually an older man, sometimes an ex-cowboy, and he was not expected to ride horseback or help with the herd, even in an emergency. His job was to see that the other members of the crew were fed.

He operated from a chuck wagon, a heavy wagon drawn by one and sometimes two teams of mules and developed especially for the needs of the roundup and the trail drive. The first chuck wagon seems to have been built by Texas rancher Charles Goodnight in 1866. According to his biographer, J. Evetts Haley, Goodnight bought the running gear from a U.S. Army wagon and took it to a Weatherford, Texas, wagon-builder, where he had it rebuilt, substituting bois d'arc and iron for the hickory and oak gear and axles and having a new bed with "the first chuck-box he had ever seen" added to it.[20] The chuck box had a hinged lid on the back that folded down to make the work table, and inside it were compartments and drawers designed to hold tin plates, cups, eating utensils, and staples: rice, beans, flour, lard, salt, baking soda, sugar, coffee, and dried or canned fruit. There was usually medicine aboard, calomel and castor oil for man, and horse liniment for beast. The bed of the wagon held bedrolls, cooking utensils, grain for the mules, a shovel, an axe, ropes and stake-pins, weapons, and, strapped to the side, a water barrel. A dried cow hide, slung under the wagon like a hammock and called the caboose or the possum-belly, carried kindling.

When the chuck wagon was set up, it became the center of the cowboy's universe. A canvas sheet stretched out above the work table might provide the only shade for miles. Nearby, dutch ovens and a coffee pot hung over hot coals smouldering in a trench created a kitchen and hearth. In spite of present day romanticizing about "chuck-wagon cooking," the diet on a trail drive was not only monotonous but also seriously deficient in calories and calcium. It generally consisted of beef, bacon, beans, biscuits, black coffee, and dried prunes or dried apples. On the trail from Texas to Kansas, the last wholesale grocery merchants were at Fort Worth. They would send salesmen out to the camping grounds west of town to tempt

trail bosses into making final purchases for their outfits, but whatever delicacies were bought were usually consumed by the time the Red River was crossed, and it was a long way across the Indian Nation and southern Kansas. Baylis Fletcher vividly described his outfit's culinary deprivation: "We bought fresh supplies at Dodge City, including a keg of pickles. During the entire trip we had tasted no vegetables other than beans, or prairie strawberries as some called them, and when the pickles were opened, the men would eat nothing else until they were devoured."[21]

"Parson" Barnard, who drove cattle across the Cherokee Outlet in the 1880s, put it more succinctly: "Breakfast: sourdough biscuits, white gravy, sowbelly, and black coffee; dinner: sowbelly, black coffee, sourdough biscuits, and white gravy; supper: black coffee, sowbelly, white gravy, and sourdough biscuits."

On the northern ranges, chuck wagons were sometimes more elaborately fitted out. Jack Potter, who went from San Antonio to Colorado in 1882 and stayed there through the summer, was amazed to see a wagon being fitted up for a horse drive to the Big Horn Ranch. It included "a big wall tent, cots to sleep on, a stove, and a number one cook."[22]

A trail drive that employed ten cowboys would have a horse herd, or *remuda*—the word means "replacement," or, more colloquially, "remount"—of sixty or seventy horses, although the size of a remuda could vary from six or eight mounts per man to the two that Charles Goodnight, the grand old man of Texas trail driving, claimed were sufficient. In Nevada and California, the remuda was called a *caballado*, "horse herd," or, in the buckaroo's Spanish, "cavayard." Whatever it was called, it was in the charge of a horse wrangler, who was frequently a boy old enough to work like a man. Wrangler was a starting job with a trail outfit and was usually given to younger or less experienced men than those who were hired as cowboys. The wrangler drove the horse herd beside the wagon, ahead of the cattle, rounded them up in a rope corral several times a day so that the cowboys could select their mounts, and saw to it that horses that were ridden hard were fed corn as well as grass when they were brought in. Although each cowboy usually owned his own horse, the pool of remounts belonged to the contractor and replacement horses were assigned to the cowboys by lot. One horse, generally the best and most sure-footed, was reserved by each cowboy as his night horse.

There were also specialized jobs among the cowboys themselves. The herd was moved in a long, strung-out line, with a cowboy on each side at the front to point the lead steers in the right direction and set the pace. This position was called the point and was occupied by the most experienced and most reliable men. Behind them, on each side of the herd, came pairs of riders called the flank, whose job was to ride back and forth along the line of the drive, seeing that cattle did not wander too far out from the main herd. At the end of the herd, always riding in a cloud of dust, came the drag, two men whose job was to push the slowest cattle forward. This was an unpleasant place to ride, and the cowboys who rode there were usually the newest or least experienced men in the group. Some men made sure they would never have to ride drag. When H. D. Gruene, who had gone to Cheyenne to deliver a herd of Texas cattle in 1870, found that the new owners wanted him to stay on and drive the cows to Salt Lake City, he agreed on the condition that he "would receive $60 a month and would not have to work at the rear of the herd."[23]

The first task of a trail outfit, once the cattle were gathered, was to road-brand them. This meant putting an additional brand on them that would mark them as part of a particular trail herd, so that they could be easily identified on the trail. This was done by driving the cattle through a long, narrow wooden chute, just wide enough for one cow and long enough for about twenty-five. Six or eight men, each with a heated branding-iron, would apply the road-brands through the slats in the chute. In this way about one thousand cattle a day could be branded.

Although cattle were driven overland from East Texas to points in eastern Kansas and southwestern Missouri before the Civil War, the great trail drives of the 1860s, 1870s, and 1880s took place over two trails, the Chisholm and the Western, with hundreds of smaller drives (in terms of numbers of cattle) moving on to the northwestern ranges from the termini of these two trails. The Chisholm Trail, named after a wagon road laid out over a portion of Indian Territory by a trader named Jesse Chisholm, ran up through central Texas west of Waco and Fort Worth, crossed the Red River at a place called Red River Station, struck across Indian Territory, ran through the sites of Caldwell and Wichita, Kansas, and met the Kansas Pacific Railroad at Abilene. The Western Trail, which began to replace the Chisholm as the main route to Kansas after 1872, crossed the Red about a hundred miles upstream from Red River Station, at Doan's Store, and cut across the far western portion of the Indian Nation to meet the Atchison, Topeka, and Santa Fe Railroad at Dodge City. Each trail began in a mass of feeder trails, reaching as far south as the Mexican border and as far east as the coastal country below Houston, and neither was by any means a well-defined highway.

The determining factors in the location of the trails from Texas to Kansas were the westward movement of farmers and the continuing quarantine legislation against the importation of Texas cattle, which carried a tick that infected local cattle with a disease that Kansas and Missouri farmers called "Texas fever." As early as 1854 Missouri had enacted a law that forbade the importation of "diseased cattle," and in 1858 Kansas followed suit. For the next twenty years each session of the Kansas legislature witnessed a three-way battle between farmers, Texas cattlemen, and cattle town promoters over the location of the quarantine line, which moved progressively westward. It was not until 1889 that scientists identified the tick *Margaropus annulatus*, and not the Texas cow herself, as the culprit.

To the men who took part in a long trail drive, it was an epic experience, never to be forgotten. Like all epic experiences, it was a mixture of fatigue, fear, monotony, and elation. A well-established daily routine provided a framework for these emotions:

> *When first put on the road the cattle are closely guarded and driven briskly for several days, until the danger of their breaking away for home is passed. For the first few days at sunset the drove is "rounded up" compactly, and half the men, relieved by the other half at midnight, ride round and round the bed-ground. This labor decreases as the cattle become more tractable, and two men at each watch are then sufficient to guard them through the night. . . . At daybreak the cattle are moved off the "bed-ground" to graze, and while the two men who were last on guard remain with them all other hands breakfast. The first to finish breakfast relieve the guards on duty and allow them to come in for their morning meal. Then, the horses being caught and saddled, and the cook having cleaned up, the drive is started again and continued until about eleven, when the cattle are allowed to graze again, and lunch or dinner is eaten. Immediately after that the men who are to stand first guard at night, and who also act as horse-herders, go ahead with the messwagon and the horses to the next camp, where they get supper, so that when the herd comes up they are ready to "graze," and hold it until the first relief of the night. The bed-ground is, when possible, on elevation, with space sufficient for all the stock to sleep. . . . The distance travelled each day is twelve to fifteen miles.*[24]

The writer of the above, an anonymous informant contributing to a special census report on the cattle industry compiled in 1880, failed to mention two occurrences that broke the routine of a trail drive so frequently that they almost became routine themselves: river crossings and stampedes. Coming up from Texas, a herd had to be put across the Brazos, Trinity, Red, Washita, Canadian, Cimarron, and Arkansas rivers and numerous creeks and branches. The rivers were normally wide, slow, and muddy—with steep cut banks and timbered bottoms, hard enough to ford a herd across in dry weather—but they became raging torrents after spring rains. Sometimes five or six separate herds would pile up on a south bank, waiting for the water to go down, become mixed, and cost their drovers a week's time sorting them out. If a drover tried to swim a

20. J. Evetts Haley, *Charles Goodnight, Cowman & Plainsman* (Boston: Houghton Mifflin Co., 1936), pp. 121–22.
21. Fletcher, *Up the Trail*, p. 46.
22. Hunter, *Trail Drivers*, 1:60.
23. Ibid., p. 136.
24. Clarence W. Gordon, "Report on Cattle, Sheep, Swine, Supplementary to Enumeration of Live Stock on Farms in 1880," in U.S. Census Office, 10th Census, 1880, *Census Reports*, 22 vols. (Washington: Government Printing Office, 1883–88), vol. 3, *Productions of Agriculture* (1883), p. 1071.

herd through high water, he risked losing both cattle and cowboys. Some rivers harbored special hazards: the South Canadian was famous for quicksand, and the Cimarron was extremely saline when it was low, so that cattle had to be driven across without being allowed to follow their natural inclination to drink. On the Loving-Goodnight Trail, special care had to be taken to keep thirst-maddened cattle from stampeding as they neared the crossing of the Pecos River.

Stampedes were the other regular hazard of the trail. They occurred most frequently during storms, when cattle would become nervous while bedded down and then be frightened by a sudden clap of thunder or bolt of lightning, but stampedes could also be artificially introduced by local residents who would then appear the next morning, slyly offering to help round up the strays for fifty cents a head. If a herd acquired the habit of stampeding early in the drive, it could run every night for a month. Drovers dreaded stampedes, not so much from the danger involved as from the loss of sleep, loss of cattle, and loss of profits.

Indians were not as much a hazard as a nuisance, at least on the Chisholm and Western Trails. Cattlemen might see Indian Territory as "one grand expanse of free grass," as Baylis Fletcher put it, but members of the Five Civilized Tribes, to whom the land had been guaranteed forever by treaty, saw the cattlemen as trespassers and felt they were entitled to some compensation for the use of their land.[25] Both the Choctaw and Cherokee legislatures passed toll acts, but individual tribal members who tried to collect the tolls were frequently met with indifference or hostility from drovers, who usually settled the matter by either making a token payment in the form of cattle or frightening the collectors away with gunplay. Of course, on the northern and western trails there was, in the 1860s and early seventies, a very real danger of attack from hostile Indians, and at least one well-known Texas cattleman, Oliver Loving, lost his life in an Indian attack.

The trail driver was constantly exposed to the elements and had to do his job in drenching rain, freezing sleet, and parching dust. Broken bones and fevers were dealt with on the trail, and few cowboys who wrote their memoirs did not recall at least one night when they went on guard so sick they could hardly stay on their horse. Homesickness, and what we would today call depression, played their part, too, as did the weight of responsibility. A remarkable insight into the daily feelings of a trail driver can be gleaned from the diary of George Duffield, who drove a herd of cattle from Texas to Iowa in 1866:

June 2nd: Hard rain & wind storm. . . . Awful night. Wet all night. Clear bright morning. Men still lost. . . . Almost starved not having a bite to eat for 60 hours.

June 14: . . . . We are now 25 miles from Ark. River & it is very high. We are water bound by two creeks & but beef and flour to eat. . . .
June 19: Good day. 15 Indians come to herd & tried to take some beeves. Would not let them. Had a big muss. . . . They are the Seminoles.[26]

Duffield may have summed up a feeling every trail driver had at least once when he wrote, on June 23, "Worked all day hard in the river trying to make the beeves swim and did not get one over. Had to go back to prairie sick and discouraged. Have *not* got the *Blues* but am in *Hel of a fix*."[27]

Once the drive reached its destination and the cattle were sold, the trail drivers split up, each going his own way. In fact, few drives seem to have reached Kansas with the same group of cowboys they left Texas with, as the memoirs constantly mention hands quitting along the way and new hands being hired to take their places. For some Texas drovers, Kansas was only the start of a longer trip to the northwestern ranges; others returned to Texas to find fall work and start the cycle again. For some, the trip home by train was as exciting and certainly more novel than the trip up on horseback. Jack Potter, a Texas boy who went up the trail in 1882 at the age of seventeen, had been around horses and cattle all of his life but had never been on a train, slept in a hotel, or taken a bath in a bathhouse. In his account of his adventures, written in the 1920s, he devotes much more space to these experiences than to the incidents of the trail. He was fascinated by the intricacies of checking his trunk and terrified by the speed of the train.[28]

The fall roundup was conducted very much like the spring roundup, except that beefs were not cut out for market. Calves born since the spring roundup were branded and castrated, and strays were cut out to be returned to their range. During the winter, most ranches let the majority of their cowboys go, telling them to come around in the spring for roundup jobs. A few men with families or some who were exceptionally good workers would be kept on for "winter work": holding cattle on a particular range, usually from a line camp. David Shirk, who went with a herd from Texas to the Snake River country of Idaho in 1867, described his winter employment in George T. Miller's camp there:

Our house was constructed by digging into the bank of the river about four feet, and consisted of one room, ten by fourteen feet. A large willow pole answered for a ridge pole, and the roof was covered with rye grass and over this dirt to the depth of six inches. The chimney was constructed of rock and dirt, while a blanket answered as a cover for the one and only door. . . . our time was mainly occupied in riding around the cattle, rounding them up and preventing them from going too far astray. Our object was to keep them near camp, and every night they were driven in. My spare time, during the winter, was occupied in trapping along the river for beaver and otter, and for coyotes on the plain. Of the latter there was no end, apparently, to the numbers, and I captured seventy-five. Of the pelts, I made two fine robes.[29]

From the yearly round of work, this constant interaction of man with horse and cow, emerged something that is loosely called the cowboy character. Reams of paper have been covered with print describing it, yet somehow it remains elusive and ephemeral. What is clear is that something about the cowboy's attitude toward his work, his fellow man, and the world at large was different from that of other nineteenth-century workers. To try to pin it down more closely at this late date may be impossible, but there are clues.

Some of them are in the attitudes that present-day cowboys—cowboys who work cattle, not the social range—have toward these same subjects, attitudes that may have been handed down through a series of informal teacher-learner relationships from the cowboys of four generations ago. Other clues lie in what perceptive observers, literate cowboys like Teddy Blue, Charlie Siringo, Gene Rhodes, and Andy Adams, wrote about the men they worked with. Sifting through these clues, several salient features emerge. The open-range cowboy was first and foremost a romantic, a refugee from industrial civilization. He was a passionate devotee of unrestricted personal freedom, and the only way that he could achieve it was by becoming so expert at his job that he had no fear of either supervision or unemployment. He obtained this expertise by careful observation of animal behavior, so that he entered into a symbiotic relationship with the cow, the animal that was, after all, his own reason for existence. Finally, because he functioned as part of an all-male work group, he became a shrewd observer of human behavior and an expert at motivating his coworkers and welding them into an efficient team. A by-product of this last talent was the understated dry wit that characterizes western humor, a wit that flows both from the cowboy's lack of need to call attention to himself and from his understanding of the role of humor in lessening tension.

The mythmakers seized on the cowboy's individualism and made it the basis for the hundreds of thousands of gaudily dressed, gun-toting, war-whooping show-offs who have ridden their way across millions of feet of film and an untold number of canvases and printed pages. Latter-day cowboys, as well as oilmen, real-estate brokers, and truck drivers from Texas to Oregon, then turned themselves into parodies of the parody, much to the disgust of sober-minded westerners. Will Rogers took cowboy humor out of its workaday context and put it on the stage and radio, but by doing so he grafted it onto the flourishing stock of "wise yokel" stories that have been the central core of American humor since the eighteenth century. Owen Wister distilled the cowboy's taciturn competence into the soft-spoken, steel-hard character he called the Virginian. William S. Hart brought it to the screen in realistic westerns like *Three-Word Brand* and Gary Cooper and John Wayne elevated it to the level of a universal western characteristic: small boys the world over know that anyone who says "yup" and "nope" and hits hard and fast is bound to be a cowboy.

Curiously, the most fundamental characteristic of the open-range cowboy never entered the myth. No film actor or novelist has ever concerned himself with the empathy with cows and the understanding of cattle that were the mark of the best cowboys. It was an attitude that was rooted in nineteenth-century agrarian philosophy and that was strengthened by years of experience with cows—a resignation to man's fate as a shepherd and herder of lower breeds. J. Frank Dobie once wrote of trail driver Ab Blocker that "he savies the cow—cow psychology, cow anatomy, cow dietetics—cow nature in general and cow nature in particular," and that was almost it, but not quite.[30] There was also an obligation to the cow. Jane Kramer, a contemporary author who has written a fine book about modern cowboys, found a West Texan who expressed it perfectly:

I'll tell you what a cowpuncher is. . . . It ain't roping and it ain't riding bronc and it ain't being smart, neither. It's thinking enough about a dumb animal to go out in the rain or snow to try to save that cow. Not for the guy who owns the cow but for the poor old cow and her calf. It's getting down in that bog—in the quicksand. . . . You tie up one leg, then the other. You tramp her out. . . . You see, this old cow, she don't know but what you're trying to kill her. But you drag her out, even if she's fighting you, and then you ride a mile yonder and find another danged old cow bogged down the same way.[31]

This is certainly not the stuff that myths are made of, but it was what enabled men to move millions of cattle across uncharted prairies, swimming them across rivers and staying with them during stampedes. It was what gave those men the attitude about themselves and their relationship to the rest of the world that created the myth. They were the final embodiment of an ideal that stretched back through the years to Thomas Jefferson. They were the last American agrarians.

25. Fletcher, *Up the Trail*, p. 31.
26. George C. Duffield, "Driving Cattle from Texas to Iowa, 1866," *Annals of Iowa* 14 (1924):252–54.
27. Ibid.
28. Hunter, *Trail Drivers*, 1:62–70.
29. Schmitt, *Cattle Drives of David Shirk*, pp. 33, 46.
30. Dobie, *Cow People*, p. 32.
31. Jane Kramer, *The Last Cowboy* (New York: Harper & Row, 1977), pp. 144–45.

WHO WAS THE COWBOY?

The range cattle industry began, matured, and collapsed in the twenty years between 1866 and 1886. In that short time nearly nine million cattle were driven in trail herds from Texas to shipping points in Kansas and new grazing ranges on the northern plains. Technological developments in transportation and refrigeration made it possible for the residents of eastern cities to consume those cattle in the form of fresh beef. At the very root of this industry was a new kind of American—the cowboy. In those twenty years, he became an object of fascination for easterners and westerners alike. He emerged as a new popular hero, symbolizing an old American ideal: unrestrained personal freedom. He inspired artists, writers, and photographers to record his unique character, and he became the foundation of a national myth. Suddenly, the open-range ranching system that gave him birth collapsed, and the cattle industry was reorganized. By 1890, the open range was gone, fenced into pastures and planted with feed crops. The day of the roundup and the trail drive had passed, but the cowboy remained. He has been part of American life, in one form or another, real and mythical, for the past century. What was he really like in his heyday?

Dinner Scene of Plateau Cow Boys W J Carpenter Telluride Colo

1-	5- Frank Leslie
2- Joe Davis	10- John Dunham
3- Ben Robinson	11- Alfred Dunham
4- Geo. Robinson	12- Harve Wallace
5- Jim Nash	13- Sam Todd
6- "Kanaki" Joe Felton	14-
7- Ike Marshall	15- Sant Bower
8- Jim Belmer	16- Nels Peterson

17- Bob Nash	24- Ruf Bloise
18-	25 Al Herndon
19- Will Belmer	26 Andy Jensen
20- Judd Pierce	27-
21- "Te He" Bill Crozier	
22- Jim Mears	
23 Billy Randall	

Akin in 1887

29

Dinner Scene of Plateau Cowboys
W. J. Carpenter (dates unknown)
Photograph, 1887

The clothing worn in nineteenth-century cow camps did not conform to modern stereotypes but instead was functional, practical, and varied. This is clearly evident in a photograph taken by W. J. Carpenter on a ranch near Telluride, probably on the range of the Naturita Cattle Company in the Plateau Basin, San Miguel County, Colorado. Although most of the men are wearing the common pocketless, pullover work shirts of the period, at least one is wearing a sweater and one a suit coat. Several are wearing vests, but the man standing next to the chuck wagon has on farmer's bib overalls. Some have on bandannas and some are wearing loosely tied neckties. Several, but not all, are wearing chaps, one pair of which is decorated with large silver conchos. Nearly all have on inexpensive wool hats, and there are no pistols in sight.

Colorado Historical Society
Denver, Colorado

Cowboys in the Texas Panhandle
Andrew Alexander Forbes (1862–1921)
Photograph, ca. 1885
Western History Collections
University of Oklahoma Library
Norman, Oklahoma

The few surviving photographs of working cowboys taken in the 1870s and 1880s confirm what contemporary written sources say about the kind of men who worked as open-range cowboys during the cattle boom. Most of the people in the photographs are Anglo-Americans, although Mexican-Americans and blacks appear with some frequency. Photographs taken in Oklahoma and Indian Territory occasionally show Indian cowboys, like the cook in a picture of an Oklahoma cowboy camp taken by A. A. Forbes. Most cowboys were in their twenties or thirties. Spending hours in the saddle required great physical stamina and was not a middle-aged or an old man's job. Few were as young as the boy in Forbes's photograph, who was probably the horse wrangler, a job often given to young and inexperienced cowboys. Camp cooks tended to be older men, often retired cowboys.

Cowboys in Camp in Western Oklahoma
Andrew Alexander Forbes (1862–1921)
Photograph, ca. 1885
Western History Collections
University of Oklahoma Library
Norman, Oklahoma

Group of Cowboys

Charles D. Kirkland (1851–1926)

Photographs, Cheyenne, Wyoming, ca. 1883

As the northwestern ranges in Colorado, Wyoming, Montana, and the Dakotas were opened to ranching in the late 1870s and early 1880s, young men from the Midwest and the Northeast as well as adventure-seeking Englishmen and other Europeans

C. D. KIRKLAND.   PHOTOGRAPHER.   CHEYENNE. WYO.

C. D. KIRKLAND.   PHOTOGRAPHER.   CHEYENNE, WYO.

drifted West to work as cowboys. These four photographs taken
in Wyoming in the 1880s, part of a set intended to show tourists
what ranch life was like, show northwestern range cowboys posing
for the camera.

Wyoming State Archives
Museums and Historical Department
Cheyenne, Wyoming

C. D. KIRKLAND.   PHOTOGRAPHER.   CHEYENNE, WYO.

C. D. KIRKLAND,   PHOTOGRAPHER.   CHEYENNE, WYO.

Driving Cattle into a Corral, Nebraska
Wood engraving after a drawing by
Valentine W. Bromley (1848–1877)
Extra supplement, *Illustrated London News*
August 21, 1875
American Folklife Center
Library of Congress

Indian Cowboys
Photographer unknown, ca. 1890
   Indian cowboys were frequently encountered tending herds in the Indian
nations or working for ranchers on the leased
lands in what is now western Oklahoma. This
group, probably Kikapoos or Caddoes, was
photographed in the Cherokee Outlet in the
late 1890s. Twenty years earlier, in 1874, the
British artist Valentine Bromley, on a tour of
the West, drew a group of Sioux driving
cattle into a corral beside the Union Pacific
tracks west of Omaha, Nebraska.
Western History Collections
University of Oklahoma Library
Norman, Oklahoma

Mounted Cowboy
John C. H Grabill (active ca. 1887–1891)
Photograph, copyright 1887
   The cowboys of the northwestern ranges in the late 1880s were
a mixture of old hands who had come up from Texas, eastern
college graduates working for the experience, British remittance
men, and midwestern farm boys. They all knew that they had
become popular heroes, however, and were proud of their trade.
In this photograph, one of more than a hundred images that
Grabill filed for copyright with the Library of Congress between
1887 and 1891, a northwestern cowboy poses in a fenced pasture.
A pistol is strapped around his waist, and he carries a rifle in a
gun case strapped to his saddle. He is wearing the dark flannel
work shirt of the period, leather chaps, and gloves. His rather
elaborate equipment includes a rubberized slicker, field glasses,
and saddle bags, and his method of holding the reins indicates
that he learned to ride in the East or in England.
Grabill Collection
Prints and Photographs Division
Library of Congress

THE COWBOY'S WORK

Ironically, the cowboy, who was so often pictured by authors and illustrators as a romantic, pastoral individualist, was in fact a link in an industrial chain that delivered refrigerated, dressed beef to the post-Civil War cities of the Northeast. In the first years of the beef industry's development, the late 1860s and early 1870s, cattle were driven from their ranges in Texas to the nearest rail shipping points in Kansas, five hundred miles north. From there they were shipped in cattle cars to Chicago slaughterhouses, where they were killed and dressed. The carcasses were then shipped in refrigerated cars to markets in the East. Later, as new ranges were opened up, herds were moved from Texas to Nebraska, Colorado, Montana, Wyoming, the Dakotas, Utah, and Nevada—anywhere that there was sufficient grass and water, and no fences—and new shipping points were created. By 1885, a government report stated that 1,365,000 square miles—44 percent of the land in the United States—were devoted to raising cattle to supply the refrigerated beef industry. At the bottom of this structure was the cowboy.

A Drove of Texas Cattle Crossing a Stream
Woodcut after a drawing by A. R. Waud (1828–1891)
Harper's Weekly, October 19, 1867
   This drawing, which appeared in the fall of the same year in which the first big cattle drives from Texas to Kansas took place, was actually executed by the artist in southwestern Louisiana and shows Texas cattle being driven to market in New Orleans. It is the first representation of a cattle drive in an American magazine.
American Folklife Center
Library of Congress

A DROVE OF TEXAS CATTLE CROSSING A STREAM.—Sketched by A. R. Waud.—[See Page 666.]

The Texas Cattle Trade, 1873

Paul Frenzeny (active 1873–1889) and Jules Tavernier (1844–1889)
Woodcut from a drawing
Harper's Weekly, May 2, 1874

In the fall of 1873, *Harper's Weekly* sent two artists West by rail to make a series of sketches of western life. Although they did not actually accompany a cattle drive up the trail, they observed the beginning of one near Denison, Texas, and the end of another at Wichita, Kansas.

This double-page woodcut done from sketches made by Frenzeny and Tavernier gave Americans their first comprehensive view of the booming cattle trade. The top center cut shows cattle being rounded up on the open range for selection of those to be driven north for sale. The cut below shows cattle being separated from the full herd to be thrown into the trail herd, with one of the cowboys using a stock whip (a holdover from pre-Civil War cattle-handling technology). The upper left-hand cut shows the trail contractor driving the trail herd through a branding chute to put the road brand on them. Below it, we see a herd, probably two or three thousand head, strung out on the trail south of Wichita. Below that is the community of Clear Water on the Ninnescah River, a supply point on the trail just south of Wichita.

The center bottom cut shows a camp on the herd grounds west of Wichita, with two cowboys coming in from night-herding while the others are having breakfast. The top right-hand cut shows cattle being loaded on the railroad cars for shipment to Chicago, having been purchased in Wichita by representatives of Chicago commission agents. Below that we see the town of Wichita, five years old at the time. The view looks north from the intersection of Douglas Avenue and Main Street. Finally, below that, we see the trail contractor and his cowboys heading back to Texas.
American Folklife Center
Library of Congress

BRANDING.

ROUND, OR ROUNDING UP CATTLE.

SHIPPING FOR THE EASTERN MARKETS.

ON THE TRAIL.

CUTTING-OUT.

WICHITA.

HALTING-PLACE ON THE NINNESCAH RIVER.

IN CAMP.

HO, FOR TEXAS!

THE TEXAS CATTLE TRADE.—Drawn by Frenzeny and Tavernier.—[See Page 383.]

The Transportation of Dressed Beef from the West
Chicago Cattle Yards and Slaughterhouses
Theodore R. Davis (1840–1894)
Woodcut from drawings, 1882
Harper's Weekly, October 28, 1882

The nonromantic, industrial aspects of the cattle trade that created trail driving and the range cattle system were illustrated by *Harper's Weekly* artist Theodore R. Davis in 1882. He visited the Chicago stockyards and one of the packing plants there, probably Swift Brothers and Co., and made a series of sketches showing its operation.

In the upper left we see buyers for the packinghouses purchasing carload lots of cattle from the commission agents, whose representatives bought them in Kansas. The upper right-hand cut shows the cattle being driven from the pens into the killing rooms, where they are dispatched by men with long spears working from the platform above. The center cut depicts the assembly-line-like butchering room, where the carcasses are dismembered as they are hauled through the room on an overhead chain. On either side of this we see meat moving from the cold-storage room, where it could be kept at temperatures below 40 degrees by mechanical refrigeration, to the refrigerated railroad cars which will take it East. The bottom three panels show the refrigerated cars which were developed by the packinghouses in the years just after the Civil War. Each one of the cars shown here could carry the equivalent of nineteen head of cattle and required a ton of ice.
American Folklife Center
Library of Congress

"Historic Sketches of the Cattle Trade of the West and Southwest"
By Joseph G. McCoy (1837–1915)
Kansas City, Missouri: Ramsey, Millett & Hudson, 1874

In 1874 the Texas-to-Kansas cattle drives were only seven years old, but they were of such importance to the economy and had attracted so much national attention that Joseph G. McCoy, one of the original promoters of the trade, was moved to write and publish a "history" of it. McCoy was a cattle commission agent who hit on the idea of building a stockyard at Abilene, Kansas, in the summer of 1867 and attracting Texas trail contractors there that fall. In this book, he credits himself with originating the post-Civil War cattle trade, and he certainly did influence the direction it took. *Historic Sketches of the Cattle Trade* did much to publicize the open-range ranching industry. Its 126 delightful, somewhat ironic illustrations, woodcuts from drawings by a Topeka, Kansas, artist named Henry Worrall, helped its readers visualize ranches and cowboys.
SF196.U5M3
Rare Book and Special Collections Division
Library of Congress

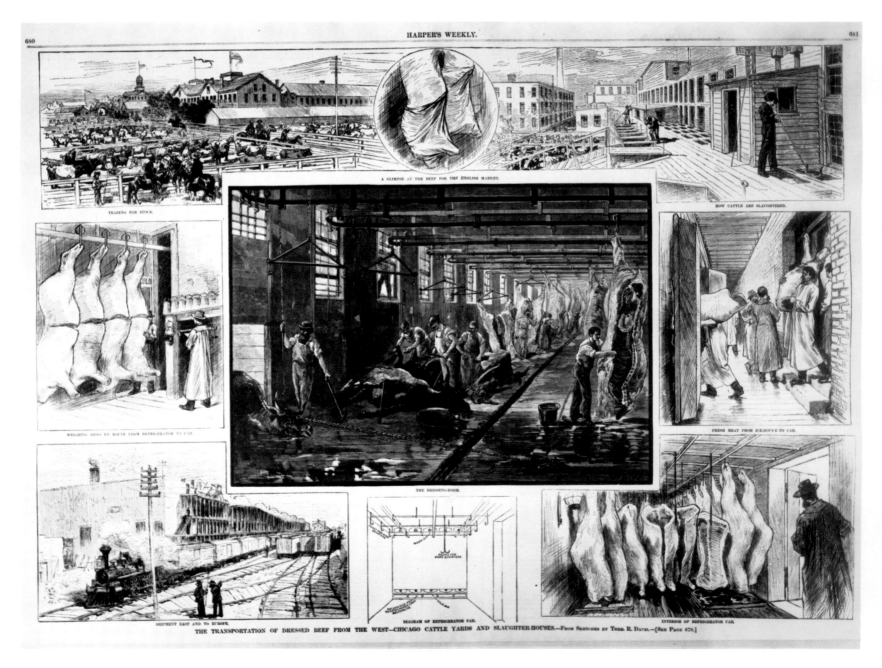

HISTORIC SKETCHES

OF THE

CATTLE TRADE

OF THE

WEST AND SOUTHWEST.

By JOSEPH G. McCOY,

THE PIONEER WESTERN CATTLE SHIPPER.

ILLUSTRATED BY PROF. HENRY WORRALL, TOPEKA, KAS.
ENGRAVED BY BAKER & CO., CHICAGO, ILL.
ELECTROTYPED BY J. T. RETON & CO., KANSAS CITY, MO.

PUBLISHED BY
RAMSEY, MILLETT & HUDSON, KANSAS CITY, MO.,
PRINTERS, BINDERS, ENGRAVERS, LITHOGRAPHERS & STATIONERS.
1874.

ABILENE IN ITS GLORY.

Abilene in Its Glory
Henry Worrall (1825–1902)
Woodcut after a drawing
In J. G. McCoy, *Historic Sketches of the Cattle Trade*, (Kansas City, Missouri: Ramsey, Millet & Hudson, 1874)
SF196.U5M3
Rare Book and Special Collections Division Library of Congress

THE BEEF BONANZA;

OR,

HOW TO GET RICH ON THE PLAINS.

BEING A DESCRIPTION OF

CATTLE-GROWING, SHEEP-FARMING, HORSE-RAISING,
AND DAIRYING

IN THE WEST.

BY

GEN. JAMES S. BRISBIN, U.S.A.,

AUTHOR OF "BELDEN, THE WHITE CHIEF," "LIFE OF GENERAL GRANT,"
"LIFE OF J. A. GARFIELD," "LIFE OF GEN. W. S. HANCOCK."

WITH ILLUSTRATIONS.

PHILADELPHIA:
J. B. LIPPINCOTT & CO.
LONDON: 16 SOUTHAMPTON ST., COVENT GARDEN.
1881.

"The Beef Bonanza; or, How to Get Rich on the Plains"
By James S. Brisbin (1837–1892)
Philadelphia: J. B. Lippincott & Co., 1881
   By 1881 the cattle boom had assumed such proportions that a flurry of books and pamphlets appeared to advise potential investors of the fortunes to be made in open-range ranching. Most of the writers overestimated the natural increase of cattle, underestimated the costs of ranching, and ignored the incidence of loss through sickness and natural disaster. James S. Brisbin's *Beef Bonanza* was one of the most optimistic, referring constantly to the alleged 25 percent annual profit that could be made. A table in the book purported to show how an initial investment of $25,000 would yield a net profit of $36,500 in five years.
SF51.B86
Rare Book and Special Collections Division Library of Congress

"Map of the United States Showing the Farm Animals in Each State"

Decatur, Illinois: H. W. Hill Co., 1878

During the late 1870s and early 1880s the northwestern range, a strip of land a thousand miles long and two hundred miles wide running east of the Rockies from Kansas to Montana, was opened to ranching and stocked with Texas cattle. In the same years, cattle from California ranges were driven into Nevada, Oregon, and Washington to stock ranges there. Thus the range cattle industry spread from California and Texas until 1885. It was estimated that there were 7.5 million cattle on the northwestern ranges alone. This 1878 map dramatically illustrates the beginning of this movement, with cattle appearing in Kansas, Colorado, and Nebraska east of the Rockies and Oregon and Nevada west of the Rockies.

Geography and Map Division
Library of Congress

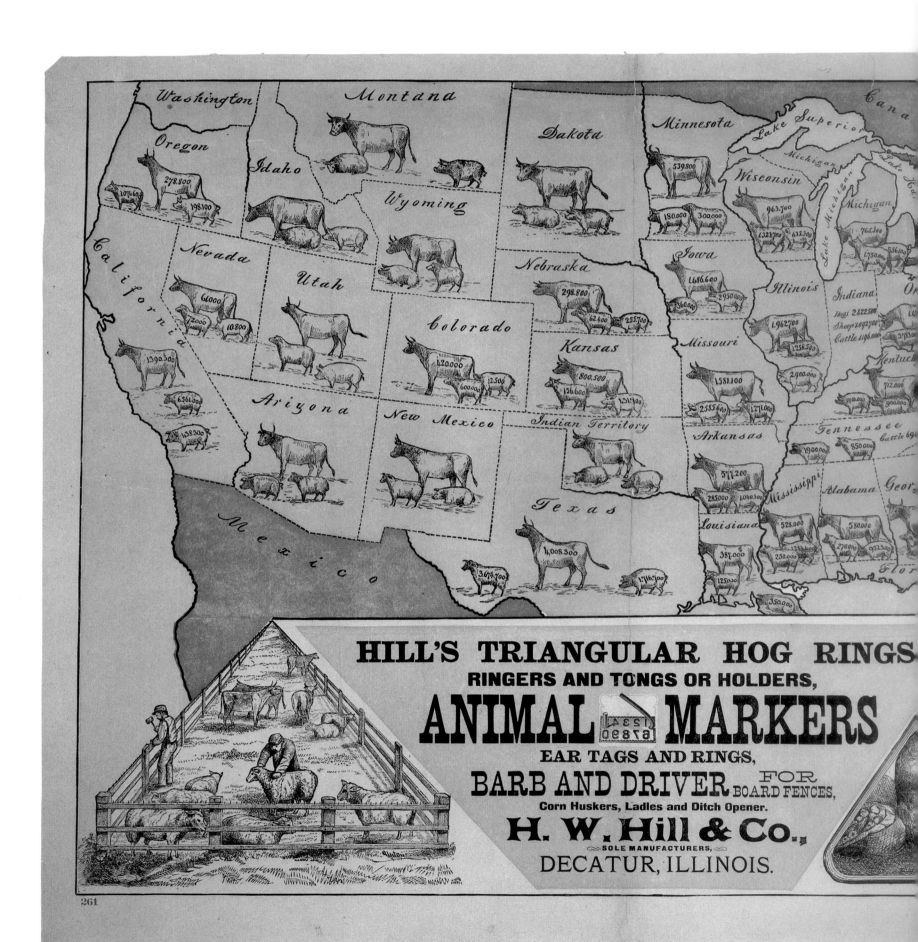

Chow Time
Charles Edward Morris (1876–1938)
Photograph, 1895
William A. Morris
(son of the photographer)
Yuma, Arizona

Covered Wagons on West Main Street, Miles City, Montana
Latcn Alton Huffmann (1854–1931)
Photograph, 1882

   As the northwestern ranges were stocked, cow towns like
Schuyler and Ogallala. Nebraska, and Pine Bluffs, Wyoming,
sprang up along the Union Pacific railroad line to serve as
shipping points. In the mid-1880s Miles City. Montana, on the
Northern Pacific Railroad, was the main shipping point for the
northern end of the Wyoming and Montana ranges. These ranges
were generally much larger than the southern ones, and their
roundup camps were more elaborate, with cook tents furnished
with iron stoves.
L. A. Huffmann Collection
Montana Historical Society
Helena, Montana

The cowboy's yearly round involved a spring roundup, during which calves were branded and stock to be sold during the summer was cut out of the herd, a summer or early fall trail drive to the nearest shipping point or delivery point, and a fall roundup. During a roundup, cowboys from neighboring ranches worked together to gather all the cattle in a particular district, separate them into herds belonging to individual ranches, and brand, earmark, and castrate the calves in each herd. A large spring roundup was a great social occasion and might involve wagons from a dozen ranches and a hundred or more cowboys.

"Cowboy Camp during the Roundup"
Charles M. Russell (1864–1926)
Oil on canvas, 1887

One of Charles Russell's first paintings was of the camp for the Judith Basin roundup at the edge of the fledgling town of Utica, Montana. The cowboys, who are camped in Sibley tents and wall tents, have just caught their horses for the morning's work. The horse herd, or *remuda*, consisting of six or seven horses for each man, is being driven out to pasture for the day. Instead of a chuck wagon, a cook tent has been set up near the town well, and the cook stands under the open flap. In the background, groups of cowboys lounge in front of two of Utica's four saloons. This picture was painted to hang in one of these saloons, and it delighted the Judith Basin cowboys, who could identify every man and every horse in it.
Amon Carter Museum
Fort Worth, Texas

Breakfast in a Roundup Camp on the Bar CC, Texas

Andrew Alexander Forbes (1862–1921)

Photograph, ca. 1885

At almost the same time that Russell painted the Judith Basin roundup camp, A. A. Forbes photographed a roundup camp in the Texas Panhandle. The Sibley tents are present, but the cook is operating from a chuck wagon, with its many-compartmented chuck box set up on the tailgate and its water barrel lashed to the side. His pots and dutch ovens have been set up over an open fire, and the horse herd has been brought up and penned in a rope corral.

Western History Collections
University of Oklahoma Library
Norman, Oklahoma

C. D. KIRKLAND,   PHOTOGRAPHER,   CHEYENNE, WYO.

C. D. KIRKLAND,   PHOTOGRAPHER,   CHEYENNE, WYO.

Roping ponies

Charles D. Kirkland (1851–1926)

Photograph, ca. 1890

   The day's work on a roundup started with each hand roping his horse from the remuda. Once mounted, the men worked in pairs, riding to the edge of the range and then working their way back toward the center, gathering loose cattle and driving them before them. When all the cattle on a range had been gathered into a herd, the work of roping and branding could begin.

Wyoming State Archives
Museums and Historical Department
Cheyenne, Wyoming

General View of Roundup

Charles D. Kirkland (1851–1926)

Photograph, Wyoming, ca. 1890

   Scattered bunches of cattle, which have been gathered on the edge of the range, are being driven in toward the main herd in the foreground. The cowboys with the main herd are holding it together.

Wyoming State Archives
Museums and Historical Department
Cheyenne, Wyoming

Moving Camp

Andrew Alexander Forbes (1862–1921)

Photograph, Texas-Oklahoma Panhandle area, ca. 1885

   When camp was moved, the tents and bedrolls were loaded on the chuck wagon and the cook was sent to make camp at a new location while the day's work went on. Here we see the bedrolls, which consisted of a canvas outer cover, called a "suggin," and a feather comforter, sometimes jocularly referred to as a "hen-skin blanket," ready to be loaded. The black man on foot, wearing suspenders, is probably the cook and wagon-driver.

Western History Collections
University of Oklahoma Library
Norman, Oklahoma

"The Big Four Brand Book . . . for the Spring Work of 1897"
By Charles V. Shepler
Kansas City, Missouri: C. V. Shepler, 1897(?)

   Once rounded up, the cattle were cut into smaller herds according to their brands, which signified their ownership. Since ownership of the brands themselves changed frequently, brand books listing the current owners and showing the position of the brand on the cow, as well as the earmarks used, were issued regularly by cattlemen's associations. The books were printed in a size that fit conveniently into a rider's vest pocket.
SF103.S54
General Collections
Library of Congress

"Brand Book Containing the Brands of the Bent County Cattle and Horse Growers' Association for the Year of 1885"
Las Animas, Colorado: Printed at the Leader Office, 1885
SF103.B47
General Collections
Library of Congress

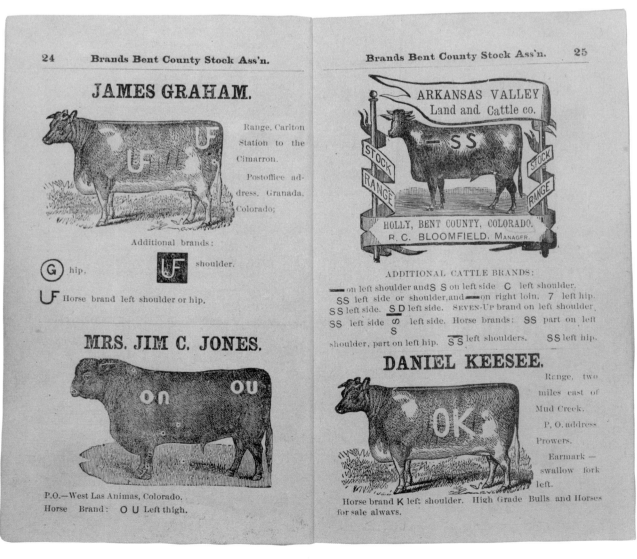

Cutting Out
Dragging a Calf from the Herd
Branding on the Prairie
Charles D. Kirkland (1851–1926)
Photographs, Wyoming, ca. 1890
    In this remarkable series of photographs,
C. D. Kirkland shows a cowboy cutting a cow
and her calf out of the main herd in order to
brand the calf with its mother's brand. In the
second photo, the calf has been roped and is
being dragged to the branding crew, and the
third photo shows the crew at work.
Wyoming State Archives
Museums and Historical Department
Cheyenne, Wyoming

"2h" Branding Iron
Registered July 7, 1874, in Wharton County, Texas,
by A. R. Hudgins
Used by Will Border, Hungerford, Texas, 1936
Dallas Historical Society
Dallas, Texas

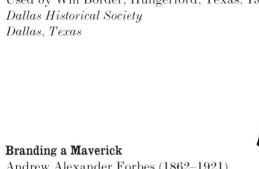

Branding a Maverick
Andrew Alexander Forbes (1862–1921)
Photograph, Texas-Oklahoma panhandle area, 1890s
   Branding crews hunting unbranded calves on the range
sometimes used running irons. These irons, either short curved
irons or circular ones, were used to draw any brand on the calf.
They were light enough to be tied to a saddle and eliminated the
necessity of carrying a number of different stamp irons. Here two
cowboys have roped a maverick and one has dismounted to brand
it with a circular running iron held between two sticks. Since no
branding fire is in evidence, the picture may have been posed for
the photographer.
Western History Collections
University of Oklahoma Library
Norman, Oklahoma

"Hog Eye" Branding Iron
Registered 1908 in Shackelford County
by John and Kathryn Honeycutt

"So far as we know, we are the only people in Texas to run the 'Hog-Eye' brand. . . . I resolved . . . to start that brand for a little red-headed girl and myself when I came back to Texas. . . . I thought then and I still think it a very noticeable and distinct brand. This brand . . . means far more to us than just something to distinguish our cattle. It is a symbol of a partnership between a man and his wife who both love their cows and their country." (John Honeycutt, Texas Centennial Exposition, 1936)
Dallas Historical Society
Dallas, Texas

The Becker Sisters Branding Calves
O. T. Davis (1840–1894)
Photograph, Walsenburg, Colorado, 1894

Although cowgirls were an invention of the Wild West shows, women did do outdoor ranch work, especially when there were no men around to do it. On the Becker ranch in the San Luis Valley of Colorado, the three Becker sisters worked alongside their father. Two of them eventually married ranchers and the third inherited her father's ranch.
Colorado Historical Society
Denver, Colorado

SCENE AT A SAN LOU'S VALLY CATTLE RANCH

Once cattle were rounded up, cut into herds, and branded, they were driven overland to market. The most famous trail drives were those from Texas to the railheads in Kansas, which lasted from six weeks to two months. Drives from Texas to the northwest ranges might last six months. One cowboy of the 1870s described such a drive as "an endless grind of worry and anxiety which only a strong physical frame could stand."

The Herd Strung Out on the Move
Erwin E. Smith (1888–1947)
Photograph, 1910
   Although there seem to be no surviving photographs of trail herds on the move during the years of the cattle boom, a series of pictures made by Texas photographer Erwin E. Smith on the Matador Ranch in the Texas Panhandle in the early 1900s captures some of the atmosphere of a long drive. This particular herd was being driven about a hundred miles to a shipping point at Lubbock, Texas.
Erwin E. Smith Collection
Prints and Photographs Division
Library of Congress

"Guide Map of the Best and Shortest Cattle Trail to the Kansas Pacific Railway: With a Concise and Accurate Description of the Route Showing Distances, Streams, Crossings, Camping Grounds, Wood and Water, Supply Stores, Etc. from the Red River Crossing to Ellis, Russell, Ellsworth, Brookville, Sabina, Solomon, and Abilene"
Kansas City: Kansas Pacific Railway Company, 1875
   By 1875, when the Kansas Pacific Railway published and distributed this map to ranchers and trail drivers, a network of trails led from the cattle ranges of Texas to the Red River, where they converged to form the Chisholm Trail, which led to Abilene and Ellsworth, Kansas. One hundred and fifty thousand cattle were driven up this trail by trailing contractors in 1875; the next year, twice that number made the trip. By 1877, a second trail, the Western Trail, had been blazed along the ninety-ninth meridian to Dodge City, Kansas, far enough west to avoid the farming settlements that had grown up around Abilene and Ellsworth. The western trail was used until 1885, when stock quarantine laws and the extension of railroads into Texas ended the Texas cattle drives.
Eugene C. Barker Texas History Center
The University of Texas at Austin
Austin, Texas

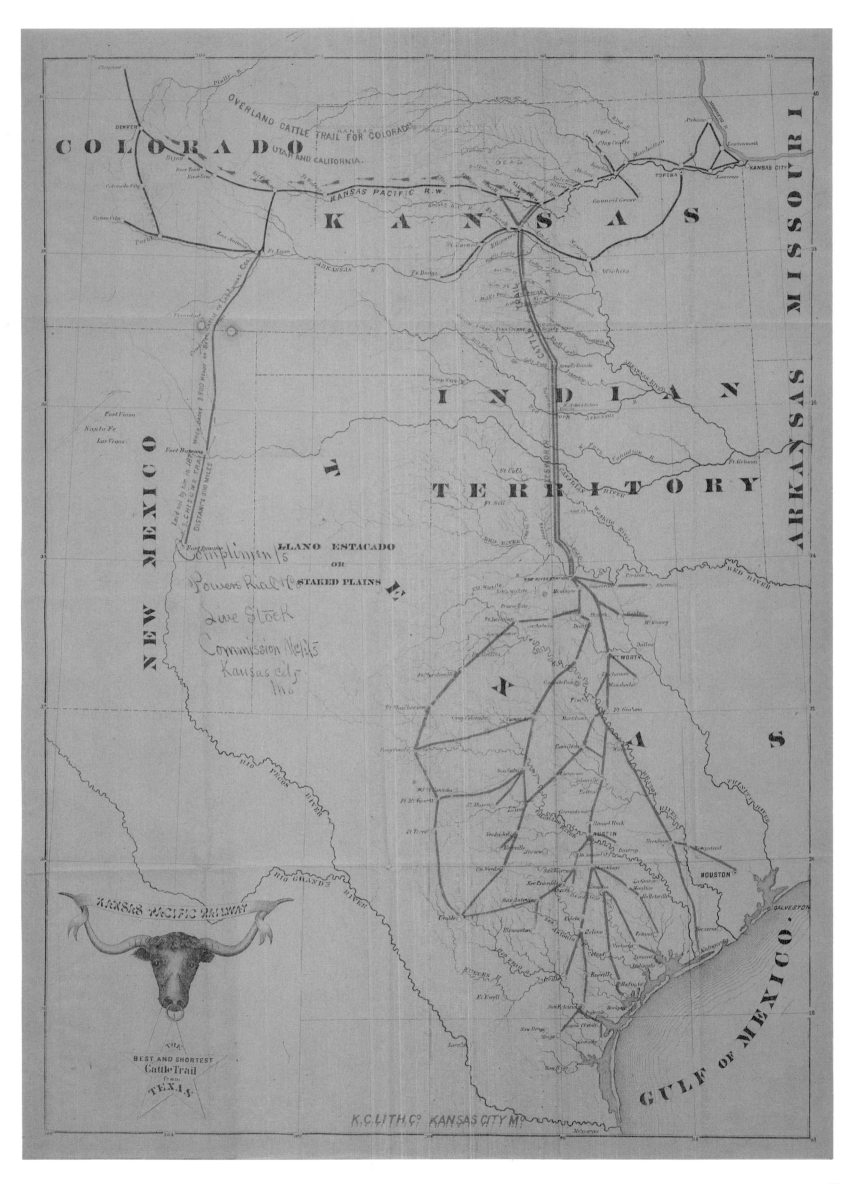

**Drag Riders at the Rear of the Herd Keeping
the Slowest Cattle Moving**
Erwin E. Smith (1888–1947)
Photograph, Matador Ranch, Texas, 1910
Erwin E. Smith Collection
Prints and Photographs Division
Library of Congress

**The Matador Horse Herd on a Well-Worn
Cattle Trail**
Erwin E. Smith (1888–1947)
Photograph, Matador Ranch, Texas, 1910
Erwin E. Smith Collection
Prints and Photographs Division
Library of Congress

**Cowboys Celebrating after Delivery of a Herd
to the Loading Pens**
Erwin E. Smith (1888–1947)
Photograph, Lubbock, Texas, 1907
Erwin E. Smith Collection
Prints and Photographs Division
Library of Congress

On the trail, the chuck wagon was the center of the cowboy's life. Albert Thompson, who trailed cattle from New Mexico to Montana in the 1880s, described this wonderful invention: "It contained the needs—and much of the worldly goods of the dozen or more men who went along with it . . . . Usually a large wagon, often a Shuttler, was used. At the rear end of this was a chuck box, an upright cabinet with its front on hinges which, when let down, formed a table. On top of the chuck box was the potrack in which all the sheet-iron kettles and generous coffee pot were carried, while beneath was the potbox, where the dutch ovens found places. Within this chuck box were compartments and drawers for the reception of bread, plates, cups, knives, forks, and spoons. One drawer was reserved for the exclusive use of the wagon boss. In this were kept his papers, brand book, and other chattels.

Compartments, too, for cans holding sugar and syrup were also in evidence. . . . on one side of the wagon between the wheels the water barrel was held in place. . . . Often camping places were made near some surface water which, though it could be used for cooking, was unfit for drinking. Within the wagon were flour, grain for the mules, camp beds, rope for lariats and staking purposes, wood for the cook's use, canned tomatoes, canned corn, and dried fruit. On the side of the chuck box was fastened a mirror before which the cowboy performed his brief toilet."

Cowboys and Chuck Wagon Currycomb Outfit
Andrew Alexander Forbes (1862–1921)
Photograph, Texas-Oklahoma Panhandle area, ca. 1885
Western History Collections
University of Oklahoma Library
Norman, Oklahoma

Making Pies
Charles D. Kirkland (1851–1926)
Photograph, ca. 1890
Wyoming State Archives
Museums and Historical Department
Cheyenne, Wyoming

The equipment of the nineteenth-century cowboy was a blend of Mexican and Anglo-American forms which first evolved in Texas and was then modified by the practices of the northwestern ranges. The Texas saddle was a modification of the Mexican vaquero's saddle; it retained the horn, which was used for securing the lariat, but it added an extra cinch. Unlike modern saddles, it had a high cantle behind the seat and a narrow fork in front. The stirrups were usually wooden, and their width reflected the Mexican influence. The lariat, made from several plaited strands of rawhide, was also borrowed from the vaquero, as were leather chaps, used to protect the legs when working in brushy country. The Anglo cowboy's spurs, however, were much smaller than the vaquero's. Rawhide hobbles, used to keep horses from wandering at night, were Mexican in origin and were the unmistakable badge of the Texas cowboy. Plaited horsehair ropes, bridles, and reins were also Mexican in origin, but many Anglo cowboys learned the craft of weaving horsehair.

Lariat
Owned by Col. Charles Goodnight
Rawhide, ca. 1866
Panhandle-Plains Historical Museum
Canyon, Texas

Chuck Box
Wood, 1866
    Charles Goodnight (1836–1929), the first rancher on the high plains of Texas and a legendary figure among cattlemen, is credited with inventing the chuck wagon. This chuck box was built in 1866 to his specifications and was used for many years on the T. S. Bugbee ranch in west Texas.
Panhandle-Plains Historical Museum
Canyon, Texas

Hobble
Rawhide, 1880
Panhandle-Plains Historical Museum
Canyon, Texas

Western Stock Saddle
Used on XIT, LE, and Other Texas Panhandle
Ranches
J. Porter and Sons, Graham, Texas
Leather, late 1880s–early 1890s
Panhandle-Plains Historical Museum
Canyon, Texas

Pair of OK-Style Spurs with Leathers
Steel and leather, ca. 1870–80
Panhandle-Plains Historical Museum
Canyon, Texas

Pair of Shotgun Chaps
Leather, undated
Panhandle-Plains Historical Museum
Canyon, Texas

Bridle
Leather, ca. 1890–1900
Panhandle-Plains Historical Museum
Canyon, Texas

Lead Rope
Horsehair, ca. 1895
Panhandle-Plains Historical Museum
Canyon, Texas

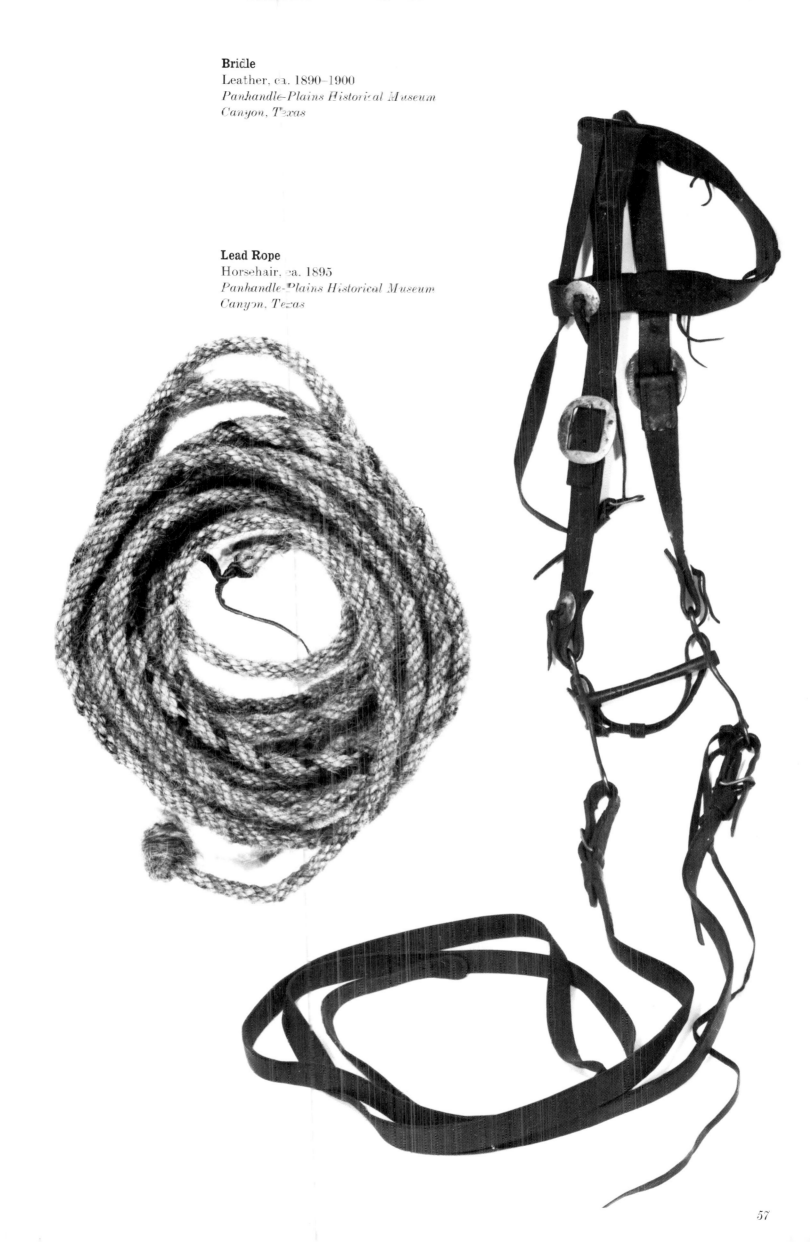

THE END OF THE OPEN RANGE

The cattle boom of the 1880s ended in disaster. Rising beef prices led to the overstocking of the range, and by the summer of 1886 there was simply not enough grass to feed the millions of cattle that were strung from Texas to Saskatchewan. The winter of 1886 dealt the range cattle industry a death blow. Deep snows and heavy winds were followed by the lowest temperatures ever recorded in the northwestern ranges. In Montana and Wyoming alone nearly half a million cattle died. The remainder were dumped on the market in poor condition the next spring, and the falling prices ruined the ranchers who had not been wiped out the previous winter.

When the ranching industry reorganized, cattle were no longer run on the open range but were kept in fenced pastures and fed during the winter. Barbed wire made effective pasture fencing possible and became symbolic of the changes that were taking place in the ranching industry. The day of the open-range cowboy was over, but his existence as a mythological hero was just beginning.

"Waiting for a Chinook"
Charles M. Russell (1864–1926)
Watercolor on paper, 1886

The winter of 1886 began on the Montana range with a week of slow rain. Then the temperature dropped below zero, covering all vegetation with ice. Two feet of snow fell. Cattle were helpless and could not find feed. A warm southern wind, called a chinook, would have melted the snow and allowed the cattle to graze, but none came, and the snow remained on the ground for eight weeks. Two hundred thousand Montana range cattle died from starvation.

At the time, Charles M. Russell was working as a cowboy on Jesse Phelps's OH Ranch. Phelps received a letter from Louis Kaufman, one of Montana's most prominent cattlemen, asking how the cattle on Phelps's range were doing. Russell painted this small watercolor to enclose in Phelps's reply and wrote "Waiting for a chinook" on it. When Phelps saw the picture, he tore up his letter and sent Kaufman the picture instead. The cow in the picture is a Bar R cow, one of Kaufman's brands.

In later years, this became one of Russell's best known pictures. The artist eventually did a larger version in watercolor, entitled *The Last of Five Thousand*, which has been reproduced many times.
Montana Stockgrowers Association
Helena, Montana

To many westerners, barbed wire symbolized the end of the open range and the modernization of the cattle industry. It was invented in the early 1870s in response to the need for fencing on the treeless prairies of the Midwest. One of the first manufacturers—and certainly the most successful—was J. F. Glidden of De Kalb, Illinois, who formed a partnership with I. L. Ellwood and Company. That firm eventually became the American Steel and Wire Company. Glidden produced ten thousand pounds of barbed wire in 1874. By 1880 his De Kalb factory was turning out eighty million pounds a year. Barbed wire enabled the rancher to segregate his cattle and improve their breed—and to control their consumption of grass. It changed the open-range country into the big pasture country.

Barbed Wire:
Kelly, 1868 (*top*)
Haish, 1875 (*center*)
Glidden, 1876 (*bottom*)
Gift of Charles Dalton
Copperas Cove, Texas

Glidden Steel Barb Wire
Artist unknown
Lithograph, ca. 1876
Shober & Carqueville Lith. Co., Chicago
Poster Plus
Chicago, Illinois

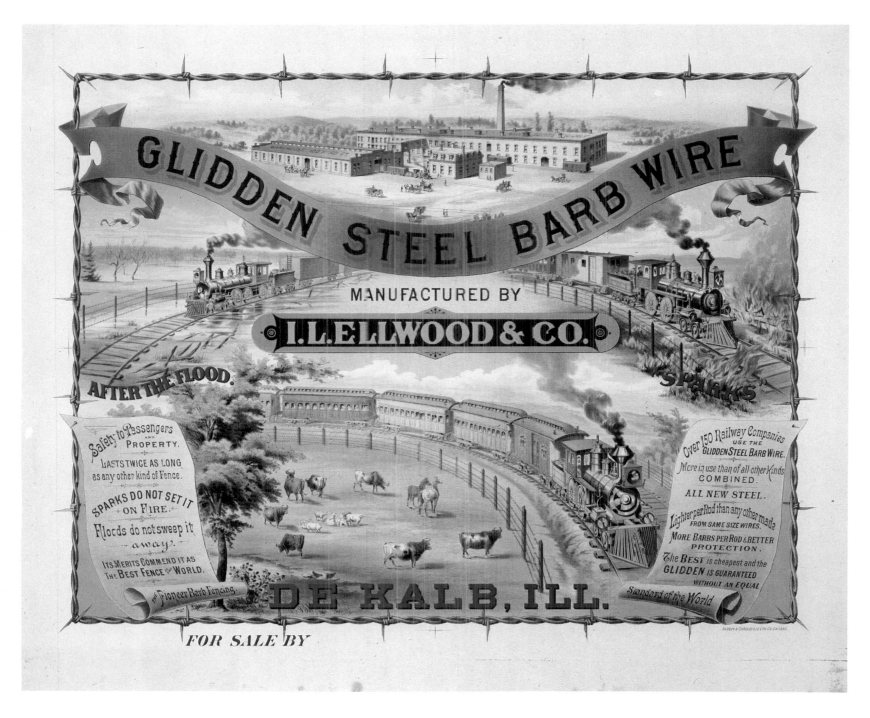

"The Fall of the Cowboy"
Frederic Remington (1861–1909)
Oil on canvas, 1895
    The barbed-wire fence did much to help the rancher hold his
cattle on their own range, and it enabled him to improve his
breed. But the cowboy regarded barbed wire and its rail gaps
as a nuisance that hindered his free passage over the plains.
Romantics like Frederic Remington, who idealized the cowboy's
freedom, saw it as a symbol of the end of the cowboy life they
admired. Remington painted this scene as an illustration for
Owen Wister's article "The Evolution of the Cowpuncher" in
Harper's Monthly Magazine, September 1895.
Amon Carter Museum
Fort Worth, Texas

LAZOOING A HORSE ON THE PRAIRIE

Eng.d by J.T.Hammon

THE COWBOY HERO: AN AMERICAN MYTH EXAMINED

Lonn Taylor

During the middle years of the nineteenth century—the four decades divided by the Civil War—a series of changes took place that profoundly altered the fabric of everyday life in America and, consequently, the way in which Americans thought about their country and its future. During those forty years, a federation of states in which life for most people was rural and agrarian became a nation whose future was irrevocably urban and industrial. This transformation, which was accelerated enormously by the war itself, was characterized by the increasing concentration of the population in urban centers, by the spread of a railroad network which linked those centers to each other and to their rural hinterlands in an interdependent economic system, and by the rise of gigantic manufacturing industries which provided that system's life's blood in the form of jobs, income, and durable goods. Within a lifetime, a pastoral nation became an industrial one, or, as we might say today, an underdeveloped nation became developed.

These changes meant that an American who had reached the age of seventy in 1890 could look backward over a youth spent in the bustling days of the Jacksonian republic; an early manhood observing, and probably participating in, the exuberant expansion of the nation from sea to sea; and a middle age marked by the sectional crises of the 1850s and the bloody horror of the Civil War. He could look forward to spending his remaining years in a country dominated by industrial monopolies, torn by open warfare between factory owners and workers, and flooded with immigrants from places he had not even imagined the existence of, who lived in slums and toiled from dawn to dusk in mills, mines, and factories.

The condition of the working class in post-Civil War America was especially bad. The Jeffersonian ideal of a nation of independent farmers had somehow gone awry. Farmers all over the nation, but especially in the South, slipped into tenancy and debt in the 1870s and 1880s. Industrial workers had even less hope of advancement and independence. In 1869 Wendell Phillips described American industrial workers as a class "that only rises to toil and lies down to rest. It is lifted by no hope, mellowed by no comfort; looks into gardens it created, and up to wealth it has garnered, and has no pleasure there; looks down into its cradle . . . there is no hope."[1]

Suddenly, in the mid-eighties, a new Jeffersonian figure burst upon America: the cowboy. As pictured in the illustrated press in the mid-eighties, he was young, heroic, independent, and relentlessly Anglo-Saxon. It is easy now, with the hindsight of a century later, to see him as yet another manifestation of that old American western hero Leatherstocking, who appeared over and over throughout the nineteenth century to glorify and explain the West, but to Americans a century ago the cowboy embodied all of the old American values, emergent once more in a new form at a time of national despair. An anonymous writer in *Harper's* summed

up the apparent contrast between the dismal realities of industrial capitalism and the cowboy's life:

The herding and breeding of cattle . . . is . . . the primitive scriptural occupation, the grand, independent, health-giving, out-of-door existence, the praises of which have been sung through all the ages. To how many a pale, thin, hard-working city dweller does the thought of "the cattle on a thousand hills," the rare dry air of the elevated plateaus and the continuing and ennobling sight of the mighty mountains bring strangely vivid emotions and longings?[2]

The first flush of the cowboy's popularity came in the 1890s, and he was endowed by his eastern admirers with all the virtues of the Progressive movement. The first mythical cowboy was manly, self-reliant, virtuous, competitive (but always fair), a free agent in the labor market, dependent only on his own skills for employment, and, above all, 100 percent Anglo-Saxon, embodying all of the alleged virtuous characteristics of that ethnic group. Once established in this manner, the mythical cowboy hero became a medium through which America's own changing social values were displayed. In the 1920s, the decade of craziness, he became a daredevil entertainer, both on the screen and, as rodeo became a national spectator sport, in the flesh—riding, roping, shooting, and, as films acquired sound, singing. In the depression-ridden thirties he became an escapist fantasy: a crooner in a fringed shirt and tooled boots, singing about a never-never land where tumbleweeds tumbled and the water was always clear and cool. In the 1940s and 1950s, as juvenile audiences swelled, he became a surrogate parent. In the 1960s and 1970s he became a corporate spokesman. We have yet to see what new forms he will take in the 1980s and 1990s.

It is hard to conceive of a time when cowboys did not occupy a niche in the average American's set of mental stereotypes, but during the first years of the cattle boom, the late 1860s and early 1870s, easterners were only dimly aware of the cowboy as a personage. Their impressions of him were vague and sometimes contradictory. It was not until the mid-1880s that these impressions began to coalesce into the single well-defined image of the cowboy hero. This heroic image first appeared in the popular press at the same time that corporate investment in the open-range cattle industry reached its peak, and it was refined in the 1890s, the years immediately following the collapse of the boom, when the cowboy, like the Indian, was thought of as a vanishing American.

Before this image coalesced, Americans got their impressions of the cowboy from a variety of sources: travel literature, dime novels, frontier melodramas, Wild West shows, and popular illustrated periodicals like the *Police Gazette* and *Frank Leslie's*. The strongest and most prevalent of these images, up to the mid-eighties, was an

1. Wendell Phillips, *Speeches, Letters, and Lectures*, 2d ser. (Boston: Lee & Shepard, 1905), p. 166.
2. *Harper's New Monthly Magazine* 59, no. 354 (November 1879): 878.

extremely negative one fostered by the illustrated press: the average cowboy was a drunken, rowdy, dangerous individual, usually a Texan, whose occupation was very close to criminal activity.

The very word *cowboy* had pejorative connotations before the Civil War. In the 1830s it was applied to gangs of Anglo-Americans in Texas who specialized in stealing cattle from Mexican ranches. James Harper Starr, a Connecticut Yankee who came to Texas in 1837 to practice medicine and stayed to become secretary of the treasury of the bankrupt republic, used the word in 1839 to record in his journal an encounter with "a company of Texas cowboys" who had stolen hundreds of cattle, mules, and horses from "the inoffensive inhabitants of Chihuahua." Fifteen years later Charles W. Webber described a character in *Tales of the Southern Border* as "a cattle-driver; or 'cow-boy,' as those men are and were termed who drove in the cattle of the Mexican rancheros of the Rio Grande border, either by stealth or by plundering and murdering the herdsmen! They were, in short, considered as banditti before the revolution, and have been properly considered so since. This term 'cow-boy' was even then—and still more emphatically, later—one name for many crimes."[3]

After the Civil War, when the great cattle drives to Kansas began and cowboys first came in contact with illustrators and writers for the eastern press, they kept this reputation for bad character, which was undoubtedly exaggerated and sensationalized by the press. During the late 1870s and early 1880s virtually every issue of the *National Police Gazette* and *Frank Leslie's Illustrated Weekly* carried at least one woodcut illustration purporting to represent an actual incident somewhere in the West, showing cowboys engaging in reckless, lawless, and frequently murderous behavior (p. 000). In some of the woodcuts the cowboys are merely being drunkenly frolicsome, but the texts accompanying the woodcuts made it clear that the activities pictured were reprehensible. *Frank Leslie's* of January 14, 1882, told its readers:

> *The cowboy of the great cattle ranges is a distinct genus. . . . he enters upon his business in life when he is seven years old. His pet is his horse, his toy a revolver. When off duty cowboys are a terror in the way they manifest their exuberance of spirits. Two or three will dash through a town, and before the people know what is going on will have robbed every store . . . and made their escape. They practice a kind of guerilla warfare during their brief and infrequent holidays in the towns. . . . Two have defied successfully a dozen constables, and a score could circumvent an entire company of militia.[4]*

The caption below a woodcut of two innocuous-looking cowboys published the next year left no doubt about *Frank Leslie's* opinion on cowboys in general: "Morally, as a class, they are foul-mouthed, drunken, lecherous, utterly corrupt. Usually harmless on the plains when sober, they are dreaded in the towns, for then liquor has the ascendency over them."[5]

Taken as a whole, this group of woodcuts—and there are literally hundreds of them—first portray the cowboy stereotypes that continued to appear in fiction, on stage, and in films up through the 1930s, and in some cases up to the present. We see cowboys riding horses into saloons; galloping down the streets of small towns, pistols blazing; shooting at the feet of traveling salesmen to make them dance; disrupting theatrical performances; and generally behaving in a reckless, rowdy, and unbecoming manner. Their context, mixed in among illustrations of child-murderers, wife-beaters, bank robbers, and occasional boxers, jockeys, and actresses, makes it clear that the editors and their readers regarded the cowboy as part of the fringes of society, if not the underworld. Yet these woodcuts, nearly all of them anonymous, are the direct ancestors of the romantic and idealized illustrations of Frederic Remington, Frank Tenney Johnson, Maynard Dixon, and their followers. They are the original western art.

The first American encounter with the cowboy, however, occurred in the 1830s and was part of the much larger encounter with the Spanish Southwest that took place in the third and fourth decades of the nineteenth century, and the first cowboys that Americans came to know were the Spanish-Mexican vaqueros of Texas and California. Their exotic costume, their superb horsemanship, and their skill with the lasso made an enormous impression on those who saw them, an impression that made its mark on visual representations and literary descriptions of the cowboy well into the 1880s.

The vaquero was first dimly perceived as a horse-hunter, a shadowy figure associated with the vast herds of wild horses that roamed the western prairies. First described by Washington Irving in *A Tour of the Prairies* (1832), these herds and the horse-hunters who followed them became a staple of every popular description of the West that followed. As American colonists pushed into Mexican Texas, they met vaqueros face to face. In 1834 the anonymous author of *A Visit to Texas* not only described the mustangs and the mustangers, he also provided a sketch to accompany his description (p. 000). That sketch, in the form of a woodcut, is probably the first American illustration of a southwestern cowboy. It shows two men on horseback, both wearing low-crowned hats and one clad in the short breeches and white leggings of the early nineteenth-century Mexican horseman. The vaquero has just roped a mustang; his lasso is taut and his horse squatting against the impact. The other rider is swinging a large loop over his head. The accompanying text explains:

> The small horses of the country, called mustangs, introduced by the Spaniards, and now numerous in the more northern prairies, run wild in droves over these parts of Texas, and are easily taken and rendered serviceable to the inhabitants. . . . This is done with a strong noosed cord, made of twisted strips of rawhide, and called a lazo, which is the Spanish word for band or bond. It has often been described, as well as the manner of throwing it, as it is in common use for catching animals, and sometimes for choking men, in the different parts of America inhabited by the descendents of the Spanish and Portugese.[6]

The lasso and its use seemed to fascinate observers as much as the vaquero himself, as it was a peculiarly Hispanic tool, its use unknown to Anglo-Americans until they crossed the Mississippi. It even insinuated itself into decorative art. At least four English potteries in the 1850s produced a china pattern intended for the American market showing a vaquero lassoing a horse or a bull. In the 1870s and 1880s, the image of the vaquero was frequently used in advertising, usually either for leather products or to indicate durability (pp. 82–83). The lariat was always a prominent part of the design, as were the broad-brimmed hat and short jacket. So deeply rooted in popular consciousness was the image that in 1887, at least a decade after realistic illustrations of Anglo-American cowboys had begun to appear, a Texan penman advertised his skill with a trade card showing a "Cow Boy" horseman in full vaquero dress even though the calligrapher lived in Gainesville, Texas, on the edge of the cattle country, and must have had the opportunity to observe the dress of Anglo-American cowboys almost daily (p. 81).

It was the California hide trade that brought the vaquero into his own as a recognizable figure with decidedly romantic associations. The trade began in the early 1820s, when Boston traders discovered that California rancheros would pay high prices in hides from their immense herds of cattle in return for manufactured goods, but it was not until the publication of Richard Henry Dana's popular *Two Years before the Mast* in 1840 that the general public began to have a clear idea of the hide trade or of the California ranches that supplied it, and of the vaqueros that roped and slaughtered the cattle on them. Dana described the dress of the ranchero and his vaqueros, consisting of a

> broad-brimmed hat, usually of a black or dark brown color, with a gilt or figured band around the crown, and lined under the rim with silk; a short jacket of silk or figured calico . . . the shirt open in the neck; rich waistcoat, if any; pantaloons open at the sides below the knee, laced with gilt, usually of velveteen or broadcloth; or else short breeches or white stockings. . . . They have no suspenders, but always wear a sash around the waist, which is generally red, and varying in quality with the means of the wearer. Add to this the never-failing poncho, or serape, and you have the dress of the Californian.

In a later passage Dana remarked on the horsemanship of the California vaqueros, saying, "they are put upon a horse when only four or five years old, their little legs not long enough to come halfway over his sides, and may be said to keep on him until they have grown to him. . . . They can hardly go from one house to another without mounting a horse."

By the end of the Civil War the vaquero had become a symbol for the old Spanish days in California, already invested with an aura of romanticism. The publication of Helen Hunt Jackson's novel of Spanish California, *Ramona*, in 1884, gave the vaquero a renewed symbolic life, but by then a new image of the cowboy had begun to coalesce, and the two went their separate ways.

In 1872 easterners got a chance to see an Anglo-American cowboy in the flesh, if only as an adjunct to a frontier melodrama. That fall the impresario Ned Buntline engaged a Virginian named John Burwell Omohundro, Jr., who had gone West after serving in Jeb Stuart's cavalry, to play Texas Jack in his three-act melodrama *The Scouts of the Prairie, or Red Deviltry As It Is*. Dressed as a scout or buffalo hunter, Texas Jack exploited the cowboy's peculiar tool, the lasso, on stage.

Omohundro had worked as a cowboy in Texas, had gone to Kansas on a trail drive, and was employed by the army as a scout at Fort McPherson. In the winter of 1870–71 he served with William F. Cody as a hunting guide for the earl of Dunraven, who described Jack as "tall and lithe, with light-brown close-cropped hair, clear laughing honest blue eyes, and a soft and winning smile. . . . [He] might have sat as a model for a typical modern Anglo-Saxon."[7] Cody was already a person of some note, having distinguished himself as an army scout, hunting guide, and buffalo hunter. He shared billing with Omohundro in *The Scouts of the Prairie* and later took over the troupe from Buntline. A third member of the cast was an Italian dancer named Giuseppina Morlacchi, who played the part of Dove Eye, an Indian maiden, who before the theater season was several months old married Texas Jack.

Buntline's play opened in Chicago in December 1872 and traveled to Saint Louis, Cincinnati, Rochester, Buffalo, Boston, and New York. No script has survived, but from a synopsis published in a New York paper it would appear that it was a thinly plotted series of skits, including a temperance lecture by Buntline, some shooting tricks, several Indian dances, a knife fight, a

3. Charles W. Webber, *Tales of the Southern Border* (Philadelphia: Lippincott, Grambo, & Co., 1853), p. 124.
4. "A Common Incident in Southwestern Life—The Capture of a Texas Town by Cowboys," *Frank Leslie's Illustrated Weekly*, January 14, 1882, p. 347.
5. "Texas—Types of Cow-Boys on the Plains," *Frank Leslie's Illustrated Weekly*, December 1, 1883, p. 229.
6. *A Visit to Texas* (New York: Goodrich and Wiley, 1834), pp. 58–60.
7. Richard Henry Dana, *Two Years before the Mast* (New York: New American Library, 1964), pp. 73–74 and 81.

dramatic rescue, a prairie fire, and "Texas Jack and His Lasso." The play was a precursor of the Wild West show. Texas Jack was the first cowboy performer and the first cowboy to gain national attention. Buntline, who knew a good thing when he saw one, kept his stars before the public during the run of the play with a dime novel entitled *Texas Jack, or Buffalo Bill's Brother*, published by DeWitt's Ten Cent Romances, and a serial story in the *New York Weekly* called "Texas Jack, the White King of the Pawnees."

The Scouts of the Prairie was a great success, as were the plays that followed it—*The Scouts of the Plains*, *Texas Jack in the Black Hills*, and *The Trapper's Daughter*. Omohundro died in Leadville, Colorado, on June 28, 1880, but the name of Texas Jack was well-known enough in 1883 that Ned Buntline thought it would be profitable to entitle a dime novel *Texas Jack's Chums; or, The Whirlwind of the West*. In 1891 Prentiss Ingraham, another dime novel virtuoso, published *Texas Jack, the Mustang King*, and in 1900 Joel Chandler Harris used Texas Jack as the central character in a number of short stories about the Civil War. Today he is forgotten, but there is no doubt that he was the first cowboy star.

The popularity of the frontier melodrama continued through the 1870s and 1880s. Beginning in 1873, Cody's troupe, the Buffalo Bill Combination, took to the road each season with a new play. Some of his plays, like *The Red Right Hand, or, Buffalo Bill's First Scalp for Custer*, were based on Cody's roles in contemporary western events, although Cody himself remarked of this particular one that it was "a five-act play, without head or tail, and it made no difference at which act we commenced the performance."[8]

Cody was by no means the only producer of frontier melodramas, but his plays set a pattern for others, most of which emphasized the scout's and the miner's frontier—rather than the cattleman's—but nevertheless played an important role in preparing the public for the cowboy hero. These plays familiarized eastern audiences with western settings and characters. Since they were didactic, attempting to contrast certain types of behavior and, by doing so, teach a system of values as well as entertain, they spent virtually no time on character development but instead identified characters as good or bad by costuming, music, or even their names—a device that later made it much easier for the public to accept a completely untarnished cowboy hero. Finally, as theatrical historian Rosmarie Bank has shown, unlike most previous American plays, they were not about "the privileged few, but the ordinary and hard-working many." Thus, "the frontier character became a symbol for a whole range of social aspirations: the desire to begin again and to succeed solely on one's merits; the ability to contribute personally to national expansion and development; the opportunity for excitement along with one's daily toil."[9] All of these aspirations eventually came to be focused on the cowboy hero.

During the same decade that the frontier melodrama was bringing easterners the flavor of the West, an older medium was introducing them to the cowboy himself. The dime novel was the culmination of a publishing trend which began in the 1830s, when the introduction of the steam rotary press, combined with new techniques in marketing and distribution, made inexpensive popular literature possible. Its first form was the weekly story paper, followed in the 1840s and 1850s by fifteen- and twenty-cent novels published in series like *Ballou's Weekly Novelette* and *Gleason's Literary Companion*. In June 1860 the House of Beadle and Adams published the first dime novel, *Maleska, the Indian Wife of the White Hunter*, which sold 65,000 copies within the first few months. By 1870, there were six major dime novel publishers in the United States, each one churning out an enormous amount of fiction.

Not all dime novels were set in the trans-Mississippi West. In fact, in the majority of them the action took place in an unspecified eastern forest, on the high seas, or in some exotic tropical or Middle Eastern setting. Like melodramas, however, they dealt with basic social problems in a didactic and entertaining way and, as Daryl Emrys Jones has perceptively noted, the protagonist was usually a figure who stood outside society and thus could serve as both a critic and a righter of wrongs: a scout, guide, or horse-hunter living with the Indians, a pirate, a spy, or a soldier of fortune. Jones goes on to point out that many dime novels explore a theme common to later western novels: the relative desirability of life in a state of nature and life in society.[10] Obviously, as popular interest in the West increased, the cowboy became an ideal dime novel hero.

Since only a fraction of the dime novels published have survived, it is impossible to identify the first dime novel cowboy hero. A survey of titles copyrighted seems to indicate that cowboy protagonists appear as early as 1870, and that the hero of *Lasso Jack, or, The Morning Star of the Commanches* was certainly one of the earliest. Others were the heroes of *Night-Hawk Kit* (1871), *The Twin Trailers* (1872), and *Hurricane Bill* (1874). Few of these novels carried any real information about ranching or cowboys. In fact, many of them were closely related to the tales of James Fenimore Cooper and the large genre of Indian captivity literature that was popular before the Civil War. On the other hand, they do carry the germs of the western romance. In Arthur Holt's *Hotspur Harry: or, The Texan Trailers*,[11] for instance, Hotspur Harry Haven and his band of cowboys are out on a roundup when a group of Comanches attack their home ranch and carry off the owner's daughter, Bessie Burke. The Comanches are led by Gerald Gordon, a rejected suitor of Bessie's who has gone to live with the Indians and is appropriately called White Weasel. With the aid of a grizzled scout named Old Whirlwind, Harry and his cowboys trail White Weasel and Bessie to the Indian camp and rescue her, hiding her in a nearby cave. White Weasel recaptures her, however. Harry trails the two and finds them, but then all three are captured by the Lipan Indians, who burn White Weasel at the stake. They are about to do the same to Harry when he and Bessie are rescued by the cowboys. They return to the ranch, where Harry marries Bessie and soon becomes, in the author's words, "a wealthy and influential cattle-king."

While the stage, dime novels, and illustrated magazines introduced the East to the cowboy and began to sketch a character for him, it was Buffalo Bill's Wild West that brought actual cowboys East and coupled their name forever with reckless, hell-for-leather horseback riding and feats of skill and daring. It also changed our attitude about cowboys forever. First organized in 1882, and in many ways the outgrowth of his stage plays, Buffalo Bill's Wild West (the word *show* was never used in his promotional material) made an impression on the popular consciousness that still endures. It toured the eastern United States and Europe from 1882 until 1916, and during those years the cry "Buffalo Bill's in town!" was enough to bring all business to a standstill. The open-air spectacle was essentially a series of riding and shooting acts, interspersed with reenactments of Indian fights and, as a grand finale, the Indian attack on the Deadwood stagecoach.

From its very first year, the show featured real cowboys, both as acrobatic riders and as rescuers of the Deadwood stage. These were the first cowboys that most easterners had seen and they set both a pattern and a standard that has influenced the portrayal of the cowboy down to the present. Buffalo Bill did not exhibit cowboys as men who worked cattle but as supermen who could ride, rope, and shoot with extraordinary skill, who could leap from galloping horses to a careening stagecoach, and who always arrived just in the nick of time to save the maiden from danger.

These have remained standard elements in the portrayal of the cowboy, even though, with the exception of riding and roping, these activities cannot have occupied much of the real cowboy's time. The influence of Buffalo Bill's Wild West was so great that Eugene Manlove Rhodes, a New Mexico cowboy who became a fine western writer, told an audience of filmmakers in 1922 that the primary causes of popular misconceptions about cowboys and the West were, first, Buffalo Bill's Wild West show, and, second, other Wild West shows.

Buffalo Bill himself invented portions of the show cowboy's costume. A fine-looking man with upturned mustache, long hair, and a goatee, he always led his troupe into the arena clad in skin-tight white trousers, thigh-high black leather boots, a wide leather belt with an oversize silver buckle, an embroidered shirt, a fringed and beaded leather jacket, enormous leather gauntlets, and a wide-brimmed, ten-gallon Stetson hat—a hat style that he introduced and that was subsequently copied by ranchers and cowboys everywhere.

Cody's show cowboys were as impressive as he was. During the first season of the Wild West, in 1883, they included Johnny Baker, the Cowboy Kid; Bronco Bill Bullock; Jim Lawson, a roping expert; and William Levi "Buck" Taylor, the King of the Cowboys.

Taylor was Buffalo Bill's star cowboy for nearly fifteen years, and during that time he was the best-known cowboy in the world. He was a native Texan, born near Fredericksburg in 1857 and orphaned when he was six years old. When he joined Cody's show he stood six feet five, but the show's literature carefully described him as "amiable as a child." Unlike Texas Jack, Buck Taylor was a cowboy first and a showman second. He never went on the stage, and when he retired he returned to ranching.

As Cody's show grew in size, he added more authentic cowboys, until his cast included Bud Ayers, Marve Beardsley, Dick Bean, Utah Frank, Con Groner, the Cowboy Sheriff, Blue Hall, Montana Joe, Jim Kid, Jim Mitchell, Jim Lawson, Bronco Charlie Miller, Antonio Esquival, and Joe Esquival. These men exhibited their skills in an act called "Cowboy Fun," which included steer roping, bronc riding, trick riding, and relay races. This act was imitated in all of the fifty-odd Wild West shows that flourished in the 1890s and survives in the modern rodeo. Another popular cowboy act was a square dance on horseback, which for many years featured Mrs. Georgia Duffy, "The Rough Rider of Wyoming," who may have been the first cowgirl. In 1891 Cody added a "Congress of Rough Riders of the World" to his show, and Antonio Esquival became the leader of a group of twenty-five vaqueros (there were also cowboys, cossacks, hussars, and lancers). The show at that time also featured a thirty-six-piece cowboy band, made up, according to a London newspaper, of "cowboys who have retired from the hardships of the plains and taken to music."

Buffalo Bill's Wild West not only introduced the cowboy to the East, it took him to Europe, where, next to the Indians, he was the leading attraction of the show. The Wild West first went to England for Queen Victoria's Golden Jubilee in 1887, taking two hundred actors and nearly three hundred head of livestock, including buffalo, elk, and deer. The English were in awe of the Indians, but they took the cowboys into their hearts, in spite of the fact that one of them, Dick Johnson, was arrested for getting into a fight in a pub with a patron who said that he "would not drink with cowboys" and a second was arrested for firing his pistol in a restaurant. The *Birmingham Daily Post* said that "the cowboy is a gentleman . . . and not to be confused with the criminals and bullies who have disgraced the name of 'cowboy' in some American states." The *Era* of London was even more effusive, saying:

8. Don Russell, *The Lives and Legends of Buffalo Bill* (Norman: University of Oklahoma Press, 1960), p. 253.
9. Rosmarie K. Bank, "Melodrama as a Social Document: Social Factors in the American Frontier Play," *Theatre Studies* 22 (1975–76):46.
10. Daryl Emrys Jones, "The Dime Novel Western: The Evaluation of a Popular Formula" (Ph.D. diss., Michigan State University, 1975), pp. 66, 95.
11. Arthur Holt, *Hotspur Harry; or, The Texas Trailers*, The Champion Library, vol. 1, no. 29 (New York, 1882).

The typical cowboy . . . is a perfect hero with respect to bearing pain and meeting danger. He has a code of honor which, half savage, as it is, he adheres to with far more rigidity than is the case in similar circumstances with the denizens of civilized districts. Absolute indifference to peril, perfect fealty to a friend, extreme amiability and openness, coupled with a readiness to shoot as soon as a certain code of civility has been transgressed . . . are, roughly speaking, the peculiarities of the cowboy's character.[12]

Buffalo Bill's Wild West went back to Europe for a four-year tour in 1889, opening at the Paris Exposition, where they played to the shah of Persia and the queen of Spain. "L'Ouest Sauvage" was an instant success, and one of its most popular acts was "l'amusement des cow-boys." The show went on to Italy, through Germany, Holland, and Belgium, and back to England. By the end of 1892 every adult and child in western Europe knew what a cowboy was.

Cody's show had numerous imitators, each with its component of cowboys. In 1893, the year of the World's Columbian Exposition, there were at least fifty Wild West shows touring the United States and Europe, and by 1900 their popularity had spread to South America, Australia, and even South Africa.

The leading show of the twentieth century was the Miller 101 Ranch Wild West Show, an outgrowth of an Oklahoma ranch empire founded in 1892 by G. W. Miller. Miller's son, Joseph C. Miller, and his brothers began producing "roundups" and rodeos for the public at their White House Ranch in the early years of the century—one held in 1905 drew 64,000 people, who arrived on special trains. In 1907 they decided to take their show on the road, where it continued until 1949. It followed and elaborated on the original format developed by Cody. One of the Miller cowboys, a black Texan named Bill Pickett, brought an innovation to "Cowboy Fun." He wrestled steers to the ground by biting into their lower lips, a technique he called bulldogging. Pickett and his "bite-'em style" were the sensation of the Miller 101 for a number of seasons, and he can rightly be called the first black cowboy star.

The Miller 101 show recognized both the symbolic and the box-office value of the cowboy, and it developed acts starring cowboys that had no relation to ranch work. Vernon Tantlinger, originally an exhibition rifle shot, learned to throw the Australian boomerang and was billed as "The Cowboy Boomerang Artist." Another crowd-pleasing act was "Cowboy Auto Polo," played by cowboys driving stripped-down model-T's equipped with primitive roll bars.

The cowgirl was enthusiastically received by audiences in the early 1900s. To make her a legitimate part of the Old West, Miller publicity claimed, quite incorrectly, that cowgirls had always assisted with roundups, trail drives, and other aspects of ranch work. The leading Miller 101 cowgirl, Edith Tantlinger, told

reporters that "the western girls' way of life made them superior to other women . . . a life in nature gave western girls such vitality that they could not be permanently injured" by bronc and steer riding. Tantlinger told reporters in 1914 that, if the United States went to war with Mexico, she would lead a company of cowgirls against the Mexicans. Philip Ashton Rollins, however, presented another view of the woman's role on the ranch:

There were, it is true, permanently living on a number of ranches women. . . . The horse being the principal and often only means of transit, many of these women and many of their daughters rode extremely well. The side-saddles and woolen riding-skirts used by most of these women, the modest divided skirts used by the few who rode astride, imparted to those quiet, unassuming courageous females of the real frontier none of the garishness which that modern invention, the buckskin-clad "cowgirl," takes with her into the circus ring. These "cowgirls" may be of Western spirit and blood, but their buckskin clothing speaks of the present-day theatre and not the ranches of long ago.[13]

The positive image of the cowboy presented by Cody was reinforced by drawings such as those William Allen Rogers published in *Harper's*, contradicting the image produced by the woodcuts in *Frank Leslie's* and the *Police Gazette*. Rogers presented instead "a merry scene familiar to the jolly rangers of the west." Significantly, the cowboys pictured in this particular drawing were on the northwestern ranges, in the Cuchara river valley of southern Colorado, rather than in the cow towns of Kansas. About them Rogers said, "The 'cow-boys' of the Rocky Mountain regions are of a race or class peculiar to that country. They bear some resemblance to the corresponding class on the southern side of the Rio Grande, but are of a milder and more original type."[14] He also pointed out to *Harper's* readers the increasingly corporate nature of the cattle business: "Probably few persons who are not immediately interested in the subject have any idea of the enormous proportions to which the cattle trade of our great West has grown. The tendency to go into business seems to be also growing. The amount of capital represented in some of the herds is sufficient to supply a national bank."[15]

It was in the year 1886—the same year that brought the downfall of the open-range cattle industry—that the cowboy was fully rehabilitated. In that year there was a flurry of articles and illustrations glorifying the cowboy, the beginning of a flood that has never stopped. After publishing his definitive study of the ranching industry in 1885, Joseph Nimmo commented in an article for *Harper's Monthly* in November 1886 that, although the original cowboy was "a Texan, armed to the teeth, booted and spurred, long haired, and covered with a broad-brimmed sombrero," who belonged to "a class of men whom persons accustomed to the usages of civilized society would characterize as ruffians of the most pronounced type," the opening of the northern ranges and the organization of the cattle trade on business principles meant:

> The cow-boy of to-day . . . is of entirely different type from the original cow-boy of Texas. . . . a new class of cow-boys has been introduced and developed. . . . Some have come from Texas . . . but the number from other States and the Territories constitutes a large majority of the whole. Some are graduates of American colleges, and others of collegiate institutions in Europe. . . . Throughout the northern ranges sobriety, self-restraint, decent behavior, and faithfulness to duty are enjoined upon the cow-boys. . . . The morale of the entire range and ranch cattle business of the United States now compares favorably with that of other large enterprises.[16]

The October 16, 1886, issue of *Harper's Weekly* carried a double-page illustration by Rufus Zogbaum entitled "Painting the Town Red," which shows four cowboys galloping abreast down the main street of a western town, firing pistols in the air. The same scene was depicted by Frederic Remington three years later, in the *Harper's Weekly* for December 21, 1889, with the title "Cowboys Coming to Town for Christmas," and, with some minor alterations, by Charles Russell in his 1909 oil painting *In Without Knocking*, and subsequently in hundreds of films, television programs, and comic books, until it has become the only acceptable way to imagine cowboys entering a town (pp. 98–99).

Zogbaum, a young South Carolinian who eventually became a well-known military artist (once described in light verse by Rudyard Kipling), was the first "western" artist to consistently romanticize the cowboy. His illustrations placed the cowboy in a much more favorable light than the woodcuts of the previous decade had. They emphasized his youth, his closeness to nature, his carefree attitude, and the loneliness of his work. Most important, they showed the cowboy in situations that were to become stereotypes, the stock-in-trade of several generations of western artists, from Remington down to the present.

The text accompanying Zogbaum's illustrations, written by G. O. Shields begins, "Cowboys as a class are brimful and running over with wit, merriment, and good humor. They are always ready for any bit of innocent fun, but are not perpetually spoiling for a fight, as has so often been said of them . . . altogether, cowboys are a large-hearted, generous class of fellows." Shields goes on to produce a perfect description of the romantic cowboy: "The constant communication with nature, the study of her broad, pure domains,

the days and nights of lonely cruising and camping on the prairie, the uninterrupted communion with and study of self which this occupation affords, tend to make young men noble and honest."[17]

Zogbaum drew the very image of Shields's romantic cowboy in his illustration "The Prairie Letter Box," which appeared in *Harper's Weekly* on April 23, 1887. The artist depicted a lone cowboy in a vast prairie of wildflowers, his distance from civilization emphasized by his act of dropping a letter into a mailbox made from a preserved beef crate, the only man-made object visible for miles. Like "Painting the Town Red," this image was popularized by many other artists. The setting and the action were adapted by Remington for his 1901 oil painting *Post Office in Cow Country*, which shows the same mailbox with three cowboys receiving their mail at it. Zogbaum's lone cowboy posting a letter was duplicated from a slightly different angle in 1906 by N. C. Wyeth for an oil painting commissioned as an advertisement by the Cream of Wheat company, apparently without any acknowledgment to Zogbaum. In Wyeth's painting, the mailbox has become a Cream of Wheat box, and Wyeth gave it the title *Where the Mail Goes, Cream of Wheat Goes*. In 1909 cowboy photographer Erwin E. Smith tried to pose a cowboy and horse in the same situation for an artistic photograph entitled "A Cowboy from the LS Outfit Mailing a Letter." The image appeared in the early 1920s on a sheet music cover, probably adapted from Wyeth's Cream of Wheat ad (pp. 97, 143). Thus a particular image proliferated, reinforcing in each manifestation the myth of the romantic cowboy.

Zogbaum's cowboy images were powerful, but his main interest was in military illustration. His contemporary Frederic Remington was a western illustrator who sometimes drew soldiers but whose real love was cowboys. "With me, cowboys are what gems and porcelains are to others," he once wrote.[18] Indeed, it was Remington, Wister, and Wister's Harvard classmate Theodore Roosevelt who launched the romantic cowboy on his mythical career: Remington through his illustrations, Wister through his writing, and Roosevelt through his political prominence. All three were upper-class easterners; all three found something symbolically American in the West in general and the cowboy in particular.

Remington was the son of an upstate New York newspaper publisher who attended Yale, tried ranching in Kansas in the early 1880s, and finally decided upon a career as a professional artist, taking classes at the Art Student's League. In 1886 he made a second trip West and sold the sketches from that trip to *Outing* magazine, which was edited by his Yale classmate Poultney Bigelow. He remained throughout his life an easterner who made visits to the West, used it shamelessly as a commodity, and may have loved it. Like many easterners of his class and generation, he felt that something essentially American was being lost in the

12. Clifford P. Westermeier, "Buffalo Bill's Cowboys Abroad," *Colorado Magazine* 52 (1975):277–98.

13. Paul L. Reddin, "Wild West Shows: A Study in the Development of Western Romanticism" (Ph.D. diss., University of Missouri, 1970), pp. 193–95; and Philip Ashton Rollins, *The Cowboy* (New York: Charles Scribner's Sons, 1930), p. 36.

14. *Harper's Weekly*, November 27, 1880, p. 759.

15. Ibid., October 2, 1880, p. 637.

16. Joseph Nimmo, "The American Cow-Boy," *Harper's New Monthly Magazine* 73 (November 1886):883–84.

17. *Harper's Weekly*, October 16, 1886, p. 671.

18. Frederic Remington, "Cracker Cowboys in Florida," *Harper's New Monthly Magazine* 91 (August 1895):339.

industrialized post-Civil War Northeast, with its large immigrant population. He was given to expressing sentiments on the subject that can only be called racist: "Jews, Injuns, Chinamen, Italians, Huns—the rubbish of the earth I hate—I've got some Winchesters and when the massacring begins, I can get my share of 'em," he wrote Poultney Bigelow in 1893.[19] He saw in the cowboy the embodiment of a lost Americanism, and he saw the cowboy passing, too, with the closing of the open range. At the same time, he could be remarkably cynical about his use of the West as a commodity. In 1902, trying to persuade Wister to collaborate with him on the portfolio *A Bunch of Buckskins*, he wrote, "I am as you know working on a big picture book—of the West and I want you to write a preface. I want a lala too, no d____ newspaper puff saying how much I weigh etc. etc. but telling the d____ public that this is the real old thing—step up and buy a copy—last chance—ain't going to be any more West etc."[20]

Remington's first large set of cowboy illustrations were the drawings he did to illustrate a series of articles by Theodore Roosevelt published in *Century* magazine in 1888 and released as a book, *Ranch Life and the Hunting-Trail*, the next year. In the text Roosevelt, who had already served as speaker of the New York State Assembly and was then a U.S. civil service commissioner, described his adventures as a gentleman rancher in the Dakotas. He attributed every virtue to cowboys, saying that they were:

> *as hardy and self-reliant as any men who ever breathed—with bronzed, set faces, and keen eyes that look all the world in the face without flinching as they flash out from under the broad-brimmed hats . . . they are quiet, self-contained men, perfectly frank and simple, and on their own ground treat a stranger with the most whole-souled hospitality. . . . They are much better fellows and pleasanter companions than small farmers or agricultural workers; nor are the mechanics and workmen of a great city to be mentioned in the same breath.*[21]

The cowboys in Remington's illustrations replicated Roosevelt's word pictures. They were hard, lean, determined men, performing difficult tasks with ease and aplomb. These drawings show the economy of line and attention to detail that distinguished Remington's later work (p. 100). Accuracy of detail became almost a fetish with him, and he brought back from his annual trips West to his studio in New Rochelle, New York, large quantities of chaps, saddles, ropes, hats, and other pieces of costume and equipment to serve as models for his paintings. In the spring of 1889 he made a trip to Mexico and brought back an embroidered charro jacket and a sombrero which he painted, rather improbably, on one of the cowboys in his monumental oil *A Dash for the Timber*. At the same time he wrote a friend in Arizona: "I have a big order for a cowboy picture and I want a lot of chaperas [*sic*]—say two or three pairs—and if you will buy them off some of the cowboys there and ship them to me COD I will be your slave."[22]

Remington's career as an artist, writer, sculptor, and illustrator spanned the last decade of the nineteenth century and the first of the twentieth. He became a sculptor in the fall of 1894 through his acquaintance with Frederick W. Ruckstall, who was working on a large equestrian statue in a tent near the Remington home. Remington became fascinated with the process, which Ruckstall suggested he try his hand at. By January 1895 he had roughed out a model, and he wrote his friend Wister, "My water colors will fade—but I am to endure in bronze—even rust douch.—I am modeling—I find I do well—I am doing a cowboy on a bucking bronco and I am going to rattle down through all the ages, unless some Anarchist invades the old mansion and knocks it off the shelf."[23]

The result was *The Bronco Buster*, which became a collector's item almost overnight. One hundred and sixty casts of it were produced in Remington's lifetime, and it was the statue that Theodore Roosevelt's Rough Riders chose to present him with at their first reunion. Remington went on to produce twenty-two bronze statues, many of them in several versions. Eight of these depicted cowboys. The most complex, and probably the most famous, is *Coming through the Rye*, which shows the Zogbaum theme of four cowboys galloping abreast, pistols firing in the air. Its most impressive version must have been the heroic plaster replica at the Saint Louis World's Fair, which was twenty feet high. It was a magnificent symbol of the romantic cowboy's popularity.

One of the most fascinating aspects of Remington's career is the fact that it popularized a subject matter as well as an artist and a style. Once Remington broke the ground, there was an enormous demand for cowboy illustrators. Of course, this went hand-in-hand with the growing popularity of cowboy novels during the first decade of the twentieth century, but one is forced to conclude that it was this artist who made the subject respectable. Without Remington to pave the way, it is difficult to see how a man like Charles Russell could have moved from being a saloon painter to becoming a nationally known illustrator and artist.

Unlike Remington, Russell was a genuine westerner, a native of Missouri and a grand-nephew of the famous Bent brothers, whose fort on the Arkansas River was the jumping-off place for the Santa Fe Trail. He went to Montana in 1880, at the age of sixteen, and stayed there the rest of his life, working as a sheep herder, cowboy, and, eventually, full-time artist. From 1880 to 1893, Russell worked on the sheep and cattle ranges, sketching and painting in his spare time and selling occasional works to friends. These were exhibited in saloons and store windows, and toward the end of the decade he became somewhat of a local celebrity, with Montana newspapers describing him as "the cowboy artist." In 1887 seven of his paintings were reproduced as a one-sheet photogravure by the Chicago Photogravure Company, under the title "A Copy of C. M. Russell's—'The Cowboy Artist's'—Last Painting," but the circumstances surrounding the production of this first Russell print are obscure.

Three years later, however, a Cascade, Montana, saddlemaker named Ben Roberts persuaded Russell to do some paintings for a printed portfolio. Russell obligingly produced a dozen paintings and Roberts arranged the printing with the Albertype Company in New York. The result was *Studies of Western Life*, a bound portfolio with twelve prints. In 1893, Russell stopped working as a cowboy and became a full-time painter, selling paintings to clients in Montana and even as far away as Saint Louis. It was not until ten years later, in 1903, that he made his first trip to New York, under the sponsorship of the illustrator John N. Marchand, whom he had met in Montana. Marchand took him to the offices of *Scribner's*, *McClure's*, *Outing*, and *Frank Leslie's*—almost the same circuit that Remington had made fifteen years previously—and introduced him to the bohemian and artistic society of New York. Russell, with his cowboy boots, red sash, and inexhaustible fund of stories, was an instant success, and on the eve of his fortieth birthday his professional career was launched. He remained a nationally known artist and illustrator until his death in 1926.

Russell's art was realistic, rather than romantic, and the situations he depicted, with a few exceptions, grew out of his own experience with cattle and horses. Some of his work, such as the "Just a Little Sunshine . . ." series (p. 105), was done for saloon decoration and is somewhat earthy. A few paintings with coin-operated mechanical devices attached were meant for the private rooms of saloons and are, as Russell biographer Frederic G. Renner tactfully puts it, "of the for-men-only variety." Many of the books he illustrated, though, were definitely romantic, and Russell must be counted among those who furthered the image of the romantic cowboy. He may have reached his broadest public through the sale of prints and reproductions of his paintings as publishers' premiums, calendars, and even placemats. It is a safe bet that there is not a cafe or tavern in the West that does not have at least one Russell print on the wall, and every car-owning citizen of Wyoming carries an adaptation of a Russell drawing on his license plate.

Remington and Russell, through their paintings, illustrations, and sculpture, had an enormous effect on the way that Americans perceive the cowboy. They standardized his costume and his poses; they made him picturesque. A peculiar example of their effect can be seen in the work of Erwin E. Smith, who is sometimes described as a documentary photographer of cowboys. Smith, who was born

in Honey Grove, Texas, in 1886, made over ten thousand photographs of cowboys on West Texas ranches between 1906 and 1916. He held his first photographic exhibition in Boston in 1908, and his pictures are still often reproduced as accurate depictions of ranch life. Many of them are, but Smith's primary aspiration was to be a sculptor and record the cowboy in bronze. He studied with Lorado Taft and Bela Lyon Pratt and took photographs primarily as a guide to anatomical accuracy in his work. These pictures were carefully posed in accordance with sketches made beforehand and show cowboys in heroic and romantic poses, many of them derived from illustrations by Remington, Russell, and Zogbaum. Smith also took truly candid pictures, showing camp work, cattle on the move, and cowboys relaxing, but it is clear that he saw cowboys through the eyes of the artist, rather than the documenter.[24]

The cowboy underwent his fullest literary development during the 1890s at the hands of Owen Wister, whose prose in *Harper's* was frequently joined with the illustrations of Frederic Remington. It was Wister, a Philadelphia-born aristocrat and Harvard graduate (summa cum laude in music, 1882) who made the cowboy acceptable to eastern readers and worthy of the attention of literary critics. Inspired by a hunting trip to Wyoming in 1891, Wister wrote his first western story, "How Lin McLean Went East," the next year and promptly sold it to *Harper's*. The story relates how a cowboy goes to Boston and decides that he prefers western forthrightness to eastern sophistication. In 1898 Lin McLean appeared again this time as the protagonist in a full-length novel entitled *Lin McLean*. Two years later another Wister collection, *The Jimmyjohn Boss*, appeared, and finally, in 1902, *The Virginian*.

The Virginian is, essentially, about a noble young cowboy, his love for an eastern schoolteacher, and their reconciliation of his sense of honor with her sense of legality. Critics have described it as a symbolic reconciliation of order and freedom, of East and West, of society and anarchy. It is a rattling good story, even if it is, as numerous critics have said, a story of "cowboys without cows." It also marks the final step in the creation of the romantic cowboy.

The Virginian firmly established the stereotyped cowboy as young, handsome, courageous, soft-spoken (who can ever forget, "When you call me that, smile?"), independent, and holding a high sense of honor. It also established him as irrevocably Anglo-Saxon—there is not a black or a Mexican in the entire book. The Virginian (he is never named in the book) is "a slim young giant, more beautiful than pictures. His broad, soft hat was pushed back, a loose-knotted dull-scarlet handkerchief sagged from his throat; and one casual thumb was hooked in the cartridge belt that slanted across his hips." He was such a paragon of virtue that a reviewer in the New York *Tribune* commented:

19. Poultney Bigelow, "Frederic Remington; with Extracts from Unpublished Letters," *New York State Historical Association Quarterly Journal* 10 (1929):46–48.
20. Frederic Remington to Owen Wister, April 1900. Wister Papers, Manuscript Division, Library of Congress.
21. Theodore Roosevelt, *Ranch Life and the Hunting-Trail* (New York: Century Co., 1888), pp. 9–10.
22. Peter H. Hassrick, *Frederic Remington* (New York: Harry N. Abrams, Inc., 1973), p. 68.
23. Remington to Wister, January 1895, Wister Papers, Manuscript Division, Library of Congress.
24. Eldon S. Branda, "Portrait of the Cowboy as a Young Artist," *Southwestern Historical Quarterly* 71 (July 1967):69–77; and J. Evetts Haley, *Life on the Texas Range* (Austin: University of Texas Press, 1952).

To some writers of fiction, especially since the time of the admirable and lamented Bret Harte, the "cow-puncher" or, as he is sometimes called, the "cowboy," seems to be an object of almost bewildering enchantment. . . . As depicted by Mr. Wister, he is a creature of such physical beauty, such mental vigor, such moral attitude, such executive equipment, and such universal genius as ought to serve as a beacon or headlight for the nation and, indeed, an example for the human race.[25]

In spite of such criticism, the book was an instant success. It sold 50,000 copies in the first two months, and Wister was deluged with letters from westerners who complimented him on the accuracy of his descriptions, often adding that they had known the Virginian.

Of course, the Virginian's path to heroism was prepared by a number of forerunners. There were dime novel cowboy heroes in the 1870s and the Live Boys in 1879 and 1880. Thomas Pilgrim, writing under the pseudonym Arthur Morecamp, published two adventure novels for boys that have been called the "first strictly cowboy fiction."[26] An Austin, Texas, attorney, Pilgrim was the son of a pioneer Texas schoolteacher. Although it is doubtful that he ever went on a cattle drive himself, he certainly got his information from people who did, and he included remarkably detailed descriptions of the cattle trail, a Kansas cow town, and Deadwood, Dakota Territory, in the *Live Boys; or, Charley and Nasho in Texas* (1879) and *Live Boys in the Black Hills* (1880). At a time when there was a good deal of animosity between Anglo-American and Spanish-speaking Texas, these books are remarkable too for their protagonists, who are, as the subtitle says, "two boys of fourteen, one a Texan, the other a Mexican." The boys decide to raise money to visit the Philadelphia Centennial Exposition by taking a herd of cattle to Kansas, and the book describes their adventures.

Another forerunner of *The Virginian* was the cowboy memoir. In 1885 a genuine Texas cowboy, Charles Siringo, published his autobiography, *A Texas Cowboy; or, Fifteen Years on the Hurricane Deck of a Spanish Pony*, a book that was reminiscent of the nautical and whaling memoirs that poured forth from American presses in the mid-nineteenth century. Siringo described his boyhood, his adoption by a wealthy New Orleans family, his running away from school, and his adventures as a cowboy on the coastal plains of Texas, where he worked for legendary cattlemen like Shanghai Pierce and Bradford Grimes. He gave a detailed account of the range cattle business, most of it accurate, written in a vivid and colorful style. Siringo judged his audience perfectly, for the public's appetite had been whetted for accurate information about cowboys. The author later claimed to have sold a million copies of his book and went on to rewrite it under three other titles, adding new anecdotes and adventures.

A second genre in addition to memoirs that popularized the cowboy in the 1890s was popular verse. Western newspapers of the nineties abounded with poems about cowboys and cattle sent in by readers, many of them in the style of Robert Service and at least some of them perhaps having their origin in the recitations given around the campfire in cow camps. A typical contributor was D. J. O'Malley, a soldier's son who became a trail driver and cowboy in Montana in the 1880s and sent a number of poems to the Miles City *Stock Grower's Journal*. O'Malley's compositions included "The Cowboy's Soliloquy," "A Busted Cowboy's Christmas," "The D2 Horse Wrangler," "When the Work's All Done This Fall," and "A Cowboy's Death." There was an O'Malley in almost every western town, and, as small town newspapers often printed exchanges from other papers, their poems got wide circulation. Some even found their way into national magazines: *Frank Leslie's* of December 14, 1893, printed a version of "The Cowboy's Dream" ("Last night as I lay on the prairie / And looked at the stars in the sky / I wondered if ever a cowboy / Would drift to the sweet by-and-by"), along with a tale about it being found in an envelope in a dead letter office.

At least two cowboy poets achieved national notice in the 1890s. Wallace Coburn, a Great Falls, Montana, rancher and a friend of Charles Russell's, brought out his *Rhymes from a Round-up Camp* in book form in 1899, with illustrations by Russell. It was an immediate success. Even more popular was Texas cattleman William Lawrence Chittenden's *Ranch Verses*, first published in 1893, which went through fourteen editions by 1918. The book contained a number of verses idealizing the cowboy ("He can sing, he can cook, yet his eyes have the look / Of a man that to fear is a stranger; / Yes, his cool, quiet nerve will always subserve / In his wild life of duty and danger.") as well as the much-printed "Cowboys' Christmas Ball."

Finally, in 1897, Alfred Henry Lewis published *Wolfville*, a book that Eugene Manlove Rhodes ranked just below Wild West shows as one of the main causes of popular misconceptions about the cowboy. Lewis has been largely forgotten now, but in his heyday he was compared to Mark Twain and Bret Harte. Like them, he was a newspaperman, the publisher and editor of a number of political journals, including the *Verdict*. He visited Arizona in the 1880s, practiced law in Cleveland and Kansas City, and wrote biographies of John Paul Jones, Aaron Burr, and Andrew Jackson. But he found his milieu in *Wolfville*, which was an immediate commercial success. It is a series of humorous short stories, held together by a narrator called the Old Cattleman, and revolving around the population of a mining and cattle town. *Wolfville* was so successful that Lewis followed it with the sequels *Wolfville Days* (1902), *Wolfville Nights* (1902), and *Wolfville Folks* (1908). In all four books, the cowboys carry pistols, ride hard and recklessly, speak in western dialect larded with outrageous oaths and similes, and spend a good deal of time playing elaborate pranks on each other.

Much of the appeal of the adventure stories, the poetry, and the memoirs lay in the public's sense that they captured the essence of a disappearing breed of men. This was especially true of *The Virginian*. A letter to Owen Wister from an admirer in Indiana began, "A dozen years ago I punched cows in the Ponca Nation; tramped through sun-blistered valleys in New Mexico and Arizona—and later spent upwards of a year in the Dakota cattle country," and went on to say, "In The Virginian I lived it all again. I lived it because your characters were *real* ones—ones that have been but are no more. . . . Your story has helped to make my dreams of those days more vivid and to preserve types that are rapidly passing away."[27] The idea that the cowboy was becoming extinct was a common theme in the 1890s and had much to do with his romanticization. It was expressed over and over again in popular magazines in articles with titles like "The Passing of the Cowboy," "Goodbye to the American Cowboy," "A Passing Race," and "The Decaying Cowboy."

The popularity of *The Virginian* was further enchanced by its production as a play in 1904. Several popular cowboy farces and melodramas had been staged in the 1890s, but this was the first serious play with a cowboy as the leading character. It opened at the Manhattan Theatre in New York on January 5, 1904, with Dustin Farnum as the Virginian, and ran for four months. The road company, which at one time included William S. Hart, kept the show open for ten years, and it was still being played as a tent show in the 1920s. The script was the basis for three films, the last made in 1946. Although Wister did not create the romantic cowboy, he did perfect him and propagate him.

The success of *The Virginian* on stage gave rise to a flood of cowboy plays, which probably did as much to fix a visual image of the romantic cowboy in the American mind as cowboy films did to fix other cowboy images in later years. The best-known and most successful was Edwin Milton Royle's play *The Squaw Man*. It opened at Wallack's Theatre in New York in October 1905 and played 222 straight performances before going on the road. In 1908 it was produced in London as *The White Man*, and the script became, like *The Virginian*'s, the basis for several films. The plot revolves around a young English aristocrat who takes the blame for another's crimes to save the family honor, flees to America, and becomes a cowboy in Utah. In the final act, his Indian bride commits suicide so that he can return to England and claim his rightful title.

A musical comedy called *The Tenderfoot*, by Richard Carle and H. L. Heertz, and David Belasco's *The Girl of the Golden West* both also opened in New York in 1905. Cowboy drama was at such a pitch on Broadway that in 1906 Joe Weber introduced a burlesque called *The Squawman's Girl of the Golden West* at Weber's Music Hall. David Belasco opened a second western drama, *The Rose of the Rancho*, that fall, and the next season brought Edmund Day's *The Round Up* and Dustin Farnum starring in Augustus Thomas's *The Ranger*. Even after the fad died out on Broadway, about 1908, cowboy plays continued to be popular with rural audiences. One of the most prolific tent show writers was a Texan, Charles Harrison, best known for *Saintly Hypocrites and Honest Sinners*, who wrote three popular cowboy melodramas: *Her Cowboy Visitor* (1905), *The Lone Star Ranch* (1911), and *A Prince of the Range* (1915). The most popular cowboy tent show of all time was not a melodrama but a "rube show," a rural comedy, called *The Girl of the Flying X*, written in 1916 by George J. Crawley and known in the theater as *Sputters*, from the name of the leading comic character. Sputters is a cowboy who stutters, and who is taught by the heroine to talk without stammering. The plot involves a horse ranch, a mysterious foreman, a rascally Mexican, and the heroine, Rose. All in all, the popularity of cowboy plays following *The Virginian* can be judged by the fact that the U.S. Copyright Office recorded only four plays with the word *cowboy* in the title between 1870 and 1899, and thirty-five such plays between 1900 and 1915.[28]

Not only did it start a Broadway fad, but the publication of *The Virginian* marked a watershed in serious western fiction. In earlier books, such as *Wolfville*, the cowboy provides local color and comic relief, but he seldom exhibits sustained heroic behavior and rarely is the center of the plot. In post-*Virginian* novels, the action revolves around a cowboy hero, who by his devotion to a code of honor, his manliness, his physical courage, and his riding and shooting skill both causes and resolves the plot action.

Some of Wister's early followers are worthy of criticism in their own right. Bertha Muzzy Sinclair, a Montana ranchwoman who wrote under the name B. M. Bower, published in 1904 a playful, almost humorous novel called *Chip of the Flying U*, illustrated by Charles Russell. Reviewers could not help comparing it favorably to *The Virginian*, one of them saying, "Few authors have come as close to duplicating Owen Wister's immortal hero." *Chip of the Flying U* was followed by several Flying U sequels and sixty other novels, many of which are still in print. The strength of Bertha Sinclair's writing was not in plots but in the fact that she knew the country and the people she wrote about.

The true flood of western fiction may have started with Clarence Mulford, whose first novel, *Bar-20*, appeared in 1907, and who published a western novel each year until his death in 1940. He was the first of a new breed of western writers, an easterner who had never known the West of the open range and the cattle boom. He relied on published accounts of the West for his details and local

25. New York *Tribune*, January 6, 1904.
26. Joe B. Frantz and Julian Choate, *The American Cowboy: The Myth and the Reality* (Norman: University of Oklahoma Press, 1955), p. 144.
27. W. H. Griffin to Wister, undated, Wister Papers, Manuscript Division, Library of Congress.
28. William Lawrence Slout, *Theatre in a Tent: The Development of a Provincial Entertainment* (Bowling Green, Ohio: Bowling Green University Popular Press, 1972), pp. 71–77; and U.S. Copyright Office, *Dramatic Compositions Copyrighted in the United States, 1870 to 1916*, 2 vols. (Washington: Government Printing Office, 1918).

color and kept voluminous card files headed "trail drives," "chuck wagons," and so on, in which he filed appropriate excerpts from Siringo and from other firsthand accounts. Mulford is best remembered today for his invention of Hopalong Cassidy.

The writer who perfected the formula western was Zane Grey, whose *Riders of the Purple Sage* appeared in 1912 and was followed by a string of romances set in a never-never West. In a perceptive essay on western fiction, W. H. Hutchinson has said, "The basic ingredients that Grey borrowed bodily from *The Virginian*, rejecting Wister's still discernible humor, and beat to a froth in *Riders of the Purple Sage* have remained unchanged ever since— virgins, villains, and varmints."[29] Grey's partner in denaturalizing the West was Frederick Schiller Faust, who between 1917 and 1944 wrote thirty million words under a dozen pseudonymns, including Max Brand. The Grey-Brand school had countless imitators, who found an outlet for their work in the dozens of pulp story magazines that sprang up in the 1920s: *Argosy*, *Adventure*, *Short Story*, *Blue Book*, *Western Story*, and *Ranch Romances*, to name only a few.

During the first decade of the twentieth century—the years Frederic Remington worked in watercolor and bronze while Owen Wister fashioned his soft-spoken hero—the romantic cowboy was defined and flourished. Curiously, it was a New York-born and Harvard-educated politician who came to symbolize the purifying force of the cowboy to the American public. Theodore Roosevelt, with his unfailing political instinct, sensed the popularity of the cowboy and frequently presented himself to the public as one. His credentials were good: he had been a ranch owner in the Dakotas in the 1880s and had certainly worked cattle. He also believed in the moral superiority of the cowboy. In *Ranch Life and the Hunting-Trail* he wrote, in a tone that foreshadowed the political philosophy of John Wayne, that

> The cowboy will not submit tamely to an insult, and is ever ready to avenge his own wrongs; nor has he an overwrought fear of shedding blood. He possesses, in fact, few of the emasculated, milk-and-water moralities admired by pseudo-philanthropists, but he does possess, to a very high degree, the stern, manly qualities that are invaluable to a nation.[30]

When the Spanish-American War broke out, Roosevelt sought to take advantage of those "stern, manly" qualities by organizing a regiment of cavalry composed solely of cowboys. The resulting First U.S. Volunteer Cavalry, called Rough Riders—a name borrowed from Buffalo Bill—eventually contained one company of elite New Yorkers as well as companies of cowboys from Texas, New Mexico, Arizona, and Colorado, but all wore a distinctive cowboy's blue-and-white bandanna in addition to regulation uniforms. The

bandanna became a Roosevelt campaign emblem in 1904, decorated with the initials *TR* joined as though on a cattle brand. Political cartoonists as early as 1899 pictured Roosevelt as a cowboy, with hat, bandanna, chaps, and, sometimes, blazing pistols, and a probably apocryphal story has Mark Hanna remarking, on hearing of William McKinley's death, "Now that damned cowboy is President of the United States." The most famous of all Roosevelt cartoons, published at the time he died, shows him ascending into heaven on horseback, waving farewell with his ten-gallon hat.

During his presidency, Roosevelt frequently presented himself, especially to his western constituents, as a cowboy. On two long tours of the West, in 1903 and 1905, he was photographed on horseback at every opportunity and participated in a trail ride and rodeo at Cheyenne, an Indian riding demonstration at Pocatello, Idaho, a "cowboy breakfast" at Hugo, Colorado, and a famous weeklong wolf hunt in Indian Territory. Roosevelt became the first person—though by no means the last—to symbolize the cowboy on a national level.

The myth of the romantic cowboy as described by Wister, pictured by Remington, and personified by Roosevelt, was in its fullest flower in the same decade that the American film industry was in its infancy. In fact, the picture often cited as the first American feature film, *The Great Train Robbery*, appeared the year after the publication of *The Virginian* and was probably inspired by a scene in Scott Marble's cowboy drama of the same title. This coincidence of media undoubtedly accounts for the continuing popularity of the cowboy myth in the United States today. Film gave the cowboy new life and added, almost immediately, another dimension to his character—or, to be more accurate, it revived an old dimension and created a new type of cowboy hero. The nature of film as a medium called for action as well as character and plot development, and for action that was visually exciting. The activities of the real cowboy—roping and branding calves and moving cattle from place to place—were repetitive and dull, but the action of the Wild West show cowboy—trick riding and roping and shooting stunts—was exciting and suited to fast-paced films. American filmmakers, after a false start with filmed versions of cowboy melodramas with titles like *The Bandit of Point Loma* and *The Rustler's Reformation*, realized the necessity of action, and a new cowboy hero was born: the fast-roping, hard-riding, and straight-shooting acrobatic cowboy.

The first actor to realize the full potential of the acrobatic cowboy hero was Gilbert Max Aaronson, known to his public as Bronco Billy Anderson. Anderson invented the "series western," a group of 376 one- and two-reelers made by his Essanay Film Company between 1908 and 1915, all starring the same hero, Bronco Billy.

The character Anderson developed was a throwback to the dime novel hero: an athlete with a boyish grin and tousled hair who saved scores of heroines from bandits, runaway horses, and fates worse than death. Bronco Billy was the ancestor of all the acrobatic cowboys—Tom Mix, Hopalong Cassidy, Johnny Mack Brown, Ken Maynard, Buck Jones, and Lash Larue, to name only a few—who have thrilled youthful audiences with their daring escapades. The acrobatic cowboy is easily distinguished from the romantic cowboy. He wears a distinctive costume that frequently looks more like a uniform than cowboy dress. He rides an identifiable horse, with a name, and has an inseparable companion. And last, he is frequently identified with some sort of gimmick, which for Lash Larue was a whip and for the Lone Ranger was a mask and silver bullet. Tom Mix, a former Wild West show performer and poolroom-keeper whose fictional autobiography almost equals in incredibility his exploits on the screen, was the epitome of the acrobatic cowboy, leaping from saloon roofs, climbing under runaway stagecoaches, and igniting dynamite caps with pistol shots. The acrobatic cowboy eventually disappeared from the screen in the 1950s, only to resurface as a rodeo hero.

This is not to say that the romantic cowboy was denied his share of screen glory. He moved off the pages of novelists onto the screen as the strong, silent man of action with an independent but impeccable moral code. William S. Hart, who had once played the Virginian on stage, first personified this type in silent films (one of Hart's immortal subtitles was, "Better a Painted Pony than a Painted Woman," and one of his best characters was a resolute cowboy known as Three-Word Brand because he seldom spoke more than three words at a time). Hart's successors in talking films include Randolph Scott, Gary Cooper, and, most recently, John Wayne.

The coming of sound to films brought with it a third type of cowboy hero, even more removed from reality than the romantic cowboy or the acrobatic cowboy: the cowboy entertainer. The cowboy entertainer, peculiarly enough, has his roots in the folksong scholarship of John A. Lomax.

Lomax became interested in collecting songs sung by cowboys while a professor of English at Texas A & M College. His initial motives are somewhat obscure. There is no question that he was caught up in the myth of the romantic cowboy. In the "Collector's Note" to the first, 1910 edition of his *Cowboy Songs* (dedicated to Theodore Roosevelt) he wrote:

That the cowboy was brave has come to be axiomatic. If his life of isolation made him taciturn, it at the same time created a spirit of hospitality, primitive and hearty as that found in the mead-halls of Beowulf. He faced the wind and the rain, the snow of winter, the

fearful dust-storms of alkalai desert wastes, with the same uncomplaining quiet . . . He played his part in winning the great slice of territory the United States took away from Mexico. He has always been on the skirmish line of civilization. Restless, fearless, chivalric, elemental, he lived hard, shot quick and true, and died with his face to the foe.

He went on to say that the Old West was disappearing, and that "the last figure to vanish is the cowboy. . . . He sits his horse easily as he rides through a wide valley, enclosed by mountains, clad in the hazy purple of a coming night—with his face turned steadily down the long, long road, 'the road that the sun goes down.' Dauntless, reckless, without the unearthly purity of Sir Galahad though as gentle to a pure woman as King Arthur, he is truly a knight of the twentieth century."

Lomax may also have been motivated by regional pride. He was a native Texan, and was raised, in fact, in a Bosque County town on the Chisholm Trail. He relates in several places how his boyhood efforts to collect songs from cowboys on the Chisholm Trail were ridiculed by an eastern-educated professor at the University of Texas, and how, as a result, he destroyed his early notebooks. In his preface to *Cowboy Songs*, he points out that "the Anglo-Saxon ballad spirit that was active in the rural districts of England and Scotland even after the coming of Tennyson and Browning" has survived equally well in the American West. He was definitely interested in proving the communal theory of ballad composition, and saw cowboy ballads as evidence of this theory. In his unsuccessful application for a Carnegie Fellowship in 1908, he wrote:

A cowboy soothes, with rythmic cry, an unquiet herd of cattle as he rides about them in the darkness. The notes are heard by his mates. They sing them also, with variations and additions. The notes take form in words; the words fall into meter and rhyme; at times a story creeps in. And there is made a ballad, as genuine, however crude and unpolished, as the best that comes from English and Scottish sources.[31]

Lomax did receive a series of Sheldon Fellowships from Harvard for his project, and between 1907 and 1910 he spent a good deal of time collecting cowboy ballads. He used two methods, making field recordings with an Edison wax-cylinder recorder and sending a letter of inquiry to newspaper editors all over the West, asking for examples of "ballads of the cattle trade and other frontier occupations." Unfortunately, only fifty-four recordings and no field notes have survived. These fifty-four recordings, according to a note accompanying them made by Lomax in 1941, "are all that

29. W. H. Hutchinson, "Virgins, Villains, and Varmints," in Eugene Manlove Rhodes, *The Rhodes Reader: Stories of Virgins, Villains, and Varmints*, 2d ed. (Norman: University of Oklahoma Press, 1975), p. x.
30. Roosevelt, *Ranch Life and the Hunting-Trail*, p. 109.
31. Lomax to the Trustees of the Carnegie Foundation, January 10, 1908, John A. Lomax Papers, Barker History Center, University of Texas at Austin.

remains of probably 250 records that I made . . . during the years 1908, 1909, 1910." They include "The Chisholm Trail," "The Cowboy's Lament," "Little Joe the Wrangler," and "Bury Me Not on the Lone Prairie," all published in *Cowboy Songs*, but they also include an even larger number of songs that have nothing to do with cowboys, including "Days of '49," "Poor Girl on the Town," "Frankie and Albert," "The Ram of Derby," and "Jerry Go Ile That Car," all sung by singers who were presumably cowboys.

Lomax's second method seems to have elicited more ballads that were topically oriented to cowboy work, as newspaper editors responded by sending clippings of verses from their papers. Subsequent scholarship has shown that many, if not most, of these ballads were the work of the "cowboy poets" of the 1890s. As one correspondent, a former cowboy and Texas Ranger, warned Lomax, "In my opinion, if you will permit me the liberty to say it, your greatest danger is to be imposed upon by imposters. Many so-called cow-boy songs reputed to be old are not over fifteen years old, and some people are singing them as old songs."[32] Lomax edited the ballads he collected, "selecting and putting together," as he said, "what seemed to be the best lines from different versions, all telling the same story."[33] He also severely bowdlerized some ballads, thinking, quite correctly, that the sexual allusions they contained would not be acceptable to any publisher. The original versions, as preserved in the Lomax Papers, offer an insight into the cowboy's attitudes toward cattle and women that *Cowboy Songs* does not. In a typescript copy of "The Old Chisholm Trail," undoubtedly a genuine cowboy song and one "with a verse for every mile of the trail," as Frank Dobie said, we find

My foot in the stirrup, my ass in the saddle
I'll bid goodbye to these God damn cattle

instead of Lomax's published

Feet in the stirrup and seat in the saddle
I hung and rattled them longhorn cattle

and

There's old Miss Annie she's a mighty fine squaw
She lives on the banks of the old Wichita
I wanted for to frig her and I offered her a quarter
Says she, "Bill Moore, I'm a gentleman's daughter"

instead of

Well, I met a little gal and I offered her a quarter
She says, "Young man, I'm a gentleman's daughter."

Verses like

I'm going down south 'fore the weather gets cold
I'm going down south to get some tallow on my pole

and

I'm going down south just whooping and yelling
If I don't get a woman I'll take a heifer yearling

didn't get into print in any form. As Lomax himself said of the song, "many stanzas are not mailable."

The point is not that Lomax was an inaccurate collector or a prude, but that *Cowboy Songs* was not a terribly accurate reflection of the song vocabulary of the average cowboy, which included many songs that had nothing to do with cattle and did not include many of the supposed songs, actually poems, included in *Cowboy Songs*. Significantly, the first edition of the book contained 112 texts and only fourteen tunes.

Cowboy Songs was uncritically accepted by the public, however, and during the next decade many of the texts in it were set to music. The English composer Liza Lehmann provided music for "The Rancher's Daughter," "The Night-Herding Song" (which was written in 1909 by a Texas A & M student named Harry Stephens), and "The Skew-Ball Black" in 1912 and University of Texas music professor Oscar Fox wrote tunes for "Rounded Up in Glory" and several others.

At almost the same time, a smattering of so-called cowboy songs written by professional songwriters began to appear. The team of Harry Williams and Egbert Van Alstyne copyrighted "San Antonio" in 1907, and at about the same time a young vaudeville actor named Will Rogers was twirling his rope on stage to a ditty called "Cheyenne."

Cheyenne, Cheyenne
Hop on my pony,
There's room for two, dear,
After the ceremony.

It was to Lomax, however, that the professional singing radio cowboys of the twenties turned for their initial material, and it was the radio cowboys who became the singing movie cowboys of the thirties. When radio programming was in its infancy, in the very early twenties, it was a poor station indeed which could not boast a Lonesome Cowboy, an Oklahoma Yodler, or a Sagebrush Sam. Their repertoire, far from being made up of songs sung by cowboys in the 1870s and 1880s (many of which could not have been sung over the air), consisted of texts taken from Lomax, like "Poor Lonesome Cowboy," "The Dying Cowboy," and "The Cowboy's Dream," supplemented by their own compositions. Carl T. Sprague, a Texas A & M track trainer and radio singer who is often referred to as the first cowboy recording star, chose D. J. O'Malley's poem, "When the Work's All Done This Fall," as given in *Cowboy Songs*, for his first recording session with Victor in 1925. Gene Autry's first recording hit, made while he was singing on radio station KV00 in Tulsa, was a song of his own composition "That Silver-Haired Daddy of Mine."

When sound came to films, in 1928, cowboy singers moved onto the screen, and in 1934, when the Ziegfeld Follies included "The Last Round-Up" as a production number, they arrived on Broadway. Judging by the sheet music filed for copyright with the Library of Congress, the thirties were the great years of the cowboy singer, whose costume, demeanor, and action on screen generally indicated that he was an entertainer first and a cowboy second, if ever. By the onset of the forties, most Americans believed that a guitar was as much a part of the cowboy's equipment as a rope or a horse.

The cowboy entertainer gained prominence through two other American institutions that grew to maturity in the twenties and thirties: the rodeo and the dude ranch. Although organized rodeos can be traced back to the 1880s, when they were given as Fourth of July entertainments, it was not until the twentieth century that rodeo became a national spectator sport. By 1915 four western rodeos had emerged as the principal two- or three-day money contest for cowboys: the California Rodeo in Salinas, Frontier Days in Cheyenne, the Calgary Stampede, and the Pendleton (Oregon) Round-Up.

In 1916 a promoter named Guy Weadick conceived the idea of taking a rodeo to the East, and he organized the New York Stampede, held at Sheepshead Bay Speedway in Brooklyn, where it ran for twelve days. A total of $50,000 in prize money was offered. and the announcer was Foghorn Clancy, who had made a career of announcing western rodeos. The events included saddle bronc riding, bareback bronc riding, trick and fancy roping, and steer roping, and the cowgirls who participated in the women's divisions attracted a great deal of attention. Although a financial failure because of a streetcar strike, the Stampede introduced New York to rodeo, setting the stage for the great Madison Square Garden rodeos of the twenties, and it marked the beginning of a new era in rodeo.

Before the Stampede, rodeos were an ancillary event to some other sort of celebration, usually a stock show or a pioneer reunion. and the participants were normally working cowboys, eager to pick up prize money by showing off their skills. After 1916, rodeos increasingly became events in themselves, and a specialized class of participants developed who came to think of themselves as professional athletes.

The twenties were the great years of spectator rodeos in the East. The World Championship Rodeo in Chicago and the Madison Square Garden Rodeo in New York became annual events. In 1924 Tex Austin, the promoter of the Chicago event, organized a rodeo at the British Empire Exposition in London. Perhaps the most publicized, and improbable, rodeo fan of the decade was Calvin Coolidge, who had to weather the criticism of the Society for the Prevention of Cruelty to Animals and the Anti-Rodeo League for both his well-publicized enthusiasm for the sport and his penchant for attending rodeos dressed in a gaudy cowboy costume.

In the early thirties, another important change took place: the use of contract riders instead of actual contestants in the more spectacular events, especially bronc riding and trick riding. By 1935, rodeos bore a strong resemblance to Wild West shows, and indeed many participants worked for both. Tad Lucas, a cowgirl trick rider, learned her skills with the California Frank Hafly Wild West Show, which toured Mexico and rural New England in the early twenties, and then participated in the Madison Square Garden Rodeo in 1923. Each season thereafter, she worked for the Miller 101 Show until the rodeo season opened, and then she went on the rodeo circuit, eventually becoming a much sought-after contract rider.

In 1936, the final step in the professionalization of rodeo was taken when the cowboys at the Boston Garden Rodeo went on strike for a fairer distribution of prize money and formed the Cowboy's Turtle Association, so-called because the members felt they had been so slow to act. The Turtle Association soon became a nationwide organization of rodeo cowboys, certifying rodeos that agreed to its conditions and rules. In 1945 it was reorganized as the Rodeo Cowboys' Association, and today it administers rodeo as a professional sport, setting contest rules and judging standards. In 1961 the R.C.A. estimated that five hundred rodeos were held each season under its auspices, and that these were seen by ten million spectators. Today's rodeo participant is unquestionably a professional athlete, the ultimate cowboy entertainer.

In another sense, however, dude ranching represented the epitome of cowboy entertainment, since it was participatory entertainment. Dude ranching, like rodeo, had its origins in the 1880s, when eastern-owned ranches in the northwest began to take paying guests. The first of these was probably the Eaton Ranch near Medora, Dakota Territory, which specialized in rehabilitating dissolute young easterners. Thirty years later. enough dude ranches had developed in the West to warrant the organization of a Dude Rancher's Association. The ranches fell into two distinct

32. S. P. Skinner, Athens, Texas, to Lomax, December 4, 1910, Lomax Papers, Barker History Center. University of Texas at Austin.
33. John A. Lomax, *Cowboy Songs and Other Frontier Ballads* (New York: Macmillan Co. 1941), p. xxix.

categories: working ranches, where guests paied to participate in actual ranch work, and larger, more elaborate establishments where portions of ranch work—such as roundups, brandings, and trail drives—were simulated to entertain the guests. These ranchers employed a "dude wrangler" to supervise the guests' activities and tactfully keep them out of trouble, and they frequently retained cowboy singers to entertain the guests around an evening campfire. They became so popular that in 1927 a dude ranch was opened in Florida, with a herd of cattle and seventy-five horses imported from Montana, and so profitable that in 1935 the University of Montana instituted a degree in "recreational ranching." Curiously enough, most dude ranch advertising did not emphasize recreational opportunities but instead extolled the scenery, the clean air, and, most of all, the authenticity of the western way of life that could be sampled. Unlike other resorts, dude ranches were places to pretend, rather than places to relax.

In the same way that Theodore Roosevelt symbolized the romantic cowboy to Americans in the first decade of the century, Will Rogers represented the cowboy entertainer to Americans of the 1920s. No one has ever been able to equal the position that Will Rogers held in American hearts—he was our first national "personality." He struck chords that predated the cowboy and went all the way back to Brother Jonathan, Artemus Ward, and the wise rube who outsmarts the city slicker. At the same time, he was an authentic cowboy, raised on a ranch in the Cherokee Nation, and a master of the lasso. His own experiences recapitulated the history of the cowboy hero: he had been a horse wrangler, a working cowboy, a Wild West performer (in South Africa), and a movie star. Unlike Theodore Roosevelt, he had access to the radio and to motion pictures, and he took advantage of both. He also wrote a syndicated political column and several books of political commentary. In those heady times, he provided just the right anchor to the American past. Paradoxically, one of his own enthusiasms was aviation, and his personal hero was Lindbergh. Will Rogers represents a transition between the world of the real cowboy and the world of the make-believe cowboy, and he is a pivotal figure in the growth of the cowboy myth.

During the last years of his life—Rogers was killed in an airplane crash in 1935—the depression curbed the activities of both organized rodeos and dude ranches, and the cowboy entertainer's stage was limited almost entirely to the movies and radio. Both media were directed primarily at juvenile audiences. As a result, the cowboy hero began to assume a fourth aspect, one he was to wear all through the 1940s and early 1950s: that of cowboy father, a moral preceptor to small children.

Filmmakers had always been aware that much of their audience was juvenile—and an early Tom Mix film shows Mix striding into a saloon and courageously ordering root beer—but it does not seem to be until the late thirties that the connection between cowboys, children, and commercial sponsors that manufactured children's products, primarily breakfast foods, was made. Ralston Purina, the Saint Louis cereal company, began sponsoring a juvenile radio show featuring Tom Mix in 1933 which was so popular that it continued until 1950, a decade after Mix's death. The sponsor invented an organization, the Tom Mix Ralston Straight-Shooters, that young listeners could belong to, and issued hundreds of premiums, available for ten cents and a Ralston box top. As William Savage says in *The Cowboy Hero*, his perceptive and biting account of the cowboy myth, "The cowboy sold the cereal, the cereal was necessary to acquire the premium, and the premium reinforced interest in the cowboy, which meant, presumably, more listening and more eating and of course more dimes."

Ralston Purina's success with Tom Mix was quickly imitated by Quaker Oats with Roy Rogers, Langendorf Bread with Red Ryder, General Mills with Hopalong Cassidy and the Lone Ranger, and Grape Nuts Flakes with Buck Jones. In order to sell food to children, however, the cowboy had to reform. He could no longer drink whiskey, chew tobacco, or swear. It may well be that William Boyd had the advantages of commercial sponsorship in mind when, in 1935, he agreed to play Hopalong Cassidy in a filmed version of one of Clarence Mulford's stories only if the part was rewritten to present Hopalong as a clean-liver.

At any rate, by the beginning of World War II, screen cowboys were advising American children over the airwaves and in personal appearances on diet, health, and behavior. During the war, when fathers were away in the service, mothers disciplined their children by saying, "What would Gene Autry say if he saw you do that?" and Gene Autry responded by codifying ten "Cowboy Commandments" as model behavioral rules for children:

1. *He must not take unfair advantage of an enemy.*
2. *He must never go back on his word.*
3. *He must always tell the truth.*
4. *He must be gentle with children, elderly people, and animals.*
5. *He must not possess racially or religiously intolerant ideas.*
6. *He must help people in distress.*
7. *He must be a good worker.*
8. *He must respect women, parents, and his nation's laws.*
9. *He must neither drink nor smoke.*
10. *He must be a patriot.*[34]

Somehow, Charlie Siringo and his fellow saddle-tramps had been turned into Frank Merriwells.

The use of the cowboy as a salesman by commercial sponsors had great ramifications for the cowboy hero. It gave him his fifth—and current—aspect, that of the commercial cowboy. The image of the cowboy had been used occasionally in the early 1900s in advertising, primarily for food products associated with the West. For instance, a canned corn label used about 1910 advertised Lasso Brand corn as "the epicurean's dream" and showed a distinctly non-epicurean cowboy serving an opened can to someone who looks suspiciously like Colonel Cody. A 1906 shipping crate label advertised Cowboy brand California prunes. But the two products that today are the greatest exploiters of the cowboy image, tobacco and alcoholic beverages, shunned cowboys almost completely until the mid-fifties.

It was Philip Morris that started the trend in 1954. Leo Burnett, president of Leo Burnett, USA, Philip Morris's advertising agency, has explained how Philip Morris wanted a masculine image to counteract the idea that its filter-tipped Marlboro cigarettes were effeminate. The Burnett agency hit on the idea of running a series of ads showing tattooed men in masculine occupations smoking Marlboros. The tattoo was a small anchor on the back of the hand. The first series of ads showed a tree surgeon, a cowboy, a lumberjack, and several other occupations, but the cowboy seemed to elicit the largest response from buyers, and he was chosen as the exclusive representative for the next series. The initial campaigns were newspaper and magazine campaigns, and nonprofessional models were used. Owen Smith, vice president of Leo Burnett, explained the shooting strategy: "To get the outdoor type for the cowboy, the suburbs were combed for healthy, manly faces. Tree surgeons, gardeners, and farmers were contacted." Eventually, however, the agency began to use real cowboys and to shoot television commercials on western locations. Ironically, one of their early cowboy models was a foreman on the Four Sixes Ranch at Gutherie, Texas, the ranch that had sponsored Theodore Roosevelt's famous wolf hunt in Indian Territory in 1905. In 1961 Darrell Winfield, a cowboy on the Quarter Circle Five ranch at Riverton, Wyoming, began posing for commercials shot on that ranch, and he has since become the best-known Marlboro Man. The tattoos and the other masculine occupations were dropped long ago, and the concept of Marlboro Country was added to the Marlboro Man, in beautiful color photographs.[35]

Historian William Savage is the only scholar who has seriously examined the commercial cowboy. He has noted that Marlboro's lead was followed in the 1970s by cowboys who "sold barbecue-flavor potato chips for Frito-Lay, motor oil for Phillips 66, trucks for Toyota, and beer for Miller and Schlitz. They sold bath soap, cigars, juice, razors, snuff, barbecue sauce, flashlight batteries, and laundry detergent." As curious as the unlikely products they sold, he goes on to say, was "the presentation of characteristics assumed to be (and evidently accepted as) typically cowboy," which he describes, in the case of a series of 1972 Falstaff Beer commercials, as "adolescent" and demonstrating "a marked preference for raising hell to working hard, or, indeed, working at all."[36]

Savage has hit on a highly significant point. The commercial cowboy was originally introduced to represent masculinity, but he has come to represent leisure and pleasure, which are frequently associated with the so-called "Southwestern way of life" that has developed in the Sunbelt. Furthermore, the men who are advertising beer and boots and men's cologne are not even movie stars who have built a reputation playing cowboy roles—they are simply male models dressed as cowboys, or as an advertising agency imagines cowboys would dress if they could afford Ralph Lauren clothing.

The current fad in western fashions is still too close to us in time to analyze completely, but its connection with the cowboy commercials of the 1960s and 1970s is obvious. For twenty years, with gathering strength, television and magazine advertising have been telling us that cowboys have more fun. A number of factors, including the popularity of the television program "Dallas," the release of the film *Urban Cowboy*, a nostalgia for the 1950s (which brought with it a revival of interest in Roy Rogers and Gene Autry films), and, perhaps, the growing economic prosperity of the Southwest, combined with this residual force to produce a fashion explosion in the East. The situation was summed up by two cartoons which appeared in the *New Yorker* in 1980. One showed an elevator in an urban office building, full of businessmen in three-button suits wearing cowboy hats. The elevator operator opened the door and said "First floor! Happy trails, gentlemen." The second showed a similarly costumed group of businessmen, each with a briefcase, standing in front of a receptionist's desk. The receptionist was speaking into an intercom, saying "Mr. Smith and his buckaroos are here to see you, sir." The clothes are expensive—embroidered silk shirts, feathered or silver-and-turquoise hatbands, thousand-dollar boots—and are associated with leisure and "dropping out" rather than with the hard work and brutal weather that they were designed for.

The future forms that the mythical cowboy will take are uncertain, but it is certain that we will continue to ring changes on him. We have recently seen the gay cowboy and the outlaw cowboy emerge as parts of American subcultures; we seem to be on the verge of the leisure cowboy. The future may hold the punk cowboy, the computer cowboy, the Third World cowboy, and the astral cowboy. None of these could be farther from reality than the series of mythical cowboys that we have already created, yet all will be equally important as reflections of ourselves and our aspirations—which is, after all, the function of a myth.

34. Quoted in David Rothel, *The Singing Cowboys* (New York: A. S. Barnes and Co., 1978), p. 17.
35. "Marlboro Won Success by Newspaper Ads," *Editor and Publisher* 91 (December 6, 1968):26; Mason Smith, "The Marlboro Man," *Sports Illustrated* 46 (January 17, 1970):59–67; and Bruce A. Lohof, "The Higher Meaning of Marlboro Cigarettes," in George H. Lewis, comp., *Side-Saddle on the Golden Calf: Social Structure and Popular Culture in America* (Pacific Palisades, Calif.: Goodyear Publishing Co., 1972).
36. William Savage, *The Cowboy Hero: His Image in American History and Culture* (Norman: University of Oklahoma Press, 1979), pp. 119–20.

"Cow Boy"

J. R. McFarren (dates unknown)

Lithograph (after a calligraphic design), 1887

This drawing by a North Texas penman of the 1880s demonstrates the tenacity of the vaquero tradition in representations of the cowboy. It shows the romanticism the cowboy has always inspired. The artist, J. R. McFarren, lived in Gainesville, Texas, only a few miles from the Chisholm Trail. He was undoubtedly familiar with Anglo-American cowboys wearing everyday work clothes, but when he set out to draw a cowboy he depicted him in the elaborate costume of the vaquero.

Popular and Applied Graphic Art Collections
Prints and Photographs Division
Library of Congress

THE IMAGE TAKES SHAPE

The cowboy first appeared to the American public as an unfocused image, a mixture of plainsman, bandit, and vaquero. Long before he was in evidence, the West and western characters had been a subject for American writers. James Fenimore Cooper had peopled the Old Northwest with buckskin-clad hunters and noble savages. As the frontier moved across the Mississippi, Mark Twain and Bret Harte added big-hatted miners, buffalo hunters, and scouts to the cast of characters. Horse-hunters and mustangers, dressed as vaqueros, appeared in early accounts of Texas and California. These figures began to merge into the cowboy in the dime novels and popular literature of the 1870s and early 1880s, particularly in the woodcut illustrations found in the "National Police Gazette." At the same time, real cowboys and actors dressed as cowboys began appearing on the eastern stage, frequently as characters in western melodramas that involved rope-throwing exhibitions or trick shooting. Finally, in 1882, Buffalo Bill Cody's Wild West brought a troupe of real cowboys East, and the image of the cowboy as a reckless, rough-riding, fast-shooting hero on horseback was forever fixed in the public mind.

Seth Norwood & Co.
Manufacturers of Fine Shoes, Beverly, Mass.
Trade card
Lithograph printed in colors, ca. 1880
   Vaqueros and their lassos were popular subjects on trade cards that advertised beef products and products whose strength and durability were being emphasized.
Popular and Applied Graphic Art Collections
Prints and Photographs Division
Library of Congress

Halstead & Co.
Beef & Pork Packers, Lard Refiners &c.
Lithograph printed in colors
H. Benke Lith., New York, N.Y.
Copyright 1886, by Halstead and Co.,
New York
   This somewhat incongruous image shows vaqueros unloading beef and hogs on a New York pier.
Popular and Applied Graphic Art Collections
Prints and Photographs Division
Library of Congress

"Testing" Clark's O.N.T. Spool Cotton
Trade card
Chromolithograph, ca. 1880
  This card compares the strength of Clark's cotton thread to that of the vaquero's rawhide lasso.
Popular and Applied Graphic Art Collections
Prints and Photographs Division
Library of Congress

Peruvian Horse Hunt
Staffordshire, transfer-printed
Manufactured by Anthony Shaw, England, ca. 1853
Collection of Petra Williams
Jeffersontown, Kentucky

The stage first brought the cowboy East. Usually he came as part of a larger cast of western characters. In 1872, Edward C. Z. Judson, who as "Ned Buntline" had popularized the exploits of Buffalo Bill Cody in several dime novels, persuaded William F. Cody to come East and appear on the stage with him in a three-act melodrama, "The Scouts of the Prairie." The cast included an Italian dancer, Giuseppina Morlacchi, and a former cowboy, John B. "Texas Jack" Omohundro. The plot was loosely constructed: Cody told stories, Morlacchi danced, Buntline delivered a temperance sermon, and Texas Jack demonstrated his skill with the lasso. For the first time, the cowboy and his unique tool appeared on stage. The costumes were those of plains hunters: fringed buckskin trousers and shirts. Later, Texas Jack married Madame Morlacchi and formed his own theatrical troupe, the Texas Jack Combination. He also became the hero of several dime novels.

For ten years Cody returned to the eastern stage each winter in a new play. The Buffalo Bill Combination was the forerunner of his Wild West show. Both troupes were widely imitated by such performers as Frank Frayne, whose act combined western drama with trick shooting.

Edward Judson "Ned Buntline" *(left)*,
William F. Cody *(center)*, **and Texas Jack Omohundro** *(right)* **in "Scouts of the Prairie"**
Burke-Koretke, Chicago
Photograph, ca. 1875
Buffalo Bill Historical Center
Cody, Wyoming

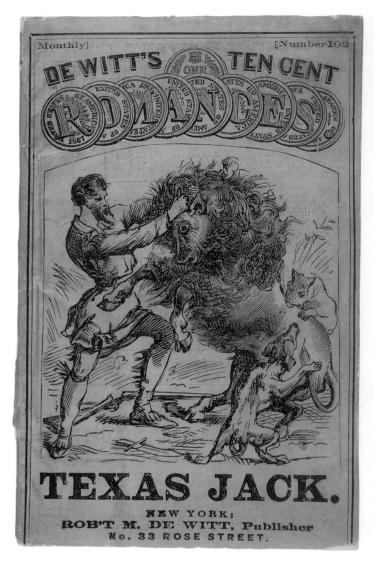

"Texas Jack"
DeWitt's Ten Cent Romances, No. 102
New York: Robert M. DeWitt, Publisher, 1872
Dime Novel Collection
Rare Book and Special Collections Division
Library of Congress

"The Scouts of the Prairie"
Playbill for Pike's Opera House
Cincinnati, Ohio
Broadside, 1875
Printer and publisher unknown
Buffalo Bill Historical Center
Cody, Wyoming

National Theater
"Si Slocum!"
Broadside, undated
Washington Chronicle Print
Thr A 15 Folio no. 21
Rare Book and Special Collections Division
Library of Congress

The Scouts Programme!

Messrs. CODY, JUDSON, OMOHUNDRO & NIXON................PROPRIETORS
Manager................Col. E. Z. C. Judson | Scenic Artist................Frank D. Skiff
Gen'l Director................J. M. Nixon | Properties and Effects................Geo. Reach
Stage Manager................W. J. Halpin | Costumer................Mrs. Beach
Armorer................W. J. Speck | Music................Carlo Patti

The New Sensation Drama, written by NED BUNTLINE, and founded on some of the most thrilling and interesting incidents of his great New York Weekly Indian Stories, entitled The

SCOUTS OF THE PRAIRIE

And Red Deviltry As It Is!

CAST OF CHARACTERS:

BUFFALO BILL—by the Original Hero................Hon. W. F. CODY
TEXAS JACK—by the Original Hero................J. B. OMOHUNDRO
CALE DURG................NED BUNTLINE
DOVE EYE................M'LLE MORLACCHI
Mormon Ben................Mr. Wentworth
Sly Mike................Mr. Walters
Phelim O'Laugherty................Harry Gilbert
Carl Pretzel................Walter Fletcher

INDIANS.

Wolf Slayer................W. J. Halpin
Big Eagle................W. H. Ferris
Ar-fi-a-ka, | | Granny Chief
As-ze-tee, | | Prairie Dog
As-sin-ah-wa, | Pawnee and Indian Chiefs, | Water Chief
Te-ko, tie-pown, | | Big Elk
Kit—kot-tona, | | Great River
Chuk-Kak, | | Seven Stars
HAZEL EYE................SENORITA ELOE CARFANO
Nat-lah................Mrs. Beach

Synopsis of Scenery and Incidents:

ACT I.—SCENE 1.—On the Plains—Cale Durg, the Trapper—Arrival of Buffalo Bill and Texas Jack—Story of the Hunt—A warning from Dove Eye—Danger—"We'll wipe the Red Skins out,"—Off on the trail—The War-Whoop.
SCENE II.—The Renegade's Camp—Mormon Ben—Phelim O'Laugherty and Sly Mike—O'Laugherty's continued Drouth—Danger to Hazel Eye!
SCENE III.—Hazel Eye's poetic tribute to Cale Durg—Hazel Eye Surprised—Cale Durg to the Rescue—The Renegade Foiled—Wolf Slayer, the Treacherous Ute—Cale Durg overpowered—Search for the Bottle—Cale Durg's Temperance Rhapsody.
SCENE IV.—Doomed to the Torture Post—Dove Eye's Appeal to the Ch'ef,—"Death to the Pale Face"—Then burn, ye cursed Dogs, burn—The blazing Faggots—Dove Eye's knife—The Severed Bonds—Cale Durg Defiant—"We'll Fight ye all"—Timely Arrival—Buffalo Bill and Texas Jack—"Death to the Redskins"—Rescue of Cale Durg.
ACT II.—SCENE I.—Mormon Ben, Sly Mike, and Phelim O'Laugherty—O'Laugherty declares "he is not a Mormon"—The Meeting with the Indians—What Mormon Ben wanted—What O'Laugherty wanted—Wolf Slayer's disdain of Fire Water,—"Its the Curse of the Red Man as well as the White"—The Departure of the Indians for the War-path—Dove Eye's invocation to the Great Spirit.
SCENE II.—Dove Eye and Hazel Eye, the two friends—Buffalo Bill Declares his Love—It is Reciprocated—Texas Jack arrives and interrupts the Meeting—"The Indians are Coming"—Buffalo Bill and Jack retire to Ambush—How Jack ropes them in—(Buffalo Bill)—"That's the kind of a man I am"—How they Scalp 'em on the Plains.
SCENE III.—Phelim O'Laugherty and Atoka—the Apache-Child of Cochise—Cale Durg to the rescue—God's Beverage—Love Scene between Texas Jack and Hazel Eye.
SCENE IV.—The Search for Hazel Eye—"The Cage is here, but the bird has flown"—The Trail—The Search and Capture of the Forest Maidens—Dove Eye's Contempt for the Renegades—Cale Durg arrives upon the scene—"Fly, Fly Your Enemies are too many"—Cale Durg Never runs—The Capture and Death of Cale Durg—The Dying Curse—The Trapper's Last Shot!
ACT III.—SCENE I.—Dove Eye and Hazel Eye—Grief for Cale Durg—Buffalo Bill and Texas Jack—Bill's Oath of Vengeance—"I'll not leave a Redskin to skim the Prairie"—Dove Eye dejected—The White Girl and Red Maiden's affections—"We'll be Sisters"—Revenge for the Slain Trapper—Vengeance or Death.
SCENE II.—The German Trader—The Loss of the Bottle—Carl Pretzel's Agony.
SCENE III.—The Scalp Dance—Eagle and Wolf Slayer—"I Come to Kill You"—The Knife Fight—Death of Wolf Slayer.
SCENE IV.—Phelim and Mormon Ben on their last legs—No prospect for the fiftieth wife, or a replenished bottle.
SCENE V.—The Trapper on the lookout—Dove Eye's faith in Manito—The Indians—Buffalo Bill's red hot reception—"Give it to them boys"—One Hundred Reds for one Cale Durg—The American Scout Triumphant—Great Heavens the

PRAIRIE ON FIRE.

Magnificent Scenic Effects; Life-like Illustrations of a Great Western Prairie, as seen when on Fire. Imposingly Grand. K. P. Railway Train in a Herd of Buffalo—Clear the Track.

To be preceded by the Short but Terribly Laughable Farce of

A KISS IN THE DARK

Mr. Pettibone................Harry Gilbert
Frank Fathom................Harry Wentworth
Mrs. Pettibone................Gussie Logan
Mary................Mrs. Beach
Unkown................Miss Jackson

MATINEES WEDNESDAY AND SATURDAY!

50 Cents................Children................25 Cents

D. H. ELLIOTT, (Gen'l West. Agent Kan. Pac. R'y.,) Trav. Agent for this Combination.

National Theater

JOHN T. FORD................Lessee
H. CLAY FORD................Manager

ONE WEEK!

WITH THE WONDERFUL

FRANK FRAYNE

RIFLE TEAM!

MRS. FRANK FRAYNE!

THE FAVORITE VOCALISTIC ACTRESS.

LITTLE FRANKY FRAYNE

FIVE YEAR OLD ACTOR AND "DEAD SHOT, Jr."

JAS. W. BUTLER!

THE DARING FRONTIERSMAN AND TALENTED ACTOR.

FRED. W. KNIGHT

THE ORIGINAL "COMANCHE FRED."

JACK, The Celebrated English Mastiff!

AND

The Real Indian Pony, HACKBERRY!

All appearing in the Greatest Sensation Play of the Century, in Five Acts, written expressly for them by C. W. Tayleure, Esq. being the most realistic picture of Wild Border Life ever presented to the public, entitled

SI SLOCUM!

SI SLOCUM, a Trapper................MR. FRANK FRAYNE
RUTH SLOCUM................MRS. FRANK FRAYNE
LITTLE FREDDIE................LITTLE FRANKIE FRAYNE
COYOTE TOBE, an Outlaw................MR. F. KNIGHT
ZAVALLA, a young Mexican................Mr. J. H. Rowe
Julian Ramires, alias Ramon Vasques................Mr. C. Hawkinson
Fuller Townsend, a New York merchant................Mr. Wm. Barton
Jake Blucane, alias Lewis Beasley................Mr. C. Walters
Wallace Foster, a Surveyor and Engineer................Mr. Geo. W. Denham
Jerry Blackburn, a Negro................Mr. Chas. Sturgis
Julius Kraatz, a German................C. Atwell
U. Bett, an Auctioneer................Mr. C. Wilson
Police Officer................Mr. L. R. Birchel
Pietro a Mexican Trapper................Mr. J. Mitchell
The Bear................Mr. J. Reddy
Jim, | | Mr. J. Monroe
Ned, | Settlers, | Miss Grace Marco
Grace Townsend................Miss Eugenia Paul
Patsey Collins................Mrs. Gonzales
Mrs. Bludsoe................Miss Kate Halpin
Pasquita.

During the Play MR. FRAYNE will shoot an apple from his wife's head by a backward rifle shot; also, rescue a hanging Negro by cutting the rope with a bullet. Mrs. Clara Butler Frayne will shoot an apple from her husband's hand. Little Frankie's wonderful shot. Terrific fight between the Dog Jack and the Bear—The most exciting Scene ever witnessed, and the wonderful performances of the Indian Pony, Hackberry.

SPECIAL.—Mr. Frayne's feat of Shooting an Apple from his Wife's Head by a backward rifle shot, hazardous as it appears, and thrilling as it is, is free from danger. Independently of the unfailing skill of the man, the Lady's head and brow is fully protected against all hazard by steel chain armor, concealed beneath her hat and handkerchief. This explanation will allay apprehensions, without detracting from the marvelous skill of the shot.

New & Beautiful Scenery!

APPROPIATE MUSIC, NEW COSTUMES, PROPERTIES, &C.

SI SLOCUM MATINEE, SATURDAY

Oct. 25, Mrs. D. P. Bowers.

WASHINGTON CHRONICLE PRINT, 914 PENNA. AVE.

The dime novel, a cheap, wrapper-bound form of fiction which first appeared in the 1860s, served as the stage did to familiarize Americans with the West. Dime novels dealt in high adventure, miraculous escapes, rescued maidens, and impossibly complex plots. Early examples were about hunters, Revolutionary war heroes, and pirates, but by the 1870s western themes began to appear in dime novels and a few even featured cowboys as heroes, rather than as men working with cattle. The cowboys were usually young, handsome, and upright and spent their time rescuing maidens from Indians or from villains disguised as Indians.

"Night-Hawk Kit"
Beadle's Dime Novels, No. 238
New York: Beadle and Company, 1871
Dime Novel Collection
Rare Book and Special Collections Division
Library of Congress

"The Twin Trailers"
Beadle's Dime Novels, No. 262
New York: Beadle and Adams, 1872
Dime Novel Collection
Rare Book and Special Collections Division
Library of Congress

Beadle's Half Dime Library
Patent Leather Joe—Always-On-Hand
Wood engraving with letterpress
Copyright 1878 by Beadle & Adams
Poster Collection
Prints and Photographs Division
Library of Congress

"Lasso Jack"
Munro's Ten Cent Novels, No. 195
New York: George Munro, Publisher, 1870
Dime Novel Collection
Rare Book and Special Collections Division
Library of Congress

"Night Riders"
The Nickel Library, No. 272
New York: Nickel Library Co., 1882
Dime Novel Collection
Rare Book and Special Collections Division
Library of Congress

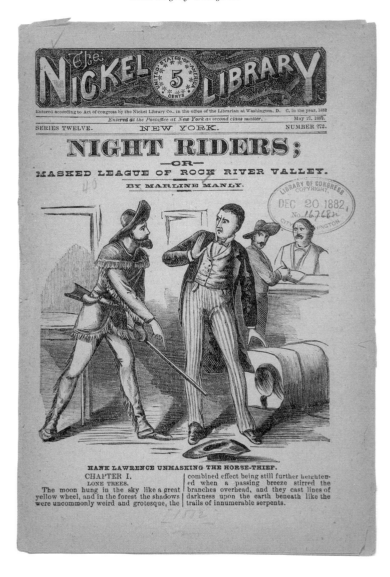

In the late 1870s and early 1880s, as the western cattle industry boomed, another image of the cowboy began to take shape in the East: that of the cowboy as a rowdy, dangerous, lawless, reckless individualist, who was constantly armed with a pistol and ready to use it. Travelers on the transcontinental railway brought back harrowing stories of the pranks played by cowboys on tourists, and at the same time the genuine lawlessness of parts of the West came to the public's attention through incidents like the Johnson County War. Between 1876 and 1888 popular illustrated magazines like the "National Police Gazette" and "Frank Leslie's Illustrated Newspaper" published hundreds of articles on the purported activities of cowboys. Many of these dealt with his criminal tendencies, and the accompanying woodcuts showed him murdering innocent settlers, tormenting dudes, and generally behaving in a reckless and antisocial manner.

He Had Him on a String
Artist unknown
Wood engraving, ca. 1887
The National Police Gazette, December 24, 1887
HV 6201.N2 Folio 51–52
Rare Book and Special Collections Division
Library of Congress

An Unpleasant Guest
Artist unknown
Wood engraving, ca. 1883
National Police Gazette, March 31, 1883
American Folklife Center
Library of Congress

AN UNPLEASANT GUEST.

A DRUNKEN COWBOY UNDERTAKES TO REFORM THE RULES OF BALL-ROOM ETIQUETTE IN LEADVILLE, COLO., AND GETS A SET BACK.

JACK DEMPSEY STILL WEARS THE DIAMOND BELT.

THE NATIONAL POLICE GAZETTE
THE LEADING ILLUSTRATED SPORTING JOURNAL IN AMERICA.

The Weir-Warren Fight.

Copyrighted for 1887 by RICHARD K. FOX, Proprietor POLICE GAZETTE PUBLISHING HOUSE, Franklin Square, New York.

RICHARD K. FOX,
Editor and Proprietor.

NEW YORK, SATURDAY, DECEMBER 24, 1887.

VOLUME LI—No. 536.
Price Ten Cents.

HE HAD HIM ON A STRING.
THE MANAGER OF A DIZZY BLONDE TROUPE IS LASSOED BY AN INDIGNANT COWBOY AT DODGE CITY, KANSAS.

Although the stage, dime novels, and popular magazines tentatively introduced the cowboy to the East, it was Buffalo Bill's Wild West that coupled him inseparably with feats of skill and daring. Organized in 1882, and in many ways an outgrowth of his stage plays, Buffalo Bill's Wild West (the word "show" was never used in its publicity) made an impression on the popular consciousness that is still discernible. It toured the eastern United States and Europe from 1882 until 1916, and during those years the cry "Buffalo Bill's in town!" was enough to bring business to a standstill. The show was essentially a series of riding and shooting acts, interspersed with a series of reenactments of Indian battles and, of course, the Indian attack on the Deadwood stagecoach. From the very beginning, the show included cowboys, both as acrobatic riders and as rescuers of the Deadwood stage. It was, in truth, the first cowboy and Indian show.

Buffalo Bill in Wild West Show Costume
Photographer unknown, ca. 1885
Buffalo Bill Historical Center
Cody, Wyoming

I Am Coming
Lithograph
Courier Litho. Co., Buffalo, N.Y.
Copyright 1900, The Courier Co.
Poster Collection
Prints and Photographs Division
Library of Congress

COL. W. F. CODY

I AM COMING

Buck Taylor—Armed with Pistol and Knife and Wearing an Embroidered Shirt, Buckskin Chaps, and Spurs—Poses with a Rawhide Lariat
Anderson Studio, New York
Photograph, ca. 1885

The first cowboy star of Buffalo Bill's Wild West was William Levi "Buck" Taylor, billed as "The King of the Cowboys." He first worked as a cowboy and then drifted north to Nebraska, where he took a job on Cody's North Platte Ranch.

The Wild West's programs were careful to state that the six-foot-five Texan was "amiable as a child," although he could throw a steer by the horns, tie him up single-handed, pick up a handkerchief from the ground while galloping by on a horse, and ride the worst bucking broncos.
Buffalo Bill Historical Center
Cody, Wyoming

Buffalo Bill's Wild West and Congress of Rough Riders of the World
Lithograph
Copyright 1896, Courier Lithography Co.
Buffalo, New York

Cody developed an act called "Cowboy Fun" that featured trick riding, steer roping, bronco riding, and races. It was this act that fixed the image of the cowboy as a daring and reckless rider in the collective American imagination and was the forerunner of all the acrobatic scenes in Hollywood westerns. Through Cody's act the cowboy and his bucking bronco became a symbol of the Wild West.
Buffalo Bill Historical Center
Cody, Wyoming

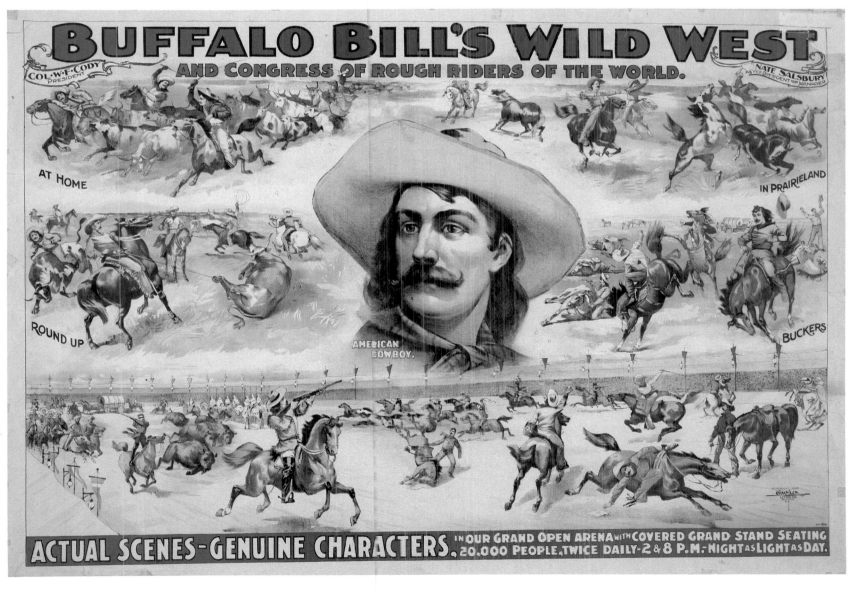

Buffalo Bill's Troupe of Cowboys

Photographer unknown, ca. 1885

This photograph shows most of the cowboys who accompanied Buffalo Bill's Wild West to London for Queen Victoria's Golden Jubilee Exposition in 1888 and on its subsequent tour of Europe. The men wore embroidered shirts and angora chaps for theatrical effect, but they had learned their skills on the open range. While they were in England, Antonio Esquivel defeated a British jockey, J. Latham, in a ten-mile relay race. Esquivel rode thirteen broncos and Latham, thirteen English thoroughbreds. In 1891, after the Wild West had added a Congress of Rough Riders of the World, Antonio Esquivel led a group of twenty vaqueros. The Congress included twenty-five cowboys and a thirty-seven-piece mounted cowboy band.

Western History Collections
University of Oklahoma Library
Norman, Oklahoma

Joe Esquival, Jim Kid, Jim Mitchell, Dick Johnson, Billy Bullock, Antonio Esquival, Tom Duffy. Lying down in front is Johnny Baker, and Billy Johnson.

GROUP OF COWBOYS WITH THE OLD TIME BUFFALO BILL'S WILD WEST SHOW

"Rough Riders—ou les Cavaliers les Plus Hardis du Monde"

Cover illustration, lithograph, 1905
French edition of *Rough Riders Magazine*, vol. 8, London: Weiners Ltd., Publisher
Buffalo Bill Historical Center
Cody, Wyoming

Buffalo Bill had many imitators. It is estimated that in 1893 there were fifty Wild West shows touring the United States. One of the most successful latter-day shows was the Miller 101 Ranch Show, which carried the tradition into the age of the motion picture and the automobile. The 101 was an Oklahoma ranch that went into show business in 1905 and was responsible for many innovations in the Wild West show before going out of business during the depression. The cowgirl was the invention of the Miller 101, which introduced the first women bronc riders in 1909.

The sport of bulldogging was popularized in the Miller 101 Ranch Show also. Bill Pickett, a black cowboy working on a Texas ranch in the 1890s, invented the method of throwing steers by biting into their lower lips. Pickett joined the Miller show in 1905 and remained until his death in 1932. He once estimated that he had thrown five thousand steers with his "bite-'em" method. The Miller show constantly introduced new acts, capitalizing on the popularity of the cowboy by developing such improbable spectacles as cowboy auto polo and cowboy boomerang throwing. The ranch also produced films, and both Tom Mix and Hoot Gibson worked for Miller before going on to careers as movie cowboys.

The Cowgirl's First Love. Bates.

Edith Tantlinger
Star Cowgirl of the Miller 101
Bates (dates unknown)
Photograph, ca. 1914
Western History Collections
University of Oklahoma Library
Norman, Oklahoma

Miller 101 Cowboy Bill Pickett
Inventor of Bulldogging
Photographer unknown, ca. 1910

Bill Pickett was a featured performer of the Miller 101 show for many years. The son of former slaves, he was born near Austin, Texas, in 1870 and worked as a cowboy on a number of central Texas ranches in the 1890s. It was there that he developed a method of throwing and holding steers by biting into their lower lip in the manner of a bulldog. In 1900 he went on the county-fair rodeo circuit with a bulldogging act. He appeared in 1904 at the Cheyenne Frontier Days celebration, one of the country's largest rodeos, which was under the management of Dave McClure. In 1905 he joined the Miller brothers and, except for a brief interval in the early twenties, he stayed with their show until it went bankrupt in 1931. He toured England and South America billed as "the dusky Demon of Oklahoma" and thrilled crowds with his "bite-'em" style of throwing cattle. By the time he retired from active performing at the age of fifty, to become a horse trainer, he estimated that he had bulldogged five thousand steers. He was killed by a horse on the Miller 101 Ranch on April 2, 1932.
Western History Collections
University of Oklahoma Library
Norman, Oklahoma

Cowboy Throwing Boomerang
Photographer unknown, date unknown
   Vernon Tantlinger, originally a trick-shooting artist, learned to throw the Australian boomerang, catching it on its return in a large net. He was featured by the Miller 101 as the "Cowboy Boomerang Artist."
Western History Collections
University of Oklahoma Library
Norman, Oklahoma

Cowboys Ready for Auto Polo
Flint (dates unknown)
Photograph, ca. 1914
   Although the program of the Miller 101 Show generally followed the format of Buffalo Bill's Wild West, it also introduced completely new acts. Cowboys used stripped-down Model T's equipped with roll bars to play auto polo.
Western History Collections
University of Oklahoma Library
Norman, Oklahoma

Boys Reading Miller 101 Advertisements
Vince Dillon (dates unknown)
Photograph, date unknown
Western History Collections
University of Oklahoma Library
Norman, Oklahoma

**Trick Riding Stunts
from the Miller 101 Show**
Emil W. Lenders (d. 1934)
Photographs, ca. 1910
Western History Collections
University of Oklahoma Library
Norman, Oklahoma

Wild West Show at a County Fair
Photographer unknown, ca. 1930

The Miller 101 Show was the last of the big Wild West shows. It went bankrupt in 1931 and was never revived, but its tradition was carried on by a number of small shows. They operated at county fairs and carnivals, or as parts of small circuses, until World War II. This photograph shows the entrance to Vern and Edith Tantlinger's Tex-Mex Wild West Show, which toured Mexico and South America in the thirties. The painted panels show some of the acts—including bronco busting, bulldogging, and the attack on the Deadwood stage, still being enacted fifty years after Buffalo Bill introduced it.
Western History Collections
University of Oklahoma Library
Norman, Oklahoma

THE ROMANTIC IMAGE

The years from 1880 to 1910 were the golden age of the cowboy in romantic illustration and fiction. The romantic image of the cowboy first appeared in popular magazines in the early 1880s in illustrations drawn by two "Harper's" artists, W. A. Rogers and Rufus F. Zogbaum. They placed their cowboys in romantic outdoor settings, rather than in the barrooms and saloons depicted in the "National Police Gazette." Their pictures emphasized the cowboy's youth, his high spirits, and, sometimes, his loneliness. Zogbaum in particular devised several settings that served as models for later illustrators.

By the mid-nineties, Frederic Remington had become America's foremost illustrator of cowboy life. His cowboys were young, reckless, daring, alive with movement, and always white. Although Remington prided himself on the accuracy with which he painted horses, horse equipment, and articles of clothing, he was highly selective in the incidents he depicted and the settings he chose. Charles M. Russell, a Montana cowboy whose work began to appear in the East after 1903, also emphasized action and skill on horseback, although he occasionally tempered them with dry western wit. Both men's pictures were immensely popular in the West as well as the East and found their way into virtually every household in America as book or magazine illustrations, prints, calendars, posters, and advertisements. Remington and Russell became the founders of a genre of western art that still flourishes, and still today presents the cowboy as a romantic, individualistic man of action.

The Prairie Letter Box
Wood engraving after a drawing by Rufus F. Zogbaum
(1849–1925)
Harper's Weekly, April 23, 1887
    Rufus Fairchild Zogbaum's treatment of cowboys was decidedly romantic. The South Carolina-born artist's illustrations of western life, done on several trips to Montana, appeared in *Harper's Weekly* between 1885 and 1887 and set the pattern for the flood of western illustrations that came in the 1890s. *The Prairie Letter Box* sought to emphasize the cowboy's isolation from civilization, the natural beauty of his surroundings, and the tenuous ties that bound him to home and loved ones. The theme was so successful that it was imitated by Frederic Remington in 1901, by N. C. Wyeth in 1906, by Erwin E. Smith in 1909, and by a sheet music publisher in the 1920s (p. 143).
American Folklife Center
Library of Congress

THE VICTOR'S PRIZE

The Victor's Prize
Guy Eurnge (dates unknown)
Color offset, 1905
Metropolitan Printing Company
Popular and Applied Graphic Art Collections
Prints and Photographs Division
Library of Congress

HARPER'S WEEKLY.
JOURNAL OF CIVILIZATION.

Vol. XXXI.—No. 1583.   NEW YORK, SATURDAY, APRIL 23, 1887.   TEN CENTS A COPY. $4.00 PER YEAR, IN ADVANCE

THE PRAIRIE LETTER-BOX.—Drawn by R. F. Zogbaum.—[See Page 295.]

Rural Delivery
"Where the Mail Goes, Cream of Wheat Goes"
N. C. Wyeth (1882–1945)
Oil on canvas, 1906
Gift of the National Biscuit Company
The Minneapolis Institute of Arts
Minneapolis, Minnesota

Cowboy from the LS Outfit Mailing a Letter
Erwin E. Smith (1888–1947)
Photograph, LS Ranch, Texas, 1909
  The Texas sculptor Erwin E. Smith, a student of Lorado Taft, became interested in photographing cowboys in the Texas Panhandle as an aid to painting and sculpting. Among the poses he chose for his subjects was this one. The fact that the mailbox is placed between the ruts of the road and the horse is shying away from it as from an unfamiliar object suggests that Smith erected the mailbox for his picture.
Erwin E. Smith Collection
Prints and Photographs Division
Library of Congress

At the turn of the century, plagued by problems of industrial strife and fearing that traditional American values were being submerged as a flood of immigrants arrived from Europe, some Americans saw the cowboy as personifying the qualities they thought of as being peculiarly American: unrestrained personal freedom, practical ability, modesty, and, when called for, reckless courage. In fact, Americans projected these values on the cowboy through a series of books, plays, and pictures that portrayed him not simply as the hard-working drifter he was but as a knight of the plains ennobled by his calling. During the 1880s, the image of the cowboy underwent a change from rogue to hero. The men most responsible for this change were easterners who idealized the West: Frederic Remington, Owen Wister, and Theodore Roosevelt.

"Painting the Town Red"
Wood engraving after a drawing
by Rufus F. Zogbaum (1849–1925)
Harper's Weekly, October 16, 1886

Rufus Zogbaum turned the criminality of the cowboy into heady playfulness. In *Painting the Town Red*, we see four youthful cowboys making a spectacular entrance at a full gallop into a western town. They are being watched with amused tolerance by some citizens and are being actively encouraged by two others. In fact, the only person who seems disturbed by their behavior is a Chinese man, who, in accordance with the racist attitudes of the period, is characterized as a comic figure. The text accompanying this drawing, written by G. O. Shields, begins, "Cowboys as a class are brimful and running over with wit, merriment, and good humor. They are always ready for any bit of innocent fun, but are not perpetually spoiling for a fight, as has so often been said of them . . . altogether cowboys are a large-hearted, generous class of fellows . . . the constant communication with nature . . . the days and nights of lonely cruising and camping on the prairie, the uninterrupted communion with and study of self which this occupation affords, tend to make young men honest and noble."

This striking image was repeated many times in the 1880s and 1890s and is still very much part of the American mental picture of the cowboy to this day.
American Folklife Center
Library of Congress

Cowboys Coming to Town for Christmas
Wood engraving after a drawing
by Frederic Remington (1861–1909)
Harper's Weekly, December 21, 1889
    By 1889 Frederic Remington was on his way to becoming
America's best known western illustrator. and he, too, used the
theme of cowboys entering a western town at full gallop. This
wood engraving appeared in the *Harper's* Christmas supplement.
American Folklife Center
Library of Congress

"The Rope Corral"
Frederic Remington (1861–1909)
Pen-and-ink drawing, 1887

Frederic Remington, the illustrator of *Ranch Life and the Hunting Trail*, was the son of an upstate New York newspaper publisher. He studied art at Yale College. In 1881 Remington made a trip West and brought back some sketches, one of which, redrawn by W. A. Rogers, was published in *Harper's Weekly*. The next year, he settled down in New York to make his living as an artist. He attended classes at the Art Students League, and in 1886 he made a second trip West to observe the Geronimo campaign. He sold the drawings he made on this trip to *Outing* magazine and launched his career as a successful western artist.

The cowboys Remington drew for Roosevelt's articles—some of them drawn from photographs the author supplied—replicated Roosevelt's word pictures. The cowboys were hard, lean, and determined men, who were shown performing a number of difficult tasks with ease and aplomb. Here we see one cowboy holding the rope to form a rope corral for the roundup remuda, while a second prepares to rope his mount.
The R. W. Norton Art Gallery
Shreveport, Louisiana

"Ranch Life and the Hunting-Trail"
By Theodore Roosevelt (1858–1919)
Illustrated by Frederic Remington (1861–1909)
New York: Century Company, 1888

In 1888, a series of articles entitled "Ranch Life and the Hunting Trail" written for *Century* magazine by Theodore Roosevelt and illustrated by Frederic Remington gave the cowboy the final stamp of respectability. The articles, in which Roosevelt described his ranching experiences in the Dakota Territory, were published by the Century Company as a book that same year.

The book's title page identifies Roosevelt, who had already served as speaker of the New York State Assembly, as *"President of the Boone and Crockett Club of New York, Honorary Member of the London Alpine Club, Etc., Etc.,"* in other words, very much a member of the eastern establishment. In the text, Roosevelt described cowboys as *"as hardy and self-reliant as any men who ever breathed—with bronzed, set faces, and keen eyes that look all the world in the face without flinching as they flash out from under the broad-brimmed hats. . . . they are quiet, self-contained men, perfectly frank and simple, and on their own ground treat a stranger with the most whole-souled hospitality."*
F596.R778
General Collections
Library of Congress

"Against the Sunset"
Frederic Remington (1861–1909)
Oil on canvas, 1906

Remington painted more Indians and soldiers than he did cowboys, but he had a special feeling that the "cow puncher," as he preferred to call him, embodied American virtues threatened by extensive immigration. Remington felt despair that the open range was disappearing and with it the cowboy he so admired. *"With me, cowboys are what gems and porcelains are to others,"* he wrote to his friend Poultney Bigelow.
Petersen Galleries
Beverly Hills, California

"Pony Tracks"
Edward Penfield (1866–1925)
Lithograph, 1895

Frederic Remington observed the West as a magazine correspondent. He returned from his summer trips of the late 1880s and early 1890s with material not only for pictures but also for magazine articles, which were published in *Harper's Weekly* and *Harper's Monthly.* Through these articles ran a theme that became a major motif in later writing about the West. It had to do with the inhospitability of the western terrain and the grim determination of the men who lived in it. Remington presented the West to eastern readers as a dangerous place—threatening even death—that produced a special spirit in the men who confronted it.

In 1895 a collection of fifteen of Remington's articles was published by Harper & Brothers in New York under the title *Pony Tracks.* In its review, the *Bookman* said that Remington had roamed *"where the American may still revel in the great red-shirted freedom which has been pushed so far to the mountain wall that it threatens soon to expire somewhere near the top."* The graphic artist Edward Penfield executed this poster to advertise the book.
Poster Collection
Prints and Photographs Division
Library of Congress

"Arizona Cowboy"
In *A Bunch of Buckskins*
Frederic Remington (1861–1909)
Lithograph printed in colors, 1901
After a drawing in pastel
Copyright by Robert Howard Russell, 1901
Popular and Applied Graphic Art Collections
Prints and Photographs Division
Library of Congress

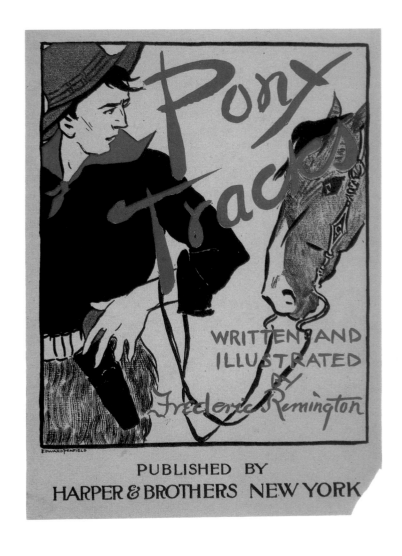

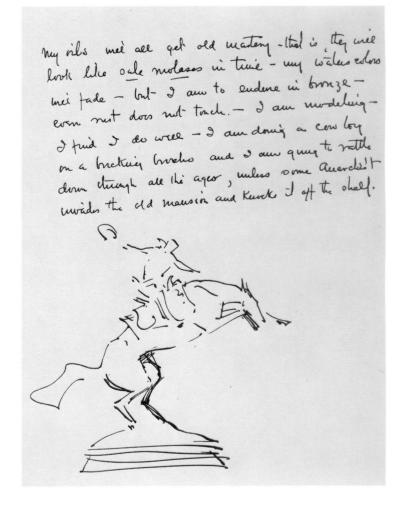

Bronco Buster
Frederic Remington (1861–1909)
Bronze, 1895
Roman Bronze Works, Greenpoint, New York
Cast No. 275
Remington Art Museum
Ogdensburg, New York

Frederic Remington to Owen Wister
Manuscript, 1895, with a sketch for
The Bronco Buster

In the summer of 1895, when Remington was thirty-four years old, he began to experiment with bronze sculpture. He had no experience with the medium but enthusiastically wrote his friend Owen Wister: *"My oils will all get old mastery—that is, they will look like Peale molasses in time—my watercolors will fade—but I am to endure in bronze . . . I am doing a cowboy on a bucking bronco and I am going to rattle down through all the ages."*

The Bronco Buster was the first of twenty-four bronzes created by Remington in the years before his death in 1909, most of them showing single equestrian figures—Indians, cavalry troopers, and cowboys.
Owen Wister Papers
Manuscript Division
Library of Congress

**"Just a Little Sunshine—Just a Little Rain
Just a Little Pleasure—Just a Little Pain"**
Charles M. Russell (1864–1926)
Watercolor on paper, ca. 1898

Many of Russell's early paintings and watercolors were done at the request of Montana saloon owners. In 1898, William Rance, proprietor of the Silver Dollar in Great Falls, Montana, asked Russell to do this series of four watercolors depicting some of the hardships of cowboy life. The bottle in the last picture contained a well-known painkiller of the period.
Amon Carter Museum
Fort Worth, Texas

"The Broken Rope"
Charles M. Russell (1864–1926)
Oil on canvas, 1904

Charles Marion Russell was a native of Missouri who went to Montana in 1880 at the age of sixteen and lived there until the end of his life. He worked as a cowboy for thirteen years before he decided to become a full-time painter. It was not until 1903 that he took his work to New York, where he found the art world eager to accept a cowboy artist. Unlike Remington, Russell was a cowboy who loved to paint, rather than a painter who loved cowboys, but he owed much of his success to the demand that Remington had created for western illustrations.

Russell's work is based on a wealth of personal experience as a working cowboy, and his images are characterized by action and detail, with a particularly strong emphasis on physical activity.
Amon Carter Museum
Fort Worth, Texas

At Rope's End
Charles M. Russell (1864–1926)
Oil on canvas, 1902
Private Collection

**Charles Marion Russell
1864–1926**
Jay Contway (b. 1935)
Bronze, 1974
*David G. Drum
Polson, Montana*

**Erwin E. Smith in
Roundup Camp, JA Ranch, Texas**
Erwin E. Smith (1886–1947)
Photograph, 1907

    The romantic view of the cowboy motivated not only painters but photographers as well. Erwin E. Smith was a native of Bonham, a farming community in north Texas. As a youth he was fascinated with cowboys and Indians. At the age of eighteen, he went to Chicago to study sculpture with Lorado Z. Taft, an American sculptor who was an art instructor at the Chicago Art Institute at the time. Two years later, Smith returned to Texas with a camera, determined to record working cowboys on the fenced ranches of the Texas Panhandle. He used photography to aid him in creating more accurate sculpture of western themes, and in the process he produced one of the great western photographic archives in the United States.
Erwin E. Smith Collection
Prints and Photographs Division
Library of Congress

**Shoe Bar Chuck Wagon, Hoodlum Wagon,
and Cowboys of the Shoe Bar Ranch, Texas**
Erwin E. Smith (1886–1947)
Photograph, ca. 1910
Erwin E. Smith Collection
Prints and Photographs Division
Library of Congress

Day Herder with the JA Outfit
JA Ranch, Texas
Erwin E. Smith (1886–1947)
Photograph, 1907
Erwin E. Smith Collection
Prints and Photographs Division
Library of Congress

Rolling Cigarette—Cowboy at Rest
Erwin E. Smith (1886–1947)
Photograph of a pencil sketch, ca. 1907

Erwin Smith's method of working was that of the artist rather than the documentary photographer. Many of his photographs were compositional studies based on sketches, with his subjects posed in romantic attitudes. In some cases, he would wait for hours with his camera until his subjects had maneuvered themselves into the positions called for in his sketch; in others, he simply posed them.
The Nita Stewart Haley Memorial Library
Midland, Texas

Frank Smith, a Cross-B Cowpuncher
Watering His Horse
Cross-B Ranch, New Mexico
Erwin E. Smith (1886–1947)
Photograph, ca. 1910
Erwin E. Smith Collection
Prints and Photographs Division
Library of Congress

**Four Cowpunchers Shooting Craps in
Roundup Camp
JA Ranch, Texas**
Erwin E. Smith (1886–1947)
Photograph, 1907
   The cowpuncher in the white shirt in this
snapshot is actually George Patullo, a writer
of western fiction who was visiting the JA
with Smith.
Erwin E. Smith Collection
Prints and Photographs Division
Library of Congress

**The Wagon Cook Is Taking a Shave
JA Ranch, Texas**
Erwin E. Smith (1886–1947)
Photograph, 1907
Erwin E. Smith Collection
Prints and Photographs Division
Library of Congress

**Injured Cowboy
Turkey Tracks Ranch, Texas**
Erwin E. Smith (1886–1947)
Photograph, 1908
   Besides taking carefully composed
pictures, Smith recorded everyday life in
more spontaneous shots. Here the photo-
grapher captured the excitement just after a
horse stepped into a prairie dog hole and
threw its rider.
Erwin E. Smith Collection
Prints and Photographs Division
Library of Congress

THE COWBOY AND THE PRINTED WORD

At the same time that the cowboy was being romantically portrayed by eastern artists and illustrators, he was making an appearance in print. At first, he was simply one among a cast of many western characters, but with the publication in 1902 of "The Virginian" by Owen Wister, he moved to center stage and held that spot through the rest of the decade amid a host of cowboy novels, cowboy memoirs, and western short stories.

In 1879 an Austin, Texas, attorney named Thomas Pilgrim published "Live Boys, or Charley and Nasho in Texas," under the pseudonym of Arthur Morecamp. "Live Boys" is an account of two Texas boys who drive cattle to Kansas in order to raise money to attend the Philadelphia Centennial Exposition. The book was primarily written for boys and lies somewhere between dime novels and serious fiction, but it has been described as the first cowboy novel. The very next year a short story in "Lippincott's Magazine" featured Bob, a California cowboy, who was distinguished by "his readiness to oblige, his kind heart, his childlike faith in human nature, his thousand and one good qualities."

"Live Boys; or Charley and Nasho in Texas"
By Arthur Morecamp (dates unknown)
Boston: Lee and Shepard, Publishers, 1879
Eugene C. Barker Texas History Center
The University of Texas at Austin
Austin, Texas

"Sargent's Rodeo"
By E. M. Osbourne (dates unknown)
Lippincott's Magazine, January 1880
Philadelphia, J. B. Lippincott and Co.
AP2.L55
General Collections
Library of Congress

BOB.

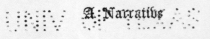

LIVE BOYS;

OR,

CHARLEY AND NASHO IN TEXAS.

A Narrative

RELATING TO TWO BOYS OF FOURTEEN, ONE A TEXAN, THE OTHER A MEXICAN: SHOWING THEIR LIFE ON THE GREAT TEXAS CATTLE TRAIL, AND THEIR ADVENTURES IN THE INDIAN TERRITORY, KANSAS, AND NORTHERN TEXAS;

EMBRACING

MANY THRILLING ADVENTURES.

TAKEN DOWN FROM CHARLEY'S NARRATIVE

BY

ARTHUR MORECAMP.

Illustrated.

BOSTON:
LEE AND SHEPARD, PUBLISHERS.
NEW YORK:
CHARLES T. DILLINGHAM.

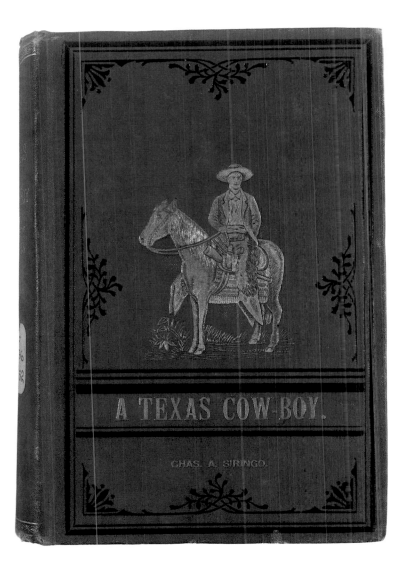

"A Texas Cow Boy; or, Fifteen Years on the Hurricane Deck of a Spanish Pony"
By Charles A. Siringo (1855–1928)
Second edition
Chicago: Siringo & Dobson, Publishers, 1886

    Charlie Siringo was born in Matagorda, Texas, in 1855. After the Civil War he learned cow work on the coastal prairies of south Texas, working for early day cattlemen like Shanghai Pierce and Bradford Grimes. Later, Siringo drove herds to Kansas and worked as a cowboy in New Mexico. In the 1880s, when cowboys became fashionable, he decided to write his memoirs. J. Frank Dobie called Siringo's book *"the first in time of all cowboy autobiographies and the first, also, in plain rolickness."* In later years many cowmen wrote their memoirs, but none were written as close in time to the events described as Siringo's, and few described the work in such detail. In his preface, Siringo gives his reason for writing the book: *"money—and lots of it."* He later claimed to have sold a million copies.
F596.S532
General Collections
Library of Congress

Representation of Life in a Cow Camp
Artist unknown
Frontispiece in
A Texas Cow Boy
F596.S532
General Collections
Library of Congress

REPRESENTATION OF LIFE IN A COW CAMP.

"Wolfville"

By Alfred Henry Lewis (1858?–1914)
Illustrated by Frederic Remington (1861–1909)
First edition
New York: Frederick A. Stokes Company, 1897

Alfred Henry Lewis, a New York journalist and active Progressive Democrat, wrote a novel that might be regarded as a transitional step between the mining camp tales of Mark Twain and Bret Harte and the cowboy novels that followed *The Virginian*. It was *Wolfville*, a series of loosely connected short stories about life in a small western town, held together by the narrator, the Old Cattleman. Lewis was by no means an exclusively western writer; he wrote biographies of Aaron Burr, John Paul Jones, and Andrew Jackson and published *Verdict*, a Democratic political journal. *Wolfville* was so successful, however, that Lewis decided to write *Wolfville Days* and *Wolfville Nights*, published in 1902, and *Wolfville Folks*, published in 1908.
Jeff Dykes
College Park, Maryland

"The Life and Adventures of the American Cowboy"

By Clark Stanley (dates unknown)
Published by Clark Stanley, 1897

By the late 1890s, the cowboy had become such a familiar part of the American landscape that his character could be appropriated to sell snake oil. Little is known of Clark Stanley beyond what he tells us in this pamphlet written to be sold at his medicine shows: that he was born in Abilene, Texas; that he first went up the trail to Kansas at the age of fourteen; that he worked as a cowboy for eleven years; and that he learned about the properties of rattlesnake oil from living with the Hopi Indians in Arizona. He includes an explanation of open-range ranching and trail driving, a description of the cowboy's costume, some advice on how to start in the cattle business ("If you have money, leave it at home"), three poems, a recipe for tanning hides, and a good deal of information about the uses of Clark Stanley's Snake Oil Liniment.
F596.S823
General Collections
Library of Congress

"Lin McLean"

By Owen Wister (1860–1938)
Illustrated by Frederic Remington (1861–1909)
New York: Harper & Brothers Publishers, 1898

Owen Wister, a Harvard classmate of Theodore Roosevelt's, made a trip to Montana in 1882 seeking the Wild West. He returned in 1891 and in that same year published his first short story, "How Lin McLean Went East," in *Harper's*. It was a straightforward, humorous story turning on the conflict between eastern sophistication and western honesty. Six years later the story reappeared as the first chapter of a western novel, *Lin McLean*. By then Wister's short stories and articles had established him as the eastern authority on the cowboy.
PS3345.L5 1898
Rare Book and Special Collections Division
Library of Congress

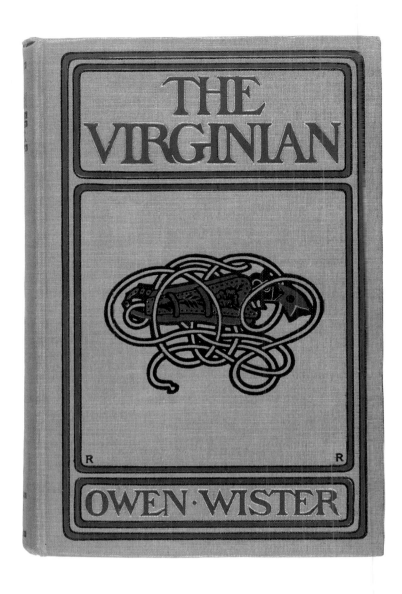

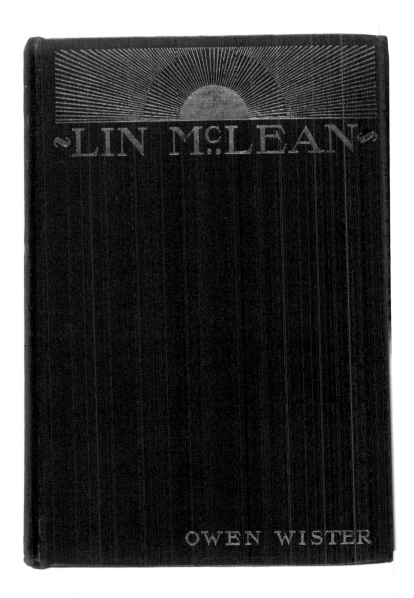

"The Virginian"
By Owen Wister (1860–1938)
First edition
New York: Macmillan Company, 1902

Magazine articles, cowboy memoirs, and cowboy poetry prepared the American public for the archetypal cowboy hero, Owen Wister's Virginian. In 1902, the Philadelphia lawyer turned writer described his hero as *"a slim young giant, more beautiful than pictures . . . his broad soft hat was pushed back; a loose-knotted, dull-scarlet handkerchief sagged from his throat; and one casual thumb was hooked in the cartridge belt that slanted across his hips. He had plainly come many miles from somewhere across the vast horizon."* He was to go on many miles, in many reincarnations, in print, on the stage, in the movies, and on television.
Lessing J. Rosenwald Collection 2305
Rare Book and Special Collections Division
Library of Congress

Publisher's Advertising Brochure for "The Virginian"
New York: Macmillan Company, 1902

The Virginian was an immense success. Fifty thousand copies were sold in the first two months after its publication. The love story of the cowboy hero—who is never given a name other than "the Virginian"—and the Vermont school teacher appealed to both easterners and westerners. Critics said that the story symbolized the reconciliation of eastern civilization and western freedom. Hundreds of western readers wrote Wister letters saying that they had known the Virginian, or someone just like him, and congratulating the author on his faithful portrayal of the cowboy. Significantly, Wister dedicated the book to President Theodore Roosevelt.
Owen Wister Papers
Manuscript Division
Library of Congress

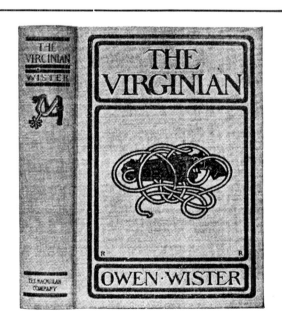

50,000 SOLD IN 2 MONTHS
Cloth, 504 pp., illustrated, $1.50

" MR. OWEN WISTER'S 'VIRGINIAN' —AN UNCOMMONLY BRILLIANT AND FASCINATING STORY-- . . . IS A BOOK OF ABSORBING INTEREST EVEN TO THOSE 'PRACTICAL' MEN WHO DO NOT ORDINARILY CARE FOR LITERATURE."
—NEW YORK TRIBUNE.

"What's your scar?" inquires one, casually, inspecting the neck of his neighbor.

"Foolishness," the other answered. "I was ~~showing off~~ displayin' myself for the benefit of the boys. One day last summer, ~~we come~~ it was. on a big snake by the Torrey Creek corral. The bettin' got pretty high ~~I~~ assured maybe my word good, ~~could'nt do it~~ so. I roped my cayuse full tilt by Mr. snake and swung down and catched him ~~by the tail~~ off the ground and cracked him same as a whip, and snapped his head off. You've seen it done?" he said to the audience.

The audience nodded, wearily.   Such a thing had never happened to me before.

"But the loose head flew ~~in~~ agin, and the fangs caught. It wouldn't occur in a hundred times, I expect. I was pretty sick for a while. But ~~we~~ had whiskey, and I used a tobacco poultice. But I'm done with snake charmin'."

Now this was coming it rather strong; but how was I to say so, when every one ~~accepted~~ received it with such silent politeness?

"An antelope knows a snake is his enemy," said another. "Ever seen a buck circlin' round and round a rattler?"

"I have always wanted to see that," said I. I knew this to be a respectable piece of truth.

"It's worth seein'," he went on. "After the buck gets close in, he gives an almighty jump up in the air, and down comes his four hoofs in a bunch on Mr. snake. Cuts him all to pieces. ~~But~~ You tell me how the buck knows that."

Of course I could not tell him. But I was very glad to meet some one who had witnessed this event. And again we sat in silence for a while; and I actually thought we were become friendly.

"A skunk'll kill you worse than a snake-bite," said another, presently. "No, I don't mean that way," he added. ~~for I had smiled.~~ "There's a brown skunk down in Arkansaw. Littler than our kind, he is. And he's mad the whole year round, same as a dog gets. Only the dog has a spell and dies; but this here Arkansaw skunk is mad right along, and it don't seem to interfere with him in other respects. Well, suppose you're campin' out, and suppose it's hot, or you're in a hurry, or anyway you haven't got inside any tent, but you're just ~~slung your blankets~~ bedded down in the open. Skunk comes travellin' along and walks on your blankets. You're warm. He likes that, same as a cat does, And he tramps with comfort, same as a cat. And you move. You get bit, that's all. And you die of hydrophobia. Ask anybody."

"Dear me!" I said. "But how do you know they're not sick skunks?"

"No, sir. They're well skunks. You'll not meet a skunk in Arkansaw that ~~ain't~~ aint robust in other respects."

I began to feel that I was being told a great many things. But now this last man went on.

"As for ~~snake bites~~ bites," he said, "See that." He held up his thumb, on which was a seamy mark.

"How did you get ~~that~~ it?" said I.

"I was huntin' owl eggs for a botanist from Boston," he answered.   Continue on (a)

WHITE HOUSE.
WASHINGTON.

personal

May 29, 1902.

Dear Dan:

I have just received the book and am immensely pleased with the dedication. It was a total surprise to me. I am glad that at least most of the chapters should be old friends, and therefore I shall not have to read the book before passing judgement; I shall not even have to tell you that I greatly admire it—for you know it already. I am genuinely proud to have my name associated with such a work. With cordial thanks,

Faithfully yours,

Theodore Roosevelt

Mr. Owen Wister,
328 Chestnut Street,
Philadelphia, Pa.

Mr. Owen Wister
c/o MacMillan & Co
New York.

Dear Sir:—

A dozen years ago I punched cows in the Ponca Nation; tramped through sun-blistered valleys in New Mexico and Arizona — and later on spent upwards of a year in the Dakota cattle country. It may be egotistical to claim that I know the west, the "Cattle Land", of that period. In the Virginian I lived it all again. I lived it because your characters were real ones — ones that have been but are no more.

Please accept my humble compliments upon your story. It has helped to make my dreams of those days more vivid and to preserve types that are rapidly passing away.

Those who knew the west owe to you a debt of gratitude for the journey back through the years.

I feel that I am one of them.

Yours very truly
W. H. Griffin

121 Sycamore St
Evansville,
Ind.

The enormous popularity of "The Virginian" opened the floodgates for a burst of cowboy fiction and memoirs. Westerners, easterners, and visiting Englishmen all contributed to defining the cowboy hero—noble, virile, quiet, modest, trustworthy, but with his own code of honor and hard as steel in a crisis. Former cowboys saw themselves in this mold, Englishmen described the "splendid fellows" they had worked with on the range, and novelists recreated the Virginian with all his virtues.

"The Log of a Cowboy"
By Andy Adams (1859–1935)
Boston: Houghton, Mifflin Company, 1903

One critic of *The Virginian* has said that the hero was "a cowboy without cattle," that is, that Wister never portrayed him working cattle. That could never be said of Andy Adams's characters. Adams was one of the few western writers of the period who portrayed the cowboy as he really was. Like his friend Charlie Siringo, Adams had worked as a cowboy in Texas and had driven cattle up the trail to Kansas. In 1898 he went to see Charles Hoyt's play, *A Texas Steer*, in which a fictional rancher-politician named Maverick Brander is satirized. As Adams put it, *"an idea came to me that if the ludicrous and false were in such demand, the real thing ought to take immensely."* He began writing plays and short stories, and in October 1902 he sent the manuscript for *The Log of a Cowboy* to Houghton Mifflin. It was the straightforward story of a cattle drive from Texas to Kansas, and it remains the best account of a trail drive ever written. Adams mixed the names and deeds of real cattlemen in with his fictional characters, and he had witnessed many of the incidents in the book. When the *Log* was published, Emerson Hough sent Houghton Mifflin a quote to be used in promoting the book: *"Andy Adams is the real thing, and the first time the real thing has appeared in print."*
American Folklife Center
Library of Congress

Cover Illustration
"Saturday Evening Post," June 19, 1915
Drawing by Harrison Fisher (1877–1934)

Western fiction underwent an important change during the first two decades of the twentieth century. Popular magazines like the *Saturday Evening Post* set the pattern for the "western story," a romance set in the West. The *Post*'s writers included some of the original formulators of the western novel: Owen Wister, Stuart Edward White, and Eugene Manlove Rhodes.
AP2.S2
American Folklife Center
Library of Congress

"The Quirt and the Spur"
By Edgar Rye (dates unknown)
Chicago: W.B. Conkey Co. Publishers, 1909
F391 R99
General Collections
Library of Congress

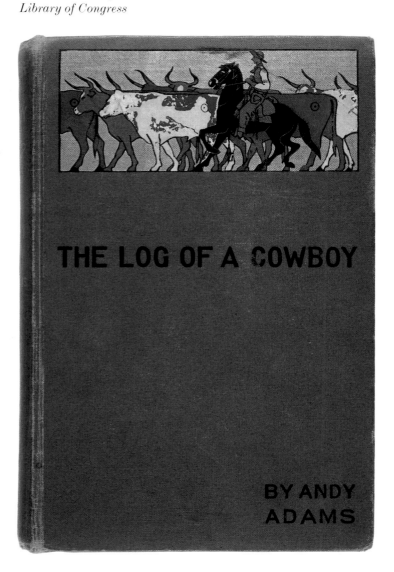

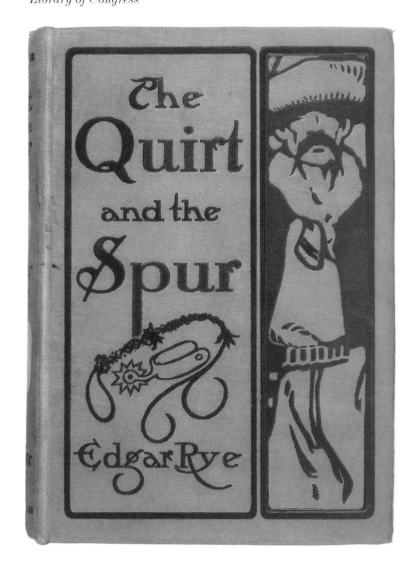

THE SATURDAY EVENING POST

An Illust[rated] [Wee]kly
Founded A°. D[...] [Benjamin Fr]anklin

JUNE 19, 1915   5cts. THE COPY

DRAWN BY
HARRISON FISHER

Queen Mary of England—By Mary Roberts Rinehart

THE COWBOY ON STAGE

In addition to being a literary hero, the cowboy emerged as a romantic stage hero at the beginning of this century. The copyright records of the Library of Congress show that in the thirty years between 1870 and 1900 four plays were filed for copyright with the word "cowboy" in the title, but in the next fifteen years thirty-five cowboy dramas were filed, including such long-forgotten thrillers as "The Cowboy Artist," "The Cowboy Detective," "The Cowboy Girl," and "The Cowpuncher: A Tale of the Country God Forgot." Not all of these plays were performed, but enough reached the stage to bring cowboy heroes in the flesh to large audiences. Unlike Buffalo Bill's cowboys, these heroes were distinguished not by feats of skill and daring but by virtuous behavior and adherence to a code of honor. They paved the way for several generations of strong, silent movie cowboys.

"A Black Sheep"
Lithograph
Strobridge Lithograph Co.
Copyright 1894

   One of the first American playwrights to use the cowboy was Charles Hoyt, the inventor of the comedy-farce. Hoyt, a newspaperman who once worked as a cowboy in Colorado, wrote seventeen comedy-farces and one comic operetta between 1883 and his death in 1899. All but one were tremendous successes. In 1886 he copyrighted a three-act play called *The Cowboy, or An American Abroad*, but it was never produced. *A Texas Steer* was a political satire built around the character of Maverick Brander, a Texas cattle king who is elected to Congress. *A Black Sheep* was set in Tombstone, Arizona, and dealt with the regenerative effects the western code of honor had on an easterner.
Poster Collection
Prints and Photographs Division
Library of Congress

"The Great Train Robbery"
Lithograph
Strobridge Lithograph Co.
Copyright 1896

Scott Marble's play "The Great Train Robbery," written in 1896, was about a western train robbery but featured a spectacle in each act. In one scene an actor dressed as a cowboy wrestled a bear (or an actor dressed as a bear). The play was still on the road in 1903 and may have been the inspiration for Edwin S. Porter's western movie of the same name.
Poster Collection
Prints and Photographs Division
Library of Congress

"The Squaw Man"
Lithograph
Courier Company Litho. Dept., Buffalo, N.Y.
Copyright 1905

One of the most successful of all cowboy melodramas was *The Squaw Man* by Edwin Milton Royle. It opened at Wallack's Theater in New York on October 23, 1905, and played 222 performances there before going on the road, its way prepared by *Arizona* and *The Virginian*. The plot involves an English nobleman who, to protect the family name, pretends to commit a crime, flees to America, and becomes a cowboy. It was a play that offered theatergoers the best of two worlds—English country houses and Utah ranches—and contrasted the nobility of the cowboy's character with the duplicity of the English aristocrat. It opened in London in 1908 under the title *The White Man*. Later, three film versions were produced.
Poster Collection
Prints and Photographs Division
Library of Congress

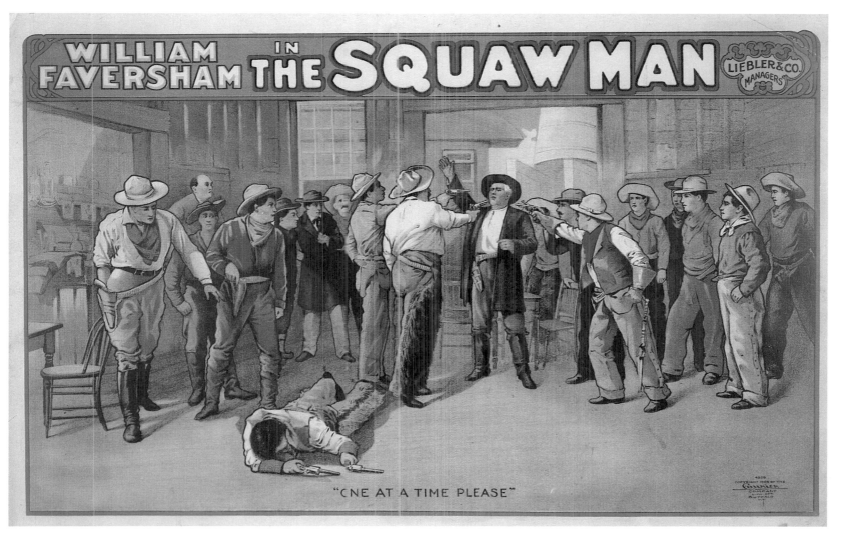

New York's leading theatrical producer, Charles Frohman, approached Owen Wister about making "The Virginian" into a play. Wister was not satisfied with Frohman's proposal and asked Augustus Thomas, a noted author of regional dramas, to write the script. Thomas considered the request but eventually abandoned the idea, whereupon Wister himself wrote a five-act version with the aid of producer Kirk La Shelle. The play opened at the Manhattan Theater in New York on January 5, 1904, starring Dustin Farnum as the Virginian. It ran about four months and then went on the road for ten years. It was still being played by stock companies in the late 1920s, and the script was the basis for three movie versions, the last one with Joel McCrae in 1946.

Dustin Farnum as the Virginian
Photographer unknown, ca. 1904
Owen Wister Papers
Manuscript Division
Library of Congress

Promotional Booklet
For the Play "The Virginian"
Issued by Kirk La Shelle, 1904
Owen Wister Papers
Manuscript Division
Library of Congress

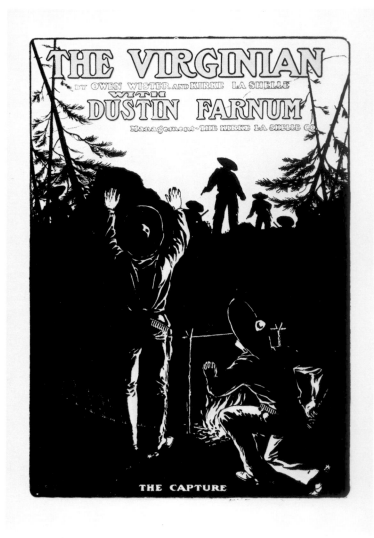

Box Office Statement

Garrick Theatre
Chicago, Illinois. May 3, 1904

The Virginian's popularity can be measured to some degree by the hundreds of box office statements found in the Owen Wister Papers at the Library of Congress. As an author receiving royalties, Wister was entitled to know the number of tickets sold for his play each night. The box office statement also listed the "opposition," that is, the performances given at other theaters in town, and it even allowed Wister to determine whether or not the weather on a given day had a bearing on the size of the audience.
Owen Wister Papers
Manuscript Division
Library of Congress

The Capture of Steve and Spanish Ed
Act 3 of "The Virginian"
Photographer unknown, ca. 1904
Owen Wister Papers
Manuscript Division
Library of Congress

THE MUSICAL COWBOY

Historians are still debating about whether or not cowboys sang to the herd. Folklorist John Avery Lomax (1867–1948) not only felt that they did, he saw their music as proof of the communal theory of ballad composition. Between 1907 and 1910 he carried an Edison recording device to ranches and cattlemen's conventions, asking former cowboys to sing the songs they knew. He also wrote to hundreds of western newspapers, asking their editors to help him collect examples of cowboy songs. It is unclear how many songs he actually recorded, but people who saw his newspaper queries sent him texts. Many of these texts were actually poems written by local balladeers for newspaper publication. In 1910 Lomax published "Cowboy Songs," containing 112 texts and 14 tunes. He edited many of the texts, "selecting and putting together," as he said, "what seemed to be the best lyrics from different versions." During the next decade, many of the texts were set to music by professional composers, and in the 1920s and 1930s they entered the repertory of cowboy radio singers and recording artists. Lomax's research thus not only documented an important song and verse tradition but paved the way for the public's acceptance of the singing cowboy.

John A. Lomax
1867–1948
S. B. Hill, Austin, Texas
Photograph, ca. 1902
Eugene C. Barker Texas History Center
University of Texas at Austin
Austin, Texas

Night-herding Song
in "Cowboy Ballads"
Collected by Prof. John A. Lomax
Music by Liza Lehman
Copyright 1912, Chappell & Co., Ltd.
M1621L
Music Division
Library of Congress

"Cowboy's Dream"
Blanche House Mulberry (dates unknown)
Manuscript, undated
Eugene C. Barker Texas History Center
University of Texas at Austin
Austin, Texas

"Rounded Up in Glory"
A Cowboy Spiritual
Music by Oscar J. Fox
Poem from John A. Lomax, *Cowboy Songs*
and Other Frontier Ballads
Sheet music copyright 1923, Carl Fisher, New York
Eugene C. Barker Texas History Center
University of Texas at Austin
Austin, Texas

Charles Goodnight to John A. Lomax
Manuscript, November 20, 1907
Eugene C. Barker Texas History Center
University of Texas at Austin
Austin, Texas

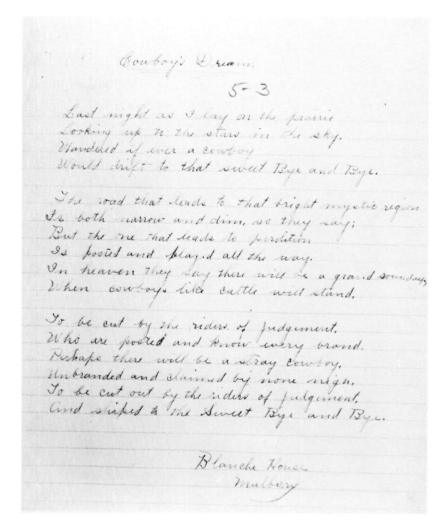

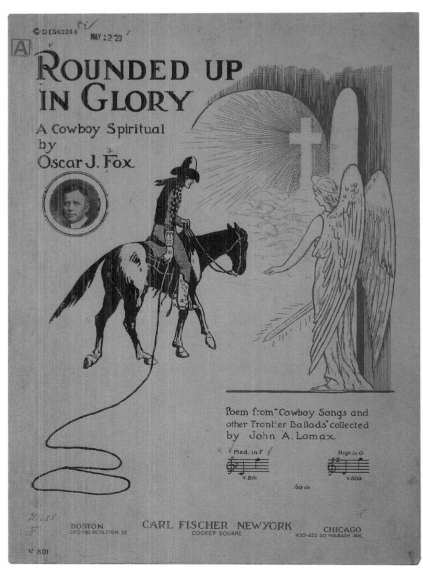

THE NATIONAL COWBOY: THEODORE ROOSEVELT

Although he was born in New York and educated at Harvard, Theodore Roosevelt (1858–1919) delighted in presenting himself to the public as a westerner. Actually, his cowboy credentials were quite sound. Between 1883 and 1886 he ranched in the Little Missouri region of Dakota Territory, where he rode on roundups, broke broncos, trailed cattle, and even served as a deputy sheriff. He returned to the Dakota Badlands on hunting trips through the 1890s. In 1898 he helped to raise a volunteer regiment of cowboy cavalry—the Rough Riders. During his presidency he traveled extensively in the West. He adopted the cowboy's bandanna as one of his campaign emblems in 1904 and kept the image of the cowboy as a man of action before the public throughout his presidency.

Teddy to the Rescue of Republicanism!
Horace Taylor (dates unknown)
Lithograph, cover illustration
Verdict, October 30, 1899
   Political cartoonists realized that the cowboy image fitted Theodore Roosevelt's impulsive political style perfectly, and they often portrayed him with a Stetson hat, bandanna, lasso, and pistols. Horace Taylor created this cover for *Verdict*, a progressive Democratic magazine published in New York, in the fall of 1899. Roosevelt had just been proposed as a presidential candidate by reform-minded western Republicans at a Rough Riders reunion in Las Vegas, New Mexico. At that time the Republican party was controlled by the conservative "Ohio Ring," led by Senator Mark Hanna. Roosevelt was the reformist governor of New York. Taylor shows him galloping recklessly toward a confrontation with the Ohio group, having disposed of a fraud scandal on the Erie Canal Board and a minor threat of labor unrest in New York.
AP2.V4
General Collections
Library of Congress

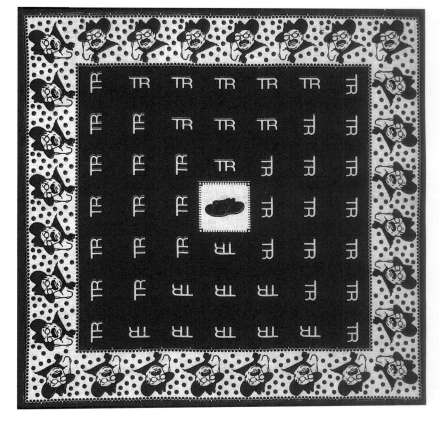

TR Campaign Bandanna
Copyright and design patented by W.A. Loftus, 1912
Made and sold exclusively by the National Kerchief Co.
New York, Chicago, and San Francisco
Cotton, ca. 1912
Susan Porter Schreiber
Takoma Park, Maryland

Colonel Theodore Roosevelt in U.S. Volunteer Uniform
Siegel-Cooper Co.
Photograph, copyright 1898
Presidential File
Prints and Photographs Division
Library of Congress

TEDDY TO THE RESCUE OF REPUBLICANISM!

**Theodore Roosevelt at a Chuck Wagon
During a Wolf Hunt in Indian Territory**
Alexander Lambert (dates unknown)
Stereograph, 1905
Stereographs—Presidents
Prints and Photographs Division
Library of Congress

Theodore Roosevelt
1858–1919
T. W. Ingersoll (dates unknown)
Photograph, ca. 1885, copyright 1910
Presidential File
Prints and Photographs Division
Library of Congress

THE MOVING PICTURE COWBOY

In 1903, the year after Owen Wister's immensely popular western novel "The Virginian" appeared, Edwin S. Porter made the first western film, "The Great Train Robbery." During the next fifty years the movies, with their enormous appeal to juvenile audiences, contributed more than any other medium to the popularization of the cowboy as an American hero. In fact, two different conceptions of the cowboy emerged from western films, both rooted in popular traditions. The romantic cowboy hero—the strong, shy, silent man of action, characterized by Wister and other writers as the ultimate embodiment of western values—dominated hundreds of thousands of feet of film in cowboy roles. He was played by William S. Hart, Randolph Scott, Gary Cooper, John Wayne, and scores of minor actors.

At the same time, the cowboy entertainer created by Buffalo Bill and his imitators—the hard-riding, crack-shooting cowboy of the Wild West show—thundered onto celluloid to perform his old tricks and use the camera to invent new ones. Tom Mix, an old Wild West performer, Hoot Gibson, Ken Maynard, William Boyd, Johnny Mack Brown, and uncounted B-western actors stopped runaway stages with leaps from galloping horses, lassoed bandits from rooftops, and wrestled badmen on the tops of speeding trains.

The advent of sound films permitted singing cowboys like Roy Rogers and Gene Autry to improve on this tradition, adding songs to the flamboyant costumes and stunt riding of their predecessors. Suddenly, in the period of national reassessment that followed the end of World War II, both the romantic cowboy and the cowboy entertainer all but disappeared from western movies, their places taken by sheriffs, marshals, and gunmen.

"Bronco Billy" Anderson
Photographer unknown, ca. 1907
(Scene shot indoors under floodlights for an early western)
    Gilbert M. Anderson (1882–1971) established a definite character for the movie cowboy and became the first cowboy film hero. Anderson, born Max Aronson, was a stage actor who had a minor role in *The Great Train Robbery* in 1903. He played in some of Selig's film melodramas but left in 1908 to form the Essanay Film Company with George K. Spoor. After shooting a group of films in Chicago, Anderson opened a West Coast studio in Niles Canyon, California, and produced the first western series focused on a cowboy hero—himself. As Bronco Billy Anderson, he produced and starred in 376 one- and two-reelers between 1908 and 1915. The character he built was one derived from dime novels and Buffalo Bill's Wild West: a quick-shooting, hard-riding hero with a boyish grin and tousled hair, who saved heroines from bandits, runaway horses, and fates worse than death. Bronco Billy was the ancestor of Tom Mix, Hopalong Cassidy, Johnny Mack Brown, and all of the other series heroes who have thrilled youthful audiences. He retired from Essanay in 1915.
Chicago Historical Society
Chicago, Illinois

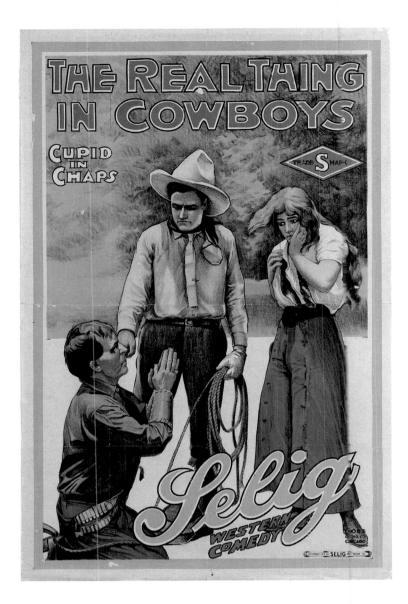

The earliest western movies tended to elaborate on the plot formula of "The Great Train Robbery" and often paralleled the structural development of the western short story of the same period: little character development, a conflict, a chase, and a resolution. The early westerns produced by William Selig were little more than melodramas with cowboy characters, although the motion picture camera permitted the inclusion of hard-riding chase scenes that could not have been enacted on stage. In "The Bandit of Point Loma" (1912), a cowboy sheriff saves an old lighthouse keeper and his daughter from a criminal disguised as a detective. In "The Rustler's Reformation" (1913), a cattle-rustler's daughter elopes with the man she loves and reforms her father through prayer. And in "The Real Thing in Cowboys" (1914), "Cupid in chaps" is at work. Nevertheless, the chase scenes in these films contained the kernel for the footage that would thrill millions of Saturday matinee fans in the 1920s, 1930s, and 1940s.

"The Real Thing in Cowboys"
Lithograph
Goes Lithography Co., Chicago
Copyright, 1914, Selig Polyscope Co.
Poster Collection
Prints and Photographs Division
Library of Congress

"The Rustler's Reformation"
Lithograph
National Printing & Engraving Co.
New York, St. Louis, Chicago
Copyright 1913, Selig Polyscope Co.
Poster Collection
Prints and Photographs Division
Library of Congress

"The Bandit of Point Loma"
Lithograph
Goes Lithography Co., Chicago
Copyright 1912
Poster Collection
Prints and Photographs Division
Library of Congress

The noble movie cowboy and the serious western movie began with
William S. Hart, a stage actor who made one of the first five-reel
westerns in 1914. From 1915 until his retirement in 1925, he
produced and starred in more than thirty films. The cowboys he
played drew their characters from Owen Wister's Virginian, a role
Hart had played successfully on stage. They were strong, silent men
of action, moved by a desire to right a wrong, save a heroine from
dishonor, or prove themselves worthy of a good woman's love. Hart
set a number of precedents for later interpreters of the cowboy: he
dressed in fairly realistic western costumes; he was closely
identified with his pinto pony, Fritz (a subtitle in one of his films
read, "Better a painted pony than a painted woman"); and his films
maintained a high moral tone, which he identified with the values
of the cowboy.

In his personal life, Hart was genuinely fascinated with the
nineteenth-century West, and he felt that his films prolonged a
heroic period in American history. His friends included Wyatt Earp,
Bat Masterson, Charlie Siringo, and Charles Russell. He was the
spiritual as well as the theatrical ancestor of other strong, silent
film cowboys: Randolph Scott, Gary Cooper, and, most particularly,
John Wayne.

**William S. Hart
1870–1946**
Charles C. Cristadoro (1881–1967)
Bronze, 1917
Gorham Co., Founders
Providence, Rhode Island
Gift of the Gorham Company
University Gallery, University of Delaware
Newark, Delaware

William S. Hart in "The Narrow Trail"
Still photograph
Artcraft Pictures Corp., 1917
   Hart, as Ice Harding, attempts to escape
the clutches of a dance hall girl on the
Barbary Coast. His faith in the woman he
believed to be good has just been shattered.
William S. Hart Collection
Prints and Photographs Division
Library of Congress

John Wayne
in "Tall in the Saddle"
Still photograph
Copyright 1944, RKO General Pictures, Inc.
Motion Picture, Broadcasting, and Recorded
Sound Division
Library of Congress

John Wayne
1907–1979
Marisol (Marisol Escobar) (b. 1930)
Wood and mixed media, 1963
Colorado Springs Fine Arts Center
Colorado Springs, Colorado

"Wagon Wheels"
Lithograph
Paramount Productions, Inc.
Copyright 1934

Randolph Scott (b. 1903), who first came to Hollywood in 1928, is an important figure in the transference of the strong, silent, man-of-action characterization of the cowboy to the western hero in general. Scott, who played a minor role in the 1929 production of *The Virginian*, made a series of westerns based on Zane Grey novels for Paramount in the 1930s. In them he played not only cowboys but badmen, outlaws, and marshals with the same soft-spoken, understated approach. In 1939 he portrayed a courageous and sympathetic lawman in *Jesse James* and Wyatt Earp in *Frontier Marshal*. In *Western Union* (1941), his outlaw became the real hero of the film. Scott presented western heroes on the screen for more than thirty years. His last film, *Ride the High Country*, was released in 1962.
Poster Collection
Prints and Photographs Division
Library of Congress

132

"Along Came Jones"
Offset
RKO Radio Pictures, Inc.
Copyright 1945

Gary Cooper (1901–1961) played cowboy roles in the tradition established by William S. Hart. To some degree the strong, silent attitude may have been natural to Cooper, who was born in Helena, Montana, in 1901 and grew up on his father's Montana ranch. One of his first film roles was that of the Virginian in the 1929 film version of Owen Wister's tale, and he carried the quiet, self-assured confidence of the Virginian into his later cowboy roles, presenting that version of the cowboy to several generations of moviegoers. The plots of his films often set eastern sophistication against western directness, as in *Saratoga Trunk* (1946) and *Along Came Jones* (1945) His most memorable performance was in *High Noon* (1952), in which he made the Virginian-like courage of Marshal Will Kane part of a national allegory.

Poster Collection
Prints and Photographs Division
Library of Congress

Tom Mix, whose film career began in 1909 and ended in 1935, was the most extravagant and the most successful of all cowboy stars. He was also the direct link between the performing cowboys of the Wild West shows and the cowboy entertainers of the movies. A consummate showman, he popularized the gaudy costume and the daring roping and riding stunts that became the trademarks of a long series of movie cowboys from Buck Jones to Roy Rogers.

Tom Mix
in "Fighting for Gold"
Photograph
Copyright 1919, Fox Studios

Mix was born in 1880 at Mix Run, Pennsylvania. At the age of ten he attended the Buffalo Bill Wild West and became fascinated by the West. Later he served in the Fourth U.S. Artillery during the Spanish-American War but, contrary to later studio publicity that placed him in the forefront at San Juan Hill, saw no action outside the States. In 1905 he joined the Miller 101 Ranch Wild West Show, and he also worked for various small Wild West shows until, in 1909, he played his first film role as a bronco buster in a Selig western.

Between 1911 and 1917, Mix starred in and directed nearly a hundred one- and two-reelers for Selig. He then moved to Fox Studios and over the next eight years made at least sixty action-packed, fast-moving feature films. They centered on chases, fights on the top of moving trains, and miraculous escapes, which Mix negotiated successfully thanks to the almost human intelligence of his horse, Tony. The studio's publicity machine ground out incredible tales of their star's Indian ancestry, his birth in a log cabin north of El Paso, his experience as a cowboy on the Texas plains, and his adventures in the Boer War and the Mexican Revolution. In the late 1920s his snow-white costumes, black boots, and enormous hats came to symbolize the cowboy. Mix retired from films in 1935, toured the country with the Tom Mix Wild Animal Circus, and was killed in an automobile accident in 1940.
Tom Mix Biographical File
Prints and Photographs Division
Library of Congress

"The Moving Picture Cowboy"
Lithograph
Goes Lithography Co., Chicago
Copyright 1914, Selig Polyscope Co.
Poster Collection
Prints and Photographs Division
Library of Congress

Spurred in part by the racial controversy surrounding "The Birth of a Nation," an independent black film industry came into being about 1916. The box office success of "horse operas" naturally led several black production companies to try westerns as part of their production schedule. The playbill for "The Bull-Dogger" promised "wild horse racing; roping and tying wild steers; fancy and trick riding by black cowboys and cowgirls proving conclusively that the black cowboy is capable of doing anything the white cowboy does."

The open range was an unlikely spot for celebrated jazz musician Louis Jordan and his "Caledonia" Tympany Band. In the early 1940s, Jordan was known as the "King of the Juke Box," and in 1946 he was featured in "Look-Out, Sister."

The black western movie genre never did establish itself with black audiences, however. This failure was attributable first to the industry's commercial dependence upon theaters located in eastern cities, whose audiences preferred films set in an urban milieu. The majority of black westerns ultimately suffered from being too consciously imitative of their white counterparts.

Louis Jordan
in "Look-Out, Sister"
Artist unknown
Offset, ca. 1946
Astor Pictures and Leo Film, 1946
American Folklife Center
Library of Congress

Bill Pickett
in "The Bull-Dogger"
Artist unknown
Lithograph, 1923
Norman Film Manufacturing Company, 1923
American Folklife Center
Library of Congress

The 1940s were the years of the B westerns, low-budget films usually made in a series and built around the adventures of a star who was immediately recognizable by some peculiarity of dress or equipment. The films were produced by a small group of companies, each of which had its own featured star. Buckskin-clad Johnny Mack Brown first made a series for Universal and then toward the end of the decade did forty-five films for Monogram. RKO featured Tim Holt. Paramount had Hopalong Cassidy. United Artists presented the Cisco Kid. Republic's star was Wild Bill Elliot, a performer with reversed gun holsters and a spectacular, fast cross-draw. And PRC featured Lash LaRue with his bullwhip.

The B western defined a standard cowboy costume that included piped shirts and trousers and pearl-buttoned cuffs. Many B westerns were set in the contemporary West and incorporated current events. Crash Corrigan and his Range Busters, for example, foiled a group of Nazis in "Cowboy Commandos." The B western institutionalized the streamlined cowboy entertainer and had an enormous effect on the way an entire generation of young movie fans thought about cowboys.

"Along the Sundown Trail"
Still photograph, 1943
Producers Releasing Corporation
Copyright 1943
Motion Picture, Broadcasting, and Recorded Sound Division
Library of Congress

MONOGRAM PICTURES Presents "COWBOY COMMANDOS" with RAY (CRASH) CORRIGAN, DENNIS MOORE, MAX (ALIBI) TERHUNE with Evelyn Finley.   Printed in U S A

"Cowboy Commandos"
with Ray (Crash) Corrigan
Still photograph, 1943
Copyright, Modern Sound Pictures Inc.
Motion Picture, Broadcasting, and Recorded Sound Division
Library of Congress

Cowboy Outfit

Worn by Mr. O. L. Nelms of Dallas, Texas
Suit: Wool and cotton with embroidery, ca. 1942–45
    Irving Thomas, Tailor, Dallas, Texas
Boots: Leather, ca. 1942–45

The elaborate costumes worn by Roy Rogers and Gene Autry
and imitated by the B-movie actors of the 1930s and 1940s
influenced the clothing worn by musicians and rodeo stars as well
as by ordinary citizens in the Southwest. The "western-cut" suit
became popular attire in the 1940s for some bankers and
businessmen; others went even further and openly imitated film
stars in their dress. This suit was made to order for a Dallas real
estate tycoon, O. L. Nelms, to wear during his trips to New York.
Linda Lavender
Denton, Texas

"Silver on the Sage"
with William Boyd

Offset
Allied Printing, Essex County, U.S.A.
Copyright 1939

The most successful of all B-western cowboy actors was
undoubtedly William Boyd (1895–1972), who began his career as
a De Mille star in the silent film era. In 1935 he was offered an
opportunity to play Hopalong Cassidy in a filmed version of
Clarence Mulford's story of the same name. He agreed to do so
only if the part was rewritten to change the lead from Mulford's
hard-drinking, heavy-smoking realistic ranch hand into a clean-
living cowboy hero. This was done, and *Hopalong Cassidy* became
the first of sixty-five Hopalong films. They all starred Boyd,
immaculately clad in a black costume and mounted on a white
horse. Toward the end of the 1940s, Boyd became a producer and
bought the seemingly worthless rights to his old films. When
television burst on the scene, Boyd had the only ready supply of
studio-produced westerns available to television. The popularity
of these old films with a new generation led to a made-for-
television Hopalong Cassidy series and a nationwide craze.
Poster Collection
Prints and Photographs Division
Library of Congress

Like Tom Mix, Gene Autry came to the movies from show business, and he projected his image as a cowboy entertainer to the public through several media. Born in Tioga, Texas, in 1907, Autry sang in Oklahoma dance halls and with a medicine show as a teenager. He launched his professional career as "Oklahoma's Singing Cowboy" on Station KVOO in Tulsa in 1928, and he recorded one of his own compositions, "That Silver-Haired Daddy of Mine," for Okeh Records in 1930. His song became an instant hit, and Autry moved to Station WLS in Chicago, where he had his own radio show for four years. He appeared in his first film in 1934 and starred in eighty-two films made by Republic and Columbia between 1935 and 1953. From 1940 to 1942 and again from 1946 to 1953, he had his own radio show, "Melody Ranch," on CBS. He continued during his film career to write and record songs, including "Back in the Saddle Again," "Mule Train," "Frosty, the Snowman," and, of course, "Rudolph, the Red-Nosed Reindeer." He was the first cowboy actor to produce and star in thirty-minute television films, which included his own "Gene Autry Show" from 1950 to 1954 as well as five other western series produced by his Flying A Productions.

Autry established the western musical as a film genre. With few exceptions, he played a fictional version of himself in his films: a radio cowboy singer named Gene Autry. His pictures were set in the present and often included gangsters, automobiles, and other trappings of contemporary life. With his guitar, his flamboyant costumes, his comic sidekick Smiley Burnette, and Champion, "the World's Wonder Horse," Gene Autry set a new standard for cowboy entertainers, one that attracted many imitators and followers.

"Songs Gene Autry Sings"
Compiled by Gene Autry, arranged by Nathan Scott
Sheet music copyright 1942, West'rn Music Publishing Co.
Hollywood, California
M1630.18.A986
Music Division
Library of Congress

"Springtime in the Rockies"
with Gene Autry and Smiley Burnette
Offset
Allied Printing, Essex County, U.S.A.
Copyright 1937
Poster Collection
Prints and Photographs Division
Library of Congress

"Roy Rogers' Album of Cowboy Songs"
Sheet music, copyright 1941,
Edward B. Marks Music Corporation
M1629. R74A6
Music Division
Library of Congress

"Sons of the Pioneers"
(Roy Rogers and Maris Wrixon)
Still photograph, 1942
Copyright, National Telefilm
Associates, Inc.,
Los Angeles, California
*Motion Picture, Broadcasting, and
Recorded Sound Division*
Library of Congress

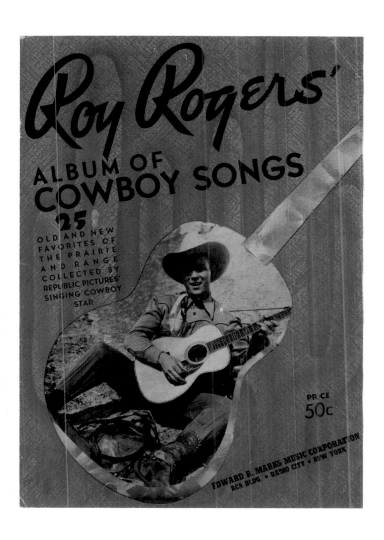

Roy Rogers, born Leonard Slye in Duck Run, Ohio, in 1911, first entered films based on his reputation as a radio singer. Slye moved to California in 1931 and sang for a Long Beach radio station with a group called the Rocky Mountaineers. After several years of singing and touring with various groups, he joined with Tim Spencer, Bob Nolan, and Hugh and Karl Marx Farr to form the Sons of the Pioneers. They sang on Station KFWB in Los Angeles and were such a success that, in 1935, they were invited to appear in the first of Gene Autry's successful westerns, "Tumbling Tumbleweeds."

Two years later Slye joined Republic Pictures as a singing cowboy, first under the name Dick Weston and then, in 1938, as Roy Rogers. From 1938 to 1942 he made B westerns that emphasized action, rather than music. But when Gene Autry left for the army in 1942, Republic promoted Rogers to stardom and launched a publicity buildup that moved the musical western into expensive, first-run, downtown theaters for the first time.

The high point in Rogers's long career came in the summer of 1943 when he was featured on the cover of "Life" magazine. At that time H. Allen Smith described the kind of cowboy that Rogers represented: "He is the protagonist in an American morality play. He is purity rampant—never drinks, never smokes, never shoots pool, never spits, and the roughest oath at his command is 'Shucks!' He never needs a shave, and when it comes to fist-fighting he seldom takes on a single opponent; he beats their brains out in a group. He always wins the girl though he doesn't kiss her. He kisses his horse. His immense public would have him no other way."

Rogers went on to follow a career that curiously paralleled Gene Autry's. He made enormously popular pictures until his retirement from film in 1952; he had his own network radio show; and he starred, with his wife Dale Evans, in a successful television series in the early 1950s. If Gene Autry invented the musical western, Roy Rogers symbolized the wholesomeness of the singing cowboy.

THE SINGING COWBOY

The singing cowboy was a product of radio, the recording industry, and the movies rather than the open range. In the 1920s when radio stations drew heavily on local talent for broadcast material, virtually every station had its "Lonesome Cowboy" or "Arizona Yodeler," usually singing songs taken from John Lomax's "Cowboy Songs" or even from southern folk song tradition. Hillbilly bands and singers adopted cowboy dress as an alternative to the poor white image and included songs with western themes in their programs. In 1925 Victor released the first hit cowboy record, which featured Carl T. Sprague, a track coach at Texas A&M College, singing "When the Work's All Done This Fall." More records followed, and when movies acquired sound in 1928 cowboy singers appeared on the screen. They also arrived on Broadway that same year when a quartet of cowboys appeared in the musical "Whoopee," which was set on a dude ranch.

During the 1930s and 1940s, the great years of the cowboy singers, most Americans believed that a guitar was as indispensable to the cowboy as a horse or a rope.

"Lonesome Cowboy Songs of the Plains and Hills"
Compiled by John White and George Shackley
Sheet music, copyright 1930, Geo. T. Worth & Co.
M 1629. W58L5
Music Division
Library of Congress

"The Sons of the Pioneers"
Words and music by Bob Nolan and Vern Spencer
Sheet music, copyright 1936, Cross & Winge, Inc.
M 1629. N75S5
Music Division
Library of Congress

"Ken Maynard's Songs of the Trails"
Sheet music, copyright 1935,
M. M. Cole Publishing Company
M 1629. M25S5
Music Division
Library of Congress

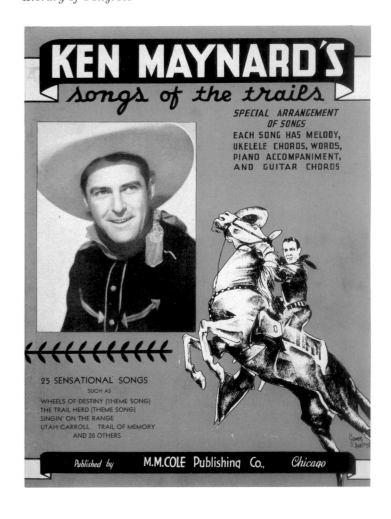

"Tumbling Tumbleweeds"
Words and music by Bob Nolan
Sheet music, copyright 1934, Sunset Music Co.
M1630.2N
Music Division
Library of Congress

"Can You Tell a Cow-Girl"
Words and music by John M. Ritter
Sheet music, copyright 1944, John M. Ritter
M1630.2R
Music Division
Library of Congress

"Patent Leather Boots"
John Klenner and Bob Miller
Sheet music, copyright 1939, Bob Miller, Inc.
M1630.2M
Music Division
Library of Congress

"Bye and Bye"
Words and music by Jimmy Wakely, Fred Rose,
and Johnny Marvin
Sheet music, copyright 1942, Leeds Music Corporation
M1630.2W
Music Division
Library of Congress

CAN YOU TELL A COW-GIRL

(WHEN YOU LOVE HER THE BEST?)

WORDS AND MUSIC
by

JOHN M. RITTER

Published by JOHN M. RITTER, Leoti, Kansas.

THE CHILDREN'S HERO

The cowboy hero has appealed to juveniles since the days of Buffalo Bill, but he has loomed especially large in children's eyes during the period from the 1930s through the early 1950s. Cowboy costumes for children first became popular in the mid-thirties, replacing soldier and sailor suits, and they remained in style until the mid-1950s. During World War II, when many fathers were away from home, cowboy actors and radio stars became surrogate fathers for American children, advising them over the air waves on diet, health, and behavior and offering their own wholesome way of life as a model. Gene Autry even codified ten "Cowboy Commandments" for children.

Child Wearing Cowboy Outfit
Photograph, ca. 1935
The Cobbs Studio
Albuquerque, New Mexico
Photo Archives
The Museum of New Mexico
Sante Fe, New Mexico

Child in Cowboy Suit
Riding a Pony
Photographer unknown, ca. 1938
Mrs. Charles B. Fahs
Oxford, Ohio

Boy in Cowboy Outfit
Photograph, 1947
Stuckey Studio
Arlington, Virginia
Private Collection

Roy Rogers Clothes Rack
Hopalong Cassidy Hat
Lone Ranger Vest
Lone Ranger Chaps
Hat, ca. 1950
Vest and chaps, ca. 1940
Hake's Americana & Collectibles
P.O. Box 1444
York, Pennsylvania 17405

Tom Mix and Child Eating Cereal
Ralston Purina child's premium photograph,
1934
Cheerios cereal box
Cisco Kid milk bottle
Lone Ranger toothbrush holder
Lone Ranger glass

Premiums: Roy Rogers sheriff's badge and
whistle, boot ring, Lone Ranger six-gun ring,
Lone Ranger pedometer, Hoppy neckerchief
slide and initial sealer "HC," Tom Mix
Ralston straight shooter signal arrowhead,
Tom Mix badge and Sheriff Dobie County
siren; Tom Mix decoder badge, Tom Mix TV,
Tom Mix gold ore watch fob, Tom Mix
lookaround ring, Tom Mix telephone

   Premiums provided a tie between cowboy
stars and their juvenile admirers. The first of
these cheaply produced items may have been
those offered by the sponsors of the Tom Mix
Ralston Straight-Shooters radio program in
the late 1930s. Like later cowboy premiums,
they were obtained through coupons
available in the sponsor's products. They
offered a fictive personal association with the
star of a radio or television program.
Through them, a child could become a
member of an elite group surrounding a
cowboy hero, communicate with its other
members in secret code, and unite with them
in helping their hero struggle against evil.
Hake's Americana & Collectibles
P.O. Box 1444
York, Pennsylvania 17405

**Roy Rogers Official Flash-Draw
Holster Outfit**
Ca. 1950–55
Hake's Americana & Collectibles
P.O. Box 1444
York, Pennsylvania 17405

Hopalong Cassidy Thermos and Box
Hopalong Cassidy Good Luck Horseshoe
Hopalong Cassidy Set of Savings Rodeo Buttons
Ca. 1950
Hake's Americana & Collectibles
P.O. Box 1444
York, Pennsylvania 17405

**Hopalong Cassidy Placemat, Cup,
Paper Plates, Knife, Fork, and Spoon, and
Wristwatch**
Ca. 1950

Between 1945 and 1955, the cowboy's role as a children's hero was reinforced by the manufacture of hundreds of children's products bearing the names and faces of cowboy stars. The commercial tie-ins, as they were called, had their origins in the popularity of Roy Rogers and Gene Autry films, and they reached their peak in the Hopalong Cassidy craze of the early 1950s. At one time, Roy Rogers estimated that nearly four hundred items bearing his name were being sold and that their distribution was second only to Walt Disney tie-ins.
Hake's Americana & Collectibles
P.O. Box 1444
York, Peansylvania 17405

RODEO

Rodeo had its origins in informal roping and riding contests on
southwestern ranches. By the 1880s, a rodeo had become standard
Fourth of July entertainment in some western towns, and during
the 1890s rodeo stunts became an integral part of Wild West shows.
The first decade of this century saw the emergence of annual rodeos
with large purses at Salinas, California; Cheyenne, Wyoming;
Calgary, Alberta; and Pendleton, Oregon, as well as many smaller
rodeos in towns all over the West. Professional rodeo promoters
began organizing rodeos as spectator sports. Riders and ropers, who
often were Wild West show performers, were paid to perform but
also held open contests. Of the rodeo promoters, the two best known
were Guy Weadick, who organized the twelve-day New York
Stampede in Brooklyn in 1916, and Tex Austin, who produced a
World Championship Rodeo in Chicago in 1920 and organized a
rodeo at the British Empire Exposition in London in 1924. During
the 1920s rodeo moved indoors and became a spectator sport,
reinforcing the movie image of the cowboy as a trick roper and rider.

Rodeo State Fair
Cowboy
Offset, 1940s
Donaldson Lithography Co., Newport, Kentucky
Poster Collection
Prints and Photographs Division
Library of Congress

Female Rodeo Performers
Erwin E. Smith (1888–1947)
Photograph, Southwest, ca. 1910
   In the first decade of the century and
through the 1920s, women participated in
rodeos to a much greater extent than they do
today. The rodeo was as responsible as the
Wild West show for the popular conception
of the cowgirl. A typical rodeo program of
the 1920s included a cowgirl trick relay race,
cowgirl bronc riding, cowgirl trick riding, and
cowgirl trick roping.
Erwin E. Smith Collection
Prints and Photographs Division
Library of Congress

Rodeo State Fair
Cowgirl
Offset, 1940s
Donaldson Lithography Co., Newport, Kentucky
Poster Collection
Prints and Photographs Division
Library of Congress

**A Rodeo Performer Has Completed
His Tie in the Calf-Roping Contest**
Erwin E. Smith (1888–1947)
Photograph, Southwest, 1920s
Erwin E. Smith Collection
Prints and Photographs Division
Library of Congress

**A Rodeo Performer Throws a Loop over a
Horse and Rider in a Rodeo Arena**
Erwin E. Smith (1888–1947)
Photograph, Southwest, 1920s
Erwin E. Smith Collection
Prints and Photographs Division
Library of Congress

A Rodeo Contestant Rides a Steer
Erwin E. Smith (1888–1947)
Photograph, Southwest, 1920s
Erwin E. Smith Collection
Prints and Photographs Division
Library of Congress

1956 Levi Buckle, World's Grand Champion Cowboy
1957 R.C.A. World's Champion Bull Rider
1959 Levi's Special Added Award, Five-Time Winner (*overleaf*)

1956 Buckle: Sterling 14k with rubies made by R. Schaezlein & Son
1957 Buckle: Sterling, made by Don Ellis Co., Seattle
1959 Buckle: Sterling 14k with rubies made by R. Schaezlein & Son

During the 1930s the first attempts were made to organize rodeo into a national sport with uniform rules and regulations. The managements of several leading rodeos formed the Rodeo Association of America, called the International Rodeo Management after 1929. In 1936 the cowboy performers at the Boston Gardens went on strike and formed the Cowboy's Turtle Association, the first organization of rodeo performers. In 1945 the name was changed to the Rodeo Cowboy Association, which today is the governing body of the rodeo world. The R.C.A. recognizes nearly five hundred rodeos, issues contest rules and judging standards, certifies national champions, and publishes *Rodeo Sports News*.

Jim Shoulders
Holder of 16 P.R.C.A. World Champion Titles
Henryetta, Oklahoma

Cowboy Wearing Bucking Belt
Photographer unknown, ca. 1929

Professional rodeo was responsible for the introduction of new cowboy equipment and some important modifications to old equipment. The bucking belt, developed to protect a rider's kidneys, was a product of bronc-riding contests rather than bronco breaking on ranches. Saddles in the 1920s were made with wide "bucking-rolls" in front to support a bronc-rider's thighs, rather than with the old "slick-fork" of the 1880s and 1890s.
American Folklife Center
Library of Congress

**Steerdogging at a Black Rodeo
in Brookshire, Texas**
Watriss-Baldwin, Houston, Texas
Photograph, 1980
Wendy Watriss and Fred Baldwin
Houston, Texas

Carte of Evolution
Dedicated to the California Rodeo of Salinas
Jo(seph) J. Mora (1876–1947)
Lithograph after a drawing
Copyright 1933, Jo Mora Publications,
Monterey, California
Carl Fleischhauer
Washington, D.C.

DUDE RANCHING

In addition to seeing cowboy film stars and rodeo performers, easterners encountered the cowboy as entertainer through the dude ranch, an institution that flourished in the 1920s and 1930s. Dude ranches first developed in the 1880s. On ranches where portions of ranch work such as roundups, brandings, and trail drives were simulated to entertain the guests, cowboy singers were often employed to sing to guests around a campfire after a supper served from a chuck wagon. Enthusiasm for dude ranches was so great in the 1920s that one was opened in Florida with a herd of cattle and horses imported from Montana. Most ranches were in the West, however, and their advertising emphasized scenery, clean air, and, most of all, the authenticity of the western way of life they offered.

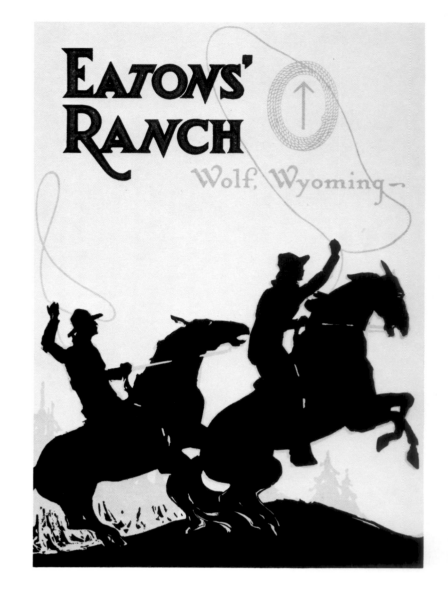

Eaton's Ranch
Artist unknown
Brochure, 1921

    The first dude ranch in the West was started by Howard Eaton, a businessman from Philadelphia, and his three brothers in 1884. The Eatons built cabins on their ranch near Medora, Dakota Territory, to accommodate paying guests and later specialized in rehabilitating dissolute young easterners. The ranch was then moved to Wolf, Wyoming, where it is still in business.
Buffalo Bill Historical Center
Cody, Wyoming

Larom's Valley Ranch
A Dude Ranch in Park County, Wyoming
Brown Studio, St. Paul, Minnesota
Photograph, ca. 1930
Buffalo Bill Historical Center
Cody, Wyoming

Irving H. "Larry" Larom, Rancher
Photographer unknown, ca. 1930
Buffalo Bill Historical Center
Cody, Wyoming

Larry Larom's Dude Ranch Outfit
Vest by Pendleton, ca. 1935
Tie by Brooks Brothers, ca. 1935
Manufacturer of shirt unknown
Buffalo Bill Historical Center
Cody, Wyoming

"Dude Wrangler"
Charles M. Russell (1864–1926)
Watercolor on paper, undated
Buffalo Bill Historical Center
Cody, Wyoming

**Cowboy Playing Polo on the
Stern Ranch, New Mexico**
T. Harmon Parkhurst (dates unknown)
Photograph, ca. 1935
Photo Archives
Museum of New Mexico
Santa Fe, New Mexico

Tex Austin's Forked Lightning Ranch
Travel brochure, ca. 1933
Illustrated by Leonard H. Grosse
   Dude ranching came to the Southwest
later than to the Northwest, and southwestern dude ranches were mainly planned as
resorts, offering polo, trail rides, and
relaxation in a western atmosphere. They
capitalized on the already established tourist
trade in the Southwest, their proximity to
Indian ruins, and the accessibility offered by
railroad lines. These dude ranches were the
forerunners of winter resorts in New Mexico
and Arizona.
History Library
Museum of New Mexico
Santa Fe, New Mexico

WILL ROGERS

To many Americans, Will Rogers symbolized the cowboy entertainer, summing up in himself the mixture of humor, common sense, and skill that came to be associated with the cowboy in the 1920s and 1930s. Rogers was born in 1879 in Indian Territory, of part-Cherokee parentage. He grew up on his father's ranch, worked as a cowboy in Texas, and transported horses to South Africa during the Boer War. He joined an American-owned Wild West show in South Africa as a trick roper. Back in the United States, he went into vaudeville with a roping act, punctuating his tricks with dry wit and political banter. By 1916 he was appearing on Broadway in the Ziegfeld Follies, and in the 1920s he starred in a dozen films. He wrote a syndicated newspaper column and several books of political commentary. In the heady twenties, he provided just the right anchor with an agrarian past, and Americans took him to heart as the Cowboy Philosopher. Paradoxically, he was fascinated with aviation, and he was killed in a crash with flier Wiley Post in 1935.

Will Rogers Souvenir Card
Postcard, ca. 1906
Will Rogers Memorial
Claremore, Oklahoma

Will Rogers
Studio portrait Naegeli, Union Square,
New York
Photograph, ca. 1905
Will Rogers Memorial
Claremore, Oklahoma

ROGERS-ISMS

The Cowboy Philosopher
on *The Peace Conference*

By WILL ROGERS

Frontispiece Portrait

NEW YORK : HARPER &
BROTHERS : PUBLISHERS

throwing two ropes at once.

THE COMMERCIAL COWBOY

Although the cowboy—and the cowgirl—were occasionally used to advertise tobacco, food, whiskey, and other products as early as the 1870s, their appearance in magazine and newspaper advertising was infrequent until the 1960s. Since then, the cowboy has sold cigarettes, beer, boots, clothing, automobiles, and even men's cologne, and his widespread use in advertising has been responsible for a revival of interest in the cowboy hero. The current advertising trend was started in 1954 by a Chicago agency, Leo Burnett USA. While looking for a way to give Marlboro filter-tip cigarettes a masculine image, the agency developed a series of advertisements showing tattooed men with outdoor occupations, among them a cowboy, smoking Marlboros. Within a few years the other occupations were dropped from the series, and the Marlboro Man was strictly a cowboy. During the 1960s and 1970s other advertisers began to use the cowboy image, and the fad spread to music, fashion, and even art.

In Repose
In Action
Photographs by Rundle, 1905
Advertisement for the A.T. Lewis & Son
Dry Goods Co. to the Stockman's Convention,
Denver, Colorado
Howard Wight Marshall Family
Columbia, Missouri

IN REPOSE

PHOTOS BY RUNDLE

COMPLIMENTS OF THE LEWIS GIRL
AND
THE A. T. LEWIS & SON DRY GOODS CO.
TO THE STOCKMEN'S CONVENTION
DENVER, COLO., 1905
POSED BY "THE LEWIS GIRL"

IN ACTION

PHOTOS BY RUNDLE

COMPLIMENTS OF THE LEWIS GIRL
AND
THE A. T. LEWIS & SON DRY GOODS CO.
TO THE STOCKMEN'S CONVENTION
DENVER, COLO., 1905
POSED BY "THE LEWIS GIRL"

A Round Up, 1877–1887
Lithograph printed in colors
Copyright 1906
Popular and Applied Graphic Art Collections
Prints and Photographs Division
Library of Congress

Bucker
Lithograph printed in colors
Schumacher and Ettlinger, New York,
New York
Copyright 1887
Tobacco Label Collection
Popular and Applied Graphic Art Collections
Prints and Photographs Division
Library of Congress

163

Westernaire Brand Yellow Free Peaches
Color offset
Copyright 1920 The Bon I. Look Stores, Co.
Denver, Colorado
Popular and Applied Graphic Art Collections
Prints and Photographs Division
Library of Congress

Cowboy Brand Prunes
Lithograph printed in colors
Mutual Label and Lith. Co.
San Francisco, California
Copyright 1906, Castle Bros. Inc.
Popular and Applied Graphic Art Collections
Prints and Photographs Division
Library of Congress

Bob Yokum's Buffalo Whiskey
Color offset, 1908
Popular and Applied Graphic Art Collections
Prints and Photographs Division
Library of Congress

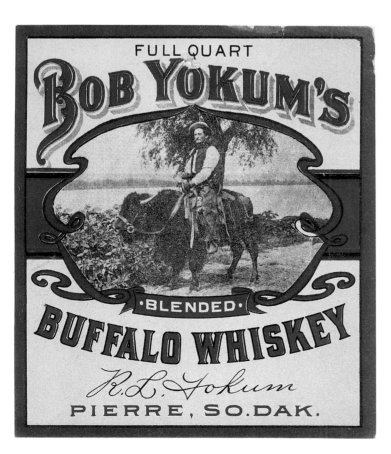

Buckaroo Brand Apples
Lithograph printed in colors, ca. 1930
Schmidt L. Co., Portland, Oregon
Carl Fleischhauer
Washington, D.C.

Libby's Ox Tongues
Color offset, 1908
Popular and Applied Graphic Art Collections
Prints and Photographs Division
Library of Congress

Lasso Brand Sweet Corn
Color offset, ca. 1900
The United States Printing Co.
Popular and Applied Graphic Art Collections
Prints and Photographs Division
Library of Congress

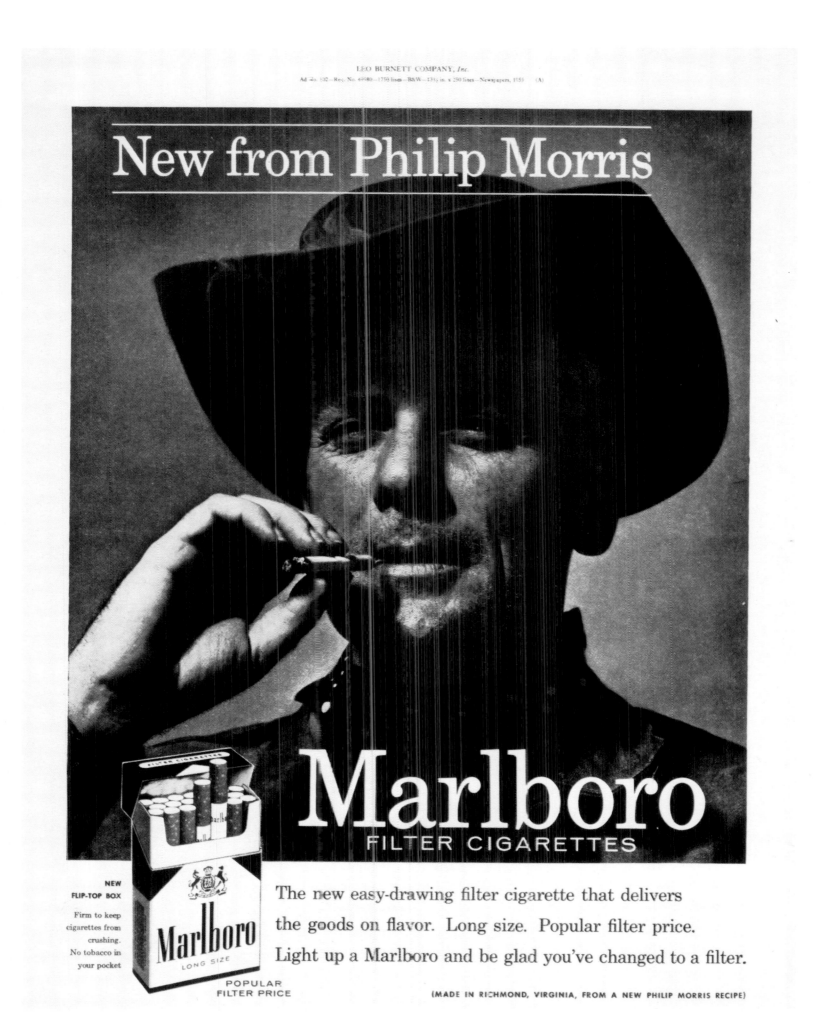

1980 Dasher Diesel
Bert Steinhauser (b. 1928)
Photographer and Art Director
Copyright 1978, Volkswagen of America
Volkswagen of America
Englewood Cliffs, New Jersey

1980 DASHER DIESEL. THE BEST MILEAGE WAGON IN AMERICA.

The VW Dasher Diesel not only gets better mileage than any other wagon in America, it gets better mileage than most other cars in America. (EPA est. 36 mpg, 49 mpg highway estimate. Use est. mpg for comparisons. Mpg varies with speed, trip length, weather.

(Actual highway mileage will probably be less.)
The Dasher Diesel wagon is big enough to hold a fair-sized calf. But the inside is so handsome, you'll want to keep the livestock elsewhere.

"Quality pervades wherever one looks, and it's pleasing to the eye as well as to the touch," says Motor Trend. "It's so nice that you'll feel as if you're driving a much more expensive car."

Breezin' by all them gas stations, you'll recollect what Car and Driver said: "It has a way of going much like that of a fine horse, precise and proud."

So, pardner, if someone tells you there ain't no way to put downright luxury together with downright economy, you can give 'em a quote from us:

"Bull."

VOLKSWAGEN DOES IT AGAIN

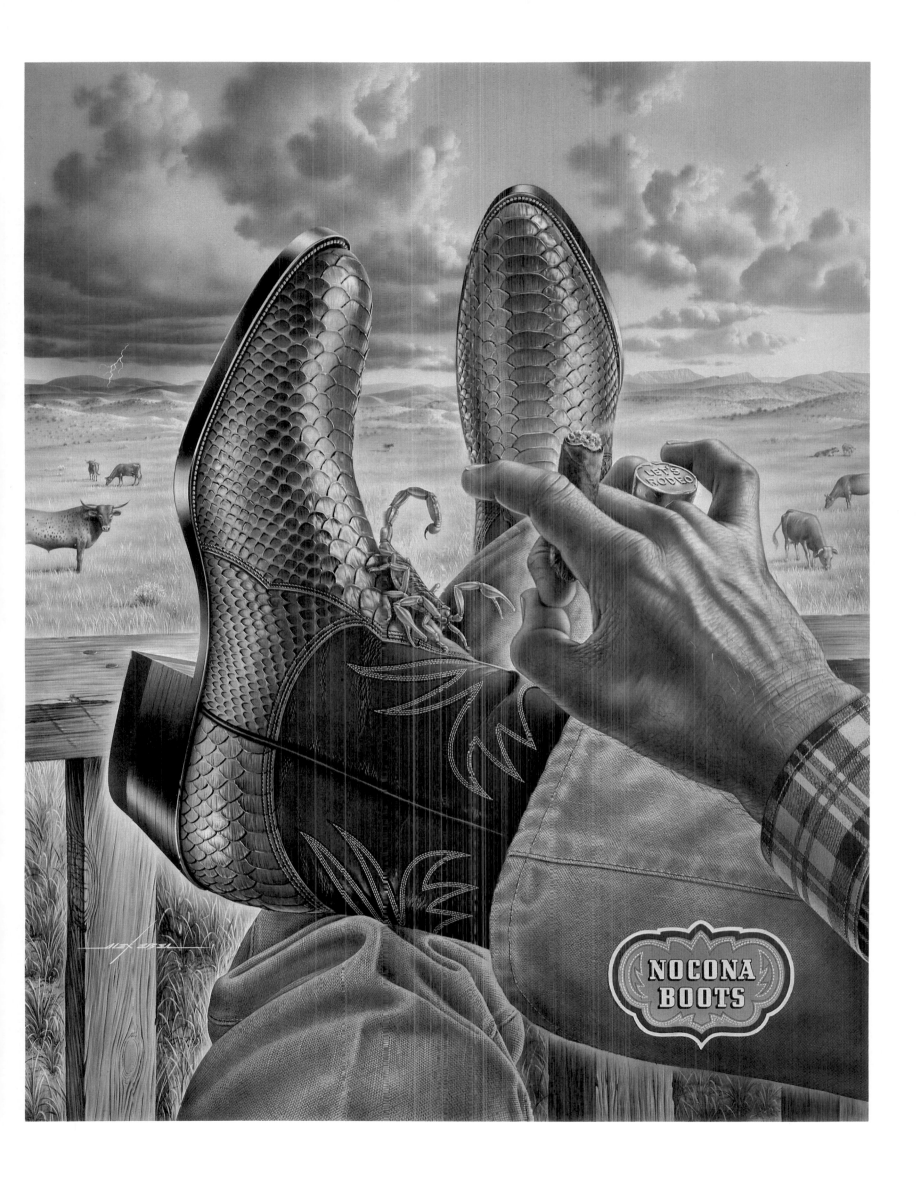

The popularity of the cowboy as an advertising image during the 1970s created a corresponding growth in the popularity of western fashions. Stetson hats and cowboy boots suddenly became as fashionable and almost as common on Wall Street as they were in Fort Worth, and designer blue jeans were a symbol of leisure everywhere.

A Holiday Tradition
Photograph by Les Goldberg
for Gregory Group Design/Advertising
Dallas, Texas, 1979
Polo/Ralph Lauren, Incorporated
New York, New York

Claude Montana
P. Roversi
Photograph, 1981
Claude Montana S.A.
Paris, France

What to wear when the sun goes down

Robes designed by
Oleg Cassini

Even if your home's not on the range, you savor slipping into something comfortable after business, after shave, after shower, after anything. But these robes are not merely comfortable. They're created by America's best-known designer, Oleg Cassini.

They make a man look as richly relaxed as he feels. Some are bold and burly; some are smooth and silky. All are tailored of the finest fabrics. Ideal for homebodies and travel, too.

From $30.00 at the country's best stores.
Robes designed by Oleg Cassini
350 Fifth Avenue, New York, N.Y 10001

What to Wear When the Sun Goes Down
Betty Gardner-Meyers, Art Director
Robert Mason, Photographer
Copyright 1979, Oleg Cassini, Inc.
Oleg Cassini Incorporated
New York, New York

Pro Rodeo Champions Choose Wrangler
Photograph by James B. Wood (b. 1935)
Copyright 1981, Blue Bell Inc.
Blue Bell Inc.
Greensboro, North Carolina

Tough customers like these ProRodeo Champions choose Wrangler western shirts.

Chaps: The New Men's Cologne
by Ralph Lauren
Advertisement designed by Kurtz & Tarlow Co., 1979
Warner Cosmetics, Incorporated
New York, New York

Taste the High Country
Gordon Snidow (b. 1936)
Gouache, 1979
Adolph Coors Company
Golden, Colorado

Chaps Cologne Cosmetic Set
Designed by Dan Kotyuk, 1979
for Primary Design Group, New York
Warner Cosmetics, Incorporated
New York, New York

The Bold Look of Kohler
Super Spa
Photograph by Pete Turner, New York
Bob Jensen, Art Director,
Campbell-Mithun Advertising Agency,
Minneapolis, Minnesota
Copyright 1981, Kohler Co., Kohler,
Wisconsin
Kohler Company
Kohler, Wisconsin

During the latter part of the decade a group of contemporary artists and craftsmen began to rediscover southwestern themes. In some cases, they viewed the cowboy's new popularity with affectionate irony; in others, the artists' enthusiasm for the material was derived from the myths of their own childhood. Their efforts have found a receptive market among Americans re-enchanted with the cowboy.

"Quemado"
Robert Shay (b. 1944)
Ceramic, multiple firings, 1981
Courtesy of the artist

Ceramic Boots
William Wilhelmi (b. 1939)
Earthenware, airbrush and gold luster, 1982
(Photograph by Marie Digatono)
William Wilhelmi-Kaffie Gallery
Corpus Christi, Texas

Cowboy
Lionel Adams (b. 1921)
Chainsaw-carved wood and house paint, 1979
Museum of International Folk Art
Museum of New Mexico
Santa Fe, New Mexico

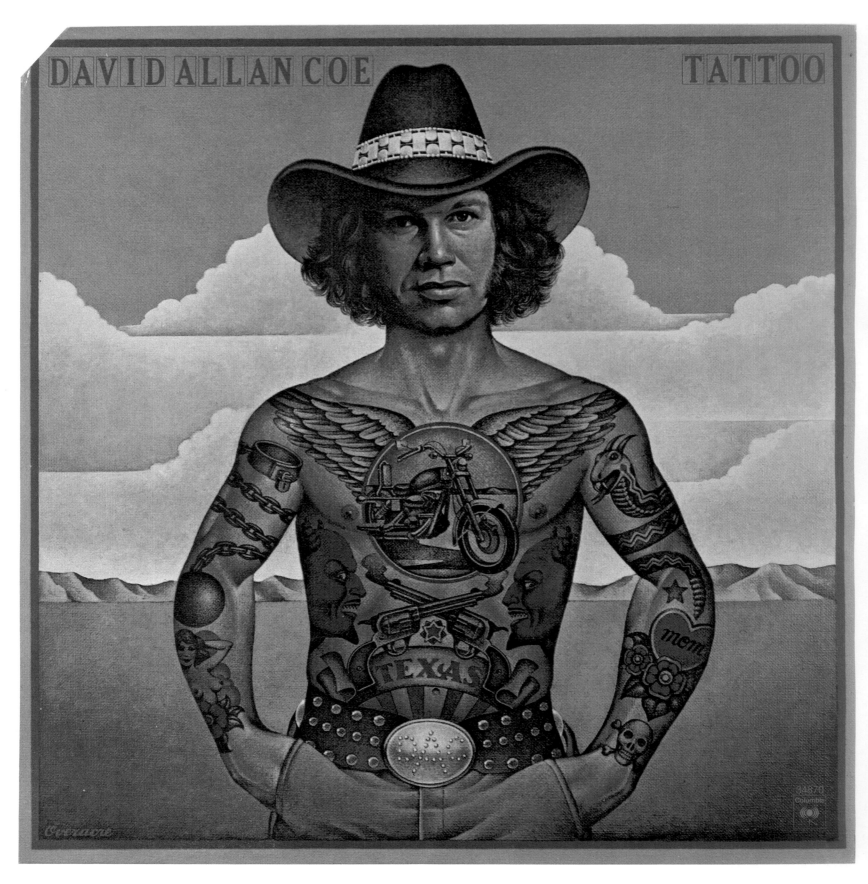

MEANWHILE, BACK AT THE RANCH

Overleaf:
Cowhand
on the Quarter Circle U Brewster-Arnold
Ranch near Birney, Montana
Arthur Rothstein (b. 1915)
Photograph, 1939
Farm Security Administration File
Prints and Photographs Division
Library of Congress

MODERN COWBOY LIFE ON THE TEXAS PLAINS

B. Byron Price

Since World War II, the life of the American cowboy has been transformed. The metamorphosis has been gradual but not uniform, and it has produced cowboys in many variations, some holdovers from an earlier day and others synthetic creations of a technological society. Classic cowpunchers, whose tools are still a rope and a branding iron, are now few in number, which contributes mightily to the pervasive but erroneous notion that cowboys are disappearing from the scene.

Because of the well-entrenched myth of the cowboy hero that has been packaged and sold for so many years by commercial advertisers, journalists, and filmmakers, Americans are almost oblivious to the cowboy's modern existence. Some who do know today's cowboy may consider him not worthy of the name, because the bulk of his work bears so little resemblance to that of the range-riding waddies of the nineteenth century.

For many years, cowboys have plied their trade on the sometimes lush, sometimes barren prairies which stretch from "Cow Town" Fort Worth to the New Mexico state line. Rooted in rich traditions, ranching there will always be measured against mammoth enterprises like the three million-acre XIT Ranch and legendary individuals such as Charles Goodnight, the first rancher in the Texas Panhandle. Like it or not, however, cowboy life today is bound together with more polyester than rawhide—even on the plains of Texas. It is a mistake to consider cattle raising only in nineteenth-century terms.

By 1900 the cumulative effects of drought, depressions, fencing, and farmers had brought an end to many of the cattle kingdoms that existed in an era when grass and men were free, or nearly so. A few giant ranches lingered on for the next four decades as a result of their tenacious leadership, economic sacrifice, and mineral wealth, but most of them gave way to smaller, more efficient operations that were closely tied to farming. Stock farmers who mixed livestock raising with crop cultivation emerged as the dominant force in a new ranching complex. With the breakup of the big outfits went the longhorns, the trail drives, and the cooperative roundups that characterized open-range ranching. The cowboy, however, survived—his numbers diminished, his duties altered, and his world smaller.

Cowboying was no longer a straight riding job and involved farming as well as ranching chores and the operation of machinery. When military draft demands of World War II depleted the cowboy population by about one-third on most of the region's ranches, the shortage of labor forced many ranchers to lease their pastures, limit their herd sizes, and trim their operations. Hard work, long hours, labor-saving devices, and patchwork crews consisting of old men, boys, and women were used to alleviate the manpower crisis. After the war, when high wages and full urban employment tempted many cowboys to seek better living and working conditions in cities and towns, ranchers intensified their dependence on technology and pooled their labor to do the ranch work. The transportation and communication revolution taking place elsewhere in America made itself felt on the plains.

The twin forces of urbanization and mechanization have continued to exert a profound influence on both the nature of ranching and the life of the cowboy. They have accelerated the prewar trend toward stock farming in the west Texas region and have contributed to the decline in the number and size of ranches and in the number of cowboys. Today even the largest ranches operate with only a quarter to a half the workforce needed in the 1930s. Only a few outfits can still boast a range that extends over a hundred thousand acres, herds that number more than a thousand head, or a regular cowboy crew that exceeds ten men.

Modernization has modified—though not eliminated—many traditional cowboy tasks and the individual skills needed to accomplish them. Today's roundups and brandings are mixtures of old-time methods and contemporary innovations. Most cow-calf ranches (ranches on which herds of mother cows are run to produce calves) still hold at least two gatherings annually, one about mid-May and the other in late September or early October. The dates of these roundups vary slightly from year to year depending on range and market conditions, but their purposes remain much the same as they were in the nineteenth century. Cattle are gathered in the spring chiefly to brand new calves, and the fall roundup is devoted to collecting stock for shipment to market or to feedlots.

Of the many factors that have altered roundup procedures in the last quarter century, none has been more important than improved transportation. When horses were the only means of travel, it often took days for a roundup crew to reach a work site. "Floating outfits" consisting of a chuck wagon, several cowboys, and a sizable remuda of extra horses were sent to far-flung ranges. These crews frequently remained out for weeks at a time without returning to headquarters.

When motorized vehicles began to appear on the plains in the early 1920s, roundups began to change. Ranchers began using pickups to ferry cowboys between the pasture and the bunkhouse every morning and evening, and soon cowboys were hauling their horses back and forth in stock trailers. By the mid-1950s only a few ranches with particularly extensive or difficult ranges could justify the expense and inconvenience of keeping a chuck wagon out for any length of time. Within another two decades chuck wagons, once deemed essential, were abandoned completely. Today a few ranches maintain them for entertainment purposes, but cowboys seldom work so far away from headquarters, home, or a nearby community that they cannot travel in to eat or sleep.

The size of a modern roundup outfit depends on the variables of land, cattle, labor, and equipment. The ranges of western Texas are diverse in topography, and each type of landform presents different demands to the cowpunchers who work there. On the relatively level and open high plains, almost anybody can be a cowboy. The mesquite- and cedar-laden breaks that characterize the rolling plains east of the Caprock Escarpment are, however, another matter. In difficult terrain, cattle tend to be more troublesome and cowboys must be skillful at finding them in the brush and retrieving them.

Modern cattle are not as wild as they were in earlier days. Alexander Mackay, the perceptive secretary of the Matador Land and Cattle Company, acknowledged the immense influence the wild cow had on the trade and on the image of the cowpuncher when he addressed a group of Scottish investors about 1890:

> *To her we are indebted for the cowboy. If she had been constituted of a gentle domestic nature with the confiding and obedient instincts of her relative at home the cowboy's occupation would have been different—and he himself would lose much of the romance which has gathered round him which is, primarily due to the dance which she leads over the western prairie.* [1]

In recent decades, improved cattle breeds and the attention given to their care and feeding have proved Mackay an astute observer. On most ranches, the summons of a pickup horn and the encouraging yell of the driver are enough to bring a herd running at feeding time.

Individual ranches and stock farms rarely employ enough full-time hands to meet the demands of the roundup. Small operations may be able to complete a roundup with as few as a half dozen men, but larger ranches with more extensive pastures and larger herds require more hands. One of the biggest roundups held in western Texas in modern times was a two-month effort on the Four Sixes Ranch in 1968. Forty to fifty cowboys and more than 125 horses were assembled to gather and work as many as twenty-five hundred cows and calves. The roundup crew was mustered from several nearby ranches, including the Pitchfork, Triangle, and Masterson. "Neighboring"—or exchanging labor among short-handed outfits—is still a well-established custom in the ranch country, and cowboys may work roundups on four or five different ranches in a single season.

Besides neighbors, there exist several additional sources of manpower. Part-time hands, so-called "weekend waddies" who take a few days off from their regular occupations to cowboy, can sometimes be secured. Their ability and experience vary widely. Some have ranching or farming backgrounds or are members of riding clubs or sheriff's posses, but others may be totally unfamiliar with handling livestock. All such help is appreciated and it is usually inexpensive. Ranchers can usually also call upon "custom cowboys." These men may be drifters or have jobs elsewhere but, with a saddle, a trailer, and a horse or two, they become temporary fixtures on the range during periods of heavy work.

Dogs and aircraft have become an important part of the labor force on stock farms and cattle ranches on the plains in recent years. Cow dogs have been used by some stock raisers of eastern Texas since the early nineteenth century. The speed and agility of highly trained canines can be a valuable asset to a stockman whose crew may be short of cowboys. Since the 1950s a handful of ranches, particularly those occupying formidable terrain with thick vegetation, have found helicopters and, to a lesser degree, airplanes to be valuable as well. Despite high operational costs, which may run to $150 or more per hour, helicopters are favored because of the visibility and versatility they afford. Proponents claim that the use of aircraft can cut the size of a roundup crew in half by eliminating miles and hours of unnecessary riding.

On the ground, however, roundup procedures vary little from ranch to ranch. Hands assemble at the headquarters or the work area at an appointed time, usually at first light or before. Neighbors and other part-time hands normally bring their own mounts loaded in trailers pulled behind pickups. Thanks to truck and trailer transportation, men and animals arrive fresh at distant pastures in a fraction of the time that was required on horseback.

It is the responsibility of the roundup boss to coordinate the gathering. He may need to pair seasoned, well-mounted cowboys with less experienced hands to ensure the success of the roundup. Motion picture portrayals notwithstanding, the roundup is by nature a silent, businesslike operation with very little verbal communication. Under the direction of the roundup boss, the crew fans out. Keeping roughly on line, horsemen sweep forward over a pasture that may be as large as forty thousand acres, although most are likely to be smaller. Pushing the cattle toward a predetermined point—usually a set of shipping or branding pens—the riders weave back and forth to cover the gaps between them and to prevent animals from slipping through the mounted cordon. Those few animals that do escape are usually not pursued by the punchers.

Rugged ground tests both men and horses. Hazardous breaks and arroyos invariably contain thick mesquite and cedar brush, which reduces visibility. Here a helicopter pilot communicating with the cowboys by means of a loudspeaker or two-way radio can make the work much easier, detecting sick or immobile animals as well as those that are in danger of escaping the roundup dragnet.

Despite modern technology, gathering cattle efficiently is still a process that requires skilled men and horses. The same may be said of branding, though it too has been touched by change. During the late nineteenth and early twentieth centuries, branding was conducted by roundup crews on the open range. Mixed herds, sometimes numbering several thousand head and containing the cattle of several ranches, were held within a perimeter of riders while the calves were roped and dragged to a nearby branding fire to be marked.

If adequate help is available, range branding is still practiced on occasion, particularly if the pasture that has been worked is not convenient to a set of branding pens. Portable corrals can be erected in the field or a herd thrown into a corner formed by the convergence of two barbed wire fences, with stock trailers, pickup trucks, and an occasional horseman forming the remainder. Bulls and cows are expertly separated from the calves and allowed to pass through the ring of vehicles, leaving only the young behind. While the herd is being separated, the branding irons are heated.

Branding fires fueled by wood or mesquite roots doused with kerosene have largely disappeared and have generally been replaced by metal racks of burners heated with liquid propane gas, a faster and cleaner fuel, or electrically heated branding irons, which maintain a constant temperature and do not need time-consuming reheating and the frequent changes that standard irons require. An effective substitute for the hot iron has not been discovered. Experiments with branding irons dipped into liquid nitrogen or a mild acid have produced scars that are less severe than those made by a hot iron but they often produce unsatisfactory brands that blot and are less readable.

When all is ready, the ropers go to work on horseback, roping the calves around their hind legs ("heeling" them) and dragging them toward the fire. On the way a pair of men known as flankers meet the animal, roll him over by the tail, and remove the lariat so that the roper may return to the herd for another catch. The calf is then stretched out and held by the flankers until the branding process, which may also include dehorning, vaccinating, earmarking, and castrating, is complete. Using a ten-man team consisting of two ropers, two sets of flankers, a pair of men marking, and a pair doctoring, the Four Sixes Ranch brands 150 calves per hour, an average of forty-eight seconds per calf. Depending on the number of men allotted to a single calf, a good branding crew typically accomplishes its tasks within thirty and sixty seconds from the time an animal is roped. The times may range as low as twenty seconds for heifer calves and twenty-five for the bull calves which require castration.

Ranchers who use the traditional rope-and-drag operations stand by the technique as the best and most efficient way of branding. As late as 1940 almost every ranch on the Texas plains still used this system, but by 1970 only about half were applying the method and

ten years later the number had dropped to about 30 percent. The decline of long-established branding practices was hastened by the widespread introduction of mechanical branding and doctoring procedures during the labor-lean years of World War II. Branding pens, when used in conjunction with devices like squeeze chutes and calf tables, offer several advantages. Foremost among these is the reduced manpower requirement, which some say is 50 to 60 percent less than the number of men necessary to run a rope-and-drag outfit. Moreover, the use of such equipment demands less energy and athletic ability than more traditional methods. No flankers or ropers are needed to secure and hold a calf because these tasks are accomplished by maneuvering the animal through a chute and into a branding table, also known as a calf table or cradle. By manipulating a series of handles and hooks the operator can secure a calf in a viselike grip and tilt him on his side so the marking and doctoring process can take place.

In the past it was sometimes necessary to rope, throw, and hold mature cattle that needed to be doctored or examined. This method was unsatisfactory, as well as dangerous, for all concerned. Today, larger cattle are worked in a squeeze chute which operates much like a calf table except that the immobilized animal remains in a stationary upright position.

Because the use of calf tables and squeeze chutes is less physically demanding than more primitive methods, older men who can wield a "hot shot" (electrical prod) or a vaccination gun or work a lever on a piece of machinery can be useful hands during branding and doctoring. The same may be said for inexperienced men who need only be able to work on foot.

Supporters of the chute method of working livestock argue that it is more sanitary and the chances of infection less than in working cattle on the ground. Detractors counter with charges that calf tables and squeeze chutes cause just as much stress in stock as does roping and point out that there are frequent instances of animals choking, breaking or straining appendages, or escaping. On the whole, today's cattle are handled more carefully than were their predecessors, and today's ranchmen are generally more attentive to unsanitary conditions and to stress factors which might bring about sickness and weight loss in animals.

Marking and treating cattle in pens and chutes and on tables has been characterized by some tradition-bound cowboys as a boring, assembly-line style of ranching. "Everybody's against using the calf table except the boss," says one.[2] Certainly such practices appear to be the antithesis of J. Frank Dobie's conception of the West as "a dream of freedom from management and, above all, of freedom from machinery."[3] In reality, however, an efficiently functioning rope-and-drag branding operation is equally standardized. The true difference is that one technique is perceived

Much of the material in this essay is based on taped interviews with West Texas cowboys in the archives of the Southwest Collection, Texas Tech University, Lubbock, Texas (S.W. Coll., TTU), and the Panhandle-Plains Historical Museum, Canyon, Texas (P²HM, Canyon), or in the possession of the author.

1. Alexander Mackay, "Cowboy Life on a Western Ranch," pp. 15–16, unpublished manuscript, photocopy, Alexander Mackay Reference File, S.W. Coll., TTU.
2. Tom Blasingame to B. Byron Price, September 20, 1975, interview, S.W. Coll., TTU.
3. As quoted in "The American Cowboy Still Dominates His Own and Other Industries," *Newsweek* 37 (June 18, 1951):58.

as being "cowboy" whereas the other is not. Ranchers are not prone to look upon the task of branding or the craft of roping in such sentimental terms. C. L. Sonnichsen's observation of the economic nature of large ranching enterprises, which ironically are those that seem to support most rope-and-drag branding operations, is as true now as when it was first published in 1950: "Their object is to make money," he wrote, "not to serve as hobbies or contribute to the welfare of any member of the human race except the stock-holders."[4] Owners who allow roping, therefore, do so because it is the most economically efficient method for their purpose. Those who would discard the lariat altogether likewise do so from the desire to run a profitable operation.

The belief of many managers that roping has no role on a modern ranch cuts deeply into a strong tradition among the cowboys of the Southwest. A cowpuncher's skill with a reata, as one cowboy-author correctly asserts, is the ability "most intimately linked with the glamorous and romantic side of the cattle business."[5] Tales of the prowess of the region's ropers are legion. Cowboys admired hands who, they claimed with typical exaggeration, could keep two or three sets of calf flankers busy around a branding fire and still have time to roll a cigarette.

Roping first developed as an art on the range. Later it became a popular, and eventually a professional, sport. Gradually, rodeo contestants in pursuit of faster times in the arena applied scientific principles and advanced technology to basic roping techniques. Their efforts in turn stimulated the production of improved equipment, which quickly benefited the working cowboy. Synthetic materials, such as nylon, dacron, and polyester, have now replaced braided rawhide, maguey fiber, and manila hemp as standard material in a cowboy's catch rope. As a result modern lariats are more durable, hold a better loop, and do not stretch as much as their predecessors.

Similarly, saddles are stronger and better fitting for both horse and rider. Costing from $750 for a plain model of split cowhide to more than $1,500 if hand stamped or decorated with silver, a cowboy's saddle is his most expensive investment. The carved leather patterns that appear on many saddles are both artistic and functional. Tooled leather wears longer and its surface provides friction that offers the rider a more secure seat than smooth leather. Saddlehorns, which are subject to abrasions caused by ropes, may be protected by a rawhide wrap, a nylon cover, or strips of rubber inner tube.

The cowboys of the Texas plains prefer double-rigged saddles with the low roping-style cantles developed for rodeo competition. Only a few working cowboys have the skill, inclination, or opportunity to become professional rodeo cowboys, but many of them do sharpen their skills at organized match and team ropings.

These events, requiring small entry fees, abound on weekends in large and small towns throughout western Texas. Some ranches even provide arenas and livestock so that their hands will have a place to rope for recreation and inexpensive entertainment.

Although roping has fewer ranch applications than before, the desire to be competent with a lariat is still very strong. Missing loops at a branding fire while flankers stand around waiting can be a very embarrassing experience. As one cowboy put it, "If your're invited to drag cattle, you durn sure want to know how." Moreover, on ranches that use roping to any degree for the working of cattle, there seems to be plenty of expertise left. During the spring of 1980, for example, one longtime cowpuncher for the Four Sixes Ranch told manager J. J. Gibson that the branding crew he had just observed at work there was the best he had seen in his fifty-year association with the ranch.[6]

Most cowboys have accepted their roles in the mosaic of contemporary ranching. There are, however, a few punchers, particularly older hands who have seen the evolution of ranch life since the 1930s, for whom mechanization will always be an anathema. The cowboy's attitude toward change stems from the way he perceives his life and work. The myths of the cowboy past, his code of conduct, and his unique life-style all influence the modern cowboy's outlook. Taking up a familiar theme, Jane Kramer's *The Last Cowboy*, a nonfiction account of cowboy life in the Texas Panhandle in the early 1970s, contrasts the heroic image of the cowboy with his contemporary and historical reality. Henry Blanton, the main figure in the book, wages a constant but losing battle against the forces of modernization. He is described as a man who "had settled into his life, but he could not settle for it. He moved in a kind of deep, prideful disappointment. He longed for something to restore him—a lost myth, a hero's West."[7]

Some years earlier author Larry McMurtry, himself the scion of a colorful West Texas ranching family, exposed another essential ingredient in the present day cowboy's character when he wrote, "Cowboys are romantics, extreme romantics, and ninety-nine out of a hundred of them are sentimental to the core. They are oriented toward the past and face the present only under duress, and then with extreme reluctance."[8] Tom Ryan, who has devoted his life to painting the life of the modern cowboy, explained a hesitance to change that he sensed among the cowboys he had met by saying, "they feel an obligation and a pride in the past."[9] But apart from sentimental expressions, there is another explanation of the cowboy's resistance to change embodied in traditional cowboy conservatism. "An old crew," said a Matador waddie, "gets their head set on working a certain way. They don't think there's any other way it can be done."[10]

Lamentations about the cowboy's loss of craft notwithstanding, one senses that at best the attitude of ranch hands toward innovation has been selective. Cowboys who enjoy roping and dragging cattle occasionally may not show the same enthusiasm for staying away from home and family for one or two months with a chuck wagon and roundup crew. One rancher, who erected a calf roping arena for his hands near headquarters, reported that the cowboys "roped like hell for about three weeks, then put their ropes down and haven't picked them up since."[11]

There may be a few uncompromising individualists lurking in the ranch community who have not come to terms with modern cowboy life, but their days are numbered. "The hand who insists he is a pure cowboy and will not touch anything but leather and hemp and animals," observed one Texas journalist in 1975, "is often a drifter, a kind of bad actor who is playing a role rather than working at a trade."[12]

The rhythm and pattern of ranching has changed so dramatically in the past three decades that to be a good cowboy it is no longer enough to know cattle, to break horses, and to be a good roper and rider. The day has passed when cowboys let their feet dangle in the stirrup the year around. Today's ranch hand spends an increasing amount of time in noncowboy tasks, particularly in the summer and winter when cow work is slack. In 1956 M. H. W. Ritchie, owner of the JA Ranch in the Texas Panhandle, described the trend that has characterized the modern era. "The old-time cowboy is doomed," he said. "Times are changing. Certainly he must ride and rope and brand but he must also be prepared to carry a wrench in his hip pocket and a sack of feed across his saddlehorn."[13] Economy requires that the contemporary cowboy be a carpenter, welder, and plumber in order to make necessary repairs and improvements on the ranch or stock farm. Even on ranches which use them in their most traditional roles, cowpunchers must sometimes assist a windmiller in laying a water pipe to a remote camp or help a fencing crew in erecting or repairing barbed barriers.

Nevertheless, one can distinguish the cowboy by his knowledge of livestock, their condition, and their needs. Cowboys are continually called upon to check the conditions of cattle, range, and water. During the course of their daily rounds, they use pickups—"cowboy Cadillacs"—instead of horses, except in special situations. These windshield cowboys must be attentive to a variety of potentially troublesome situations. They look for cattle that have bogged, cows that need milking or help with calving, and calves that are not "mothered up" or acclimating themselves to a new range. Fortunately disease is not as serious a problem as it once was. Scientists have helped control—and in some cases eradicate—such formidable afflictions as screwworms, hoof-and-mouth disease, and brucellosis. It is still necessary to spray or dip cattle to rid them of ticks, lice, and flies, and occasionally an animal on the range

requires medical attention. Treatment would have been administered on the spot in times past, but now it is common to load the animal into a vehicle and carry it to headquarters where its recovery can be monitored. In an emergency a cowboy can usually summon help by two-way radio.

Ranchers must keep a careful watch on grass and water conditions. Permanent surface water is scarce and thus windmills are of critical importance on the plains. Several large ranches employ a separate windmiller or windmilling crew whose sole responsibility is to make certain that sufficient water is available. This is no small chore, since a ranch of 250 sections may have more than a hundred windmills. Even when a full-time windmiller is employed, cowboys may be called upon to assist him periodically. On smaller ranches, a cowboy himself may be responsible for the windmills. During the winter, he must clear ice from water tanks and thaw out mills at the point where the pump rod goes into the ground. When the wind is too light to pump enough water for stock needs, the ranch hand may hook up an auxiliary motor to the pump.

If grass on the range is poor—as it often is in western Texas, particularly during the summer and winter months—the cowboy must move cattle to a new pasture where vegetation is more plentiful or onto fields with a forage crop like winter wheat. Otherwise hay, corn, or other feed supplements must be delivered to the pastures and scattered from the rear of a pickup. This practice dates back to the 1920s or before, when cattle on the southern plains of Texas were fed cottonseed cake from mule-drawn wagons.

Fencing requires constant attention too. Though a separate crew is usually contracted with to erect fence, the job of mending it often falls to the cowboy. This task has never been greeted with enthusiasm. Says one puncher, "A little bit of fencing makes you really appreciate being horseback."[14] A posthole digger, fence staples, wire stretchers and a hammer may be carried in a pickup toolbox for minor repairs like replacing "water gaps" and fencing washed away in low places after a rain. Eventually the effects of weather, age, and cattle will combine to make total replacement necessary.

On large ranches the daily supervision of the land and the cattle often falls to camp men. Each lives on a particular section of the ranch and is responsible for its day-to-day maintenance, with occasional assistance from a floating crew sent from headquarters. The Pitchfork Ranch, for example, currently maintains three such camps in pastures ranging in size from twenty to thirty thousand acres. Camp men on the Four Sixes Ranch care for pastures averaging forty thousand acres each. On many smaller properties rapid transportation has eliminated the need to maintain separate camps. Responsibilities can be easily handled from headquarters—or even from town, if a ranch has no cowboy in residence.

4. C. L. Sonnichsen, *Cowboys and Cattle Kings: Life on the Range Today* (Norman: University of Oklahoma Press, 1950), p. 156.
5. John Erickson, "Pasture Roping over the Years," part 1, *Cattleman* 66 (October 1979):49.
6. Jim I. Williams to Elizabeth Shrank, interview, n.d. [1979], S.W. Coll., TTU; J. J. Gibson to B. Byron Price, December 4, 1980, interview, notes in the possession of the author.
7. Jane Kramer, *The Last Cowboy* (New York: Harper & Row, 1977), p. viii.
8. Larry McMurtry, *In a Narrow Grave* (Austin, Texas: The Encino Press, 1978), p. 149.
9. As quoted in Dean Krakel, *Tom Ryan: A Painter in Four Sixes Country* (Flagstaff, Arizona: Northland Press, 1971), p. 51.
10. Tutt Garnett to Jeff Townsend, November 21, 1973, interview, S.W. Coll., TTU.
11. Gibson to Price, December 4, 1980.
12. Bill Porterfield, "In Search of the Modern Cowboy," *Texas Monthly* 3 (October 1975):57.
13. As quoted in Frank Farmer, "The Vanishing Cowboy," *Collier's* 137 (May 25, 1956):35.
14. Mike Hobbs, as quoted in Chan Bergen, "Mike Hobbs: A Proud Way to Live," *Western Horseman* 45 (April 1980):57.

The breaking and training of horses remains a traditional cowboy occupation providing a break from the prosaic and routine duties of the summer and winter months. Even though other forms of transportation have supplanted them, horses remain important to the cowboy both as tools of his trade and as a part of his identity.

Except for the custom cowboy, who usually provides his own mount, most punchers still depend on ranches for the horse flesh. Most outfits, in fact, do not allow a cowboy to keep a personal mount. The day when ranches supported large remudas and when a cowboy's string of horses might include a dozen or more is gone, however, and today's strings rarely exceed half a dozen. The best animals are still coveted and in many places are still assigned on the basis of seniority.

The specialized animal bred for cow work is the quarter horse. These mounts are famous for their ability to accelerate quickly and to maintain speed over short distances. They are characterized by strength, stamina, and an intangible ability to anticipate the movement of cattle when cutting. They come in all colors and sizes, but most average fifteen hands tall and weigh about 1,250 pounds. Besides being larger and better bred than their scrawny nineteenth-century ancestors, modern ranch horses are also more expensive. A single animal can bring several thousand dollars on the market.

Realizing this, some ranchers have engaged in ambitious breeding programs in which cowboys are involved in breaking and training horses not only for ranch use but also for sale as show or performance animals for racing and rodeos. Unregulated pasture breeding has given way to strictly controlled artificial insemination. Modern horse training programs differ significantly from earlier ones. Although training philosophies vary widely, it can be generally stated that horses are brought along more quickly but with gentler treatment than when they were cheap, plentiful, and ill-bred.

The making of a good cow horse still takes five or six years. Some cowboys think that the number and quality of ranch horses has declined because they are not worked enough. As one rider put it "They don't learn very much in a trailer."[15] It is the opinion of at least some trainers, however, that the fault lies in the declining skill of cowboys to ride and manage their mounts properly. They say that after a year of training for ranch service, a horse can be ruined in two hours if ridden improperly.

Like their riders, horses have different personalities, temperaments, and physical abilities. Most are excellent all-purpose animals, although some are naturally better at cutting or roping than others. Their individual natures are the source of rich folklore and still figure heavily in cowboy conversation. Cowpunchers have always looked upon being well mounted as a virtue, and the contemporary cowboy is no exception. They measure themselves in part by the performance of their horses. "To be a cowboy," said Larry McMurtry, "meant, first of all to be a horseman."[16]

"Being set afoot," according to E. C. "Teddy Blue" Abbott, was one of "only two things that the old-time cowpuncher was afraid of." The other was "a decent woman."[17] The majority of working cowboys during the late nineteenth and early twentieth centuries were single. Ranchers preferred unattached men because they could be hired cheap, and they would work at jobs that required long absences from family and home. Today cowboys are likely to be married and more permanent than their predecessors. This relatively recent phenomenon reflects the social and technological revolutions that have altered cowboy life and work. It also represents a basic change in the philosophy of ranch management.

Automobiles and pickups gave young, single cowboys greater mobility and enhanced their natural tendency toward independence. At the same time they also reduced the cowboy's working hours and the necessity for him to remain in remote areas for long periods of time. Only five or six days are now required to do work that formerly took seven to accomplish. As a result, contemporary cowboys normally have a day off each week. They also have a wider range of social and recreational opportunities, although the rural nature of their work continues to be somewhat isolating.

Single drifting cowboys were still common around west Texas ranches as late as the early 1970s. Richard Bolt, a longtime cowboy and cook for outfits like the Waggoner, Pitchfork, Matador, and Four Sixes, stated in 1972 that few cowboys stayed on one job very long and that an entire crew might turn over two or three times a year. Today a few drifters still wander from outfit to outfit and there is a certain amount of turnover associated with seasonal help, but it is not nearly as pronounced as in the past. Bolt's estimates can be contrasted with the longevity of the Pitchfork crew, which in 1979 had men who served the ranch for periods ranging from four to twenty years. A few cowboys have always exhibited uncommon pride in a single ranch and loyalty to it. The story is told of Doc Gustafson, an old SMS Ranch cowboy, who was approached by a camp meeting evangelist and asked if he would "work for Jesus." He replied that "he believed not—he had a real good job with the Swenson brothers and he reckoned on staying there till he died."[18]

Cowboys themselves say that management and living conditions are the two most important factors in the retention of ranch personnel. Leadership and managerial ability remain cornerstones to a successful operation whether it is corporately or individually owned. The paths to ranch management are diverse. Some managers are graduates of college and university programs in agricultural economics, animal science, or range management, but others have risen to such positions after long years of experience as cowboys. Whatever the route, most of those who are successful administrators of personnel are also good cowboys themselves. They usually exhibit leadership qualities that inspire confidence and on-the-job discipline in their hired hands. The advice of good managers is unthreatening and tempered with common sense, and those who are highly regarded do not ask cowboys to do things they have not done or would not do themselves.

Inevitably there are a few owners and administrators who do not respect the independence and pride which characterize the cowboy's approach to his job. According to rancher John Stevens, ownership that does not appreciate or cannot be convinced of this fact usually has problems. "They end up running all their good help off and working a lower grade of help and changing every thirty days."[19]

Ranchers have also realized that improved working conditions are essential to maintaining a quality labor force. As a result, cowboy wages, housing, and even food have improved significantly in recent years. In part these developments are a response to the economic competition offered by urban centers. During and immediately following World War II, the booming economy, the shortage of manpower, and the near total employment rate drove wages upward for all workers. Cowboys were no exception, though it was with reluctance that ranchers accustomed to paying between $25 and $50 per month for a cowpuncher's services acceded to paying two or three times that amount for the same work. "We'll just leave the damn things [cattle] in the brush," is said to have been manager John Mackenzie's indignant declaration at the suggestion that the salaries of Matador cowboys be raised above $100 per month.[20]

The characteristic frugality of ranchers notwithstanding, wages did rise, but they still lagged well behind those of most urban workers. This lag continues to have an effect as potential cowboys join other rural Texans in a steady migration to cities and towns. Typical pay in the early 1970s was $225 to $350 a month plus board. By mid-decade it had jumped to between $500 and $700 depending on previous experience, marital status, and additional benefits. A married hand on a well-paying ranch today may expect to receive $600 to $700 for an entry level position and as much as $900 to $1,000 per month if he is experienced. A different sort of salary arrangement usually applies to cowboys who are employed by absentee owners to care for small stocks of cattle. Such a cowboy may receive a share in the herd or be paid a certain amount per head for his help.

Wages are not, however, the only consideration. Modern ranches, particularly the larger ones, offer a wide range of benefits that may include life and health insurance, a retirement plan, and occasionally a percentage bonus figured from the ranch's yearly gross. In addition, some outfits furnish pickups for their hands or pay a monthly expense allowance if a cowboy uses his personal vehicle on ranch business. Full-time married employees who live at the ranch are typically furnished a modest house, utilities, and beef. At one time their grocery bills were paid as well, but this practice has been generally discontinued in favor of higher salaries.

Single cowboys usually occupy a bunkhouse at the ranch headquarters and take their meals at a mess hall. On large outfits this structure may resemble a college dormitory. Rooms are comfortable but not spacious or elegant, and a few modern amenities such as televisions and clothes washers and driers are standard in most.

In contrast, camp men and their families live a more isolated existence, which until very recently was more primitive as well. A few are still without electricity and running water. The Campbell Creek Camp, located on a 20,000-acre pasture in the Palo Duro Canyon, nine miles but an hour-and-a-half drive from the JA Ranch headquarters, has few modern conveniences. Tom Blasingame, the eighty-two-year-old cowboy who lives there alone, hauls in his own drinking water, cooks with propane gas, and lights the frame structure with kerosene lamps.

With old-timers like Blasingame becoming more and more scarce, ranch owners and managers frequently complain of the shortage of experienced ranch hands. The foreman of the Masterson Ranch felt that the problem had reached such proportions in the early 1970s that some sort of "cowboy college" was needed to teach essential occupational skills. Various explanations are offered for this unsettling situation. Conservative voices in the ranch community blame welfare, food stamps, unemployment insurance, and other social programs. Others berate a younger generation for exhibiting neither the willingness nor the fortitude of their rugged forebears to endure adverse working conditions for low pay and little chance of advancement.

The observation that a cowhand has "about as much chance to become a cattleman as a rustler has of getting to Heaven" is still valid.[21] The cost of land, cattle, and interest on borrowed money has risen sharply in the past quarter century, putting the prospect of a cowboy being able to own his own property farther out of reach. Once in a while a small ranch owner will cowboy for another outfit or manage a herd for an absentee proprietor, but these cases are limited.

Urban centers offer the modern ranch hand and his family greater social, economic, and educational opportunities than a rural environment does. Modern transportation allows many of today's cowboys to move to town and yet retain their employment on a ranch. Tax laws which allow the deduction of expenses incurred in driving to work have even encouraged some punchers to relocate.

Smaller towns in western Texas also present attractive

15. Gibson to Price, December 4, 1980.
16. McMurtry, *In a Narrow Grave*, p. 147.
17. E. C. ("Teddy Blue") Abbott and Helena Huntington Smith, *We Pointed Them North* (Norman: University of Oklahoma Press, 1954), p. 8.
18. Mary W. Clarke, *The Swenson Saga and the SMS Ranches* (Austin, Texas: Jenkins Publishing Co., 1976), p. 316.
19. John Stevens to David Murrah, June 29, 1971, interview, S.W. Coll., TTU.
20. As quoted in Alvin Durham to Jeff Townsend, August 16, 1972, S.W. Coll., TTU.
21. Sonnichsen, *Cowboys and Cattle Kings*, p. 96.

employment alternatives in livestock-related industries. Young men who in another day and time might have become ranch hands may now take jobs as pen riders in modern cattle feedlots. Since the early 1960s the growth of livestock feeding, particularly in the panhandle-plains region, has been impressive. Today virtually all cattle are grain-fed to maturity in a feedyard before slaughter. Almost 4.5 million head were marketed from Texas feedlots in 1979 alone. The largest of the more than one thousand feedlots in Texas are located on the plains adjacent to areas of irrigated farming. Some of these giant concerns have a capacity for fifty thousand head of cattle, employ as many as ten to fifteen pen riders, and cover hundreds of acres of ground. During a normal stay of 120 to 180 days, yearling cattle are fattened on processed grain, roughage, and protein supplements while they are under the constant supervision of feedlot cowboys.

The majority of this new breed of cowboy are in their twenties. Some are ex-ranch hands but many come to the job from high school or college and have little or no experience with livestock. In dress they do not differ greatly from their range-riding counterparts and their duties are more similar than one might expect.

If, by definition, the primary responsibility of a working cowboy is caring for cattle from horseback, then the pen riders of the modern feedlot surely qualify for the title. Pen riders practice their craft not on the open range but in a maze of corrals, alleys, gates, and chutes. Spending as many as sixty hours a week in the saddle, they must be every bit as hardy as their counterparts who toil on the range. They must also be reasonably good horsemen and be well mounted on animals with quiet dispositions and adequate reining ability. Since periodic changes of horses are necessary in the conduct of a pen rider's daily routine, some feedlots provide extra animals. Unlike men on larger ranches, pen riders may also keep and use personal mounts, which are boarded free at the yard.

Normally one pen rider is allotted to each five thousand head of cattle in the lot, so that a large feedlot may employ as many cowboys as a large ranch. Every morning the pen riders begin winding their way through their assigned sections of pens, each of which may contain as many as two hundred head. Pen checks can take as little as ten minutes or as long as half an hour depending on the problems that are encountered. The riders check water levels and stay alert for stock that may have escaped their proper corral or become entangled trying to do so. Most importantly the pen rider must notice any animals that are sick, injured, or not gaining weight as they should. Illness among feedlot cattle is most prevalent during the thirty-day period that is required for them to become fully acclimated to their new surroundings. Infection, shortness of breath, drooping heads, and other characteristics of sick stock are reported at once to the management. The afflicted animals are cut out of their pen and carried to a "hospital" area for treatment by "feedlot doctors" or veterinarians.

Occasionally pen riders must brand cattle or tag the ears of stock with a lot number for more convenient identification. They may also have to use their skills as horsemen to prepare cattle for weighing and shipment to the slaughterhouse. A great deal of finesse is required to negotiate a herd through the corrals to its appointed destination, and rough handling of the cattle is strictly forbidden. The process is accomplished with almost no roping and as little cutting on horseback as is possible, because the stress induced would cause the cattle to lose weight.

Pen riding is a straight riding job with no fences to mend or windmills to climb. Depending on the size of the yard, hands can start at a salary of $750 to $800 per month and eventually reach $1,000 or more. Yet some ranch hands who have done both find the life of a feedlot cowboy to be monotonous and unsatisfying. The drudgery is probably best expressed by a man who returned to ranch work after two years at a Hereford, Texas, yard: "The routine of the place was beginning to take too much out of me. In a feedlot you don't look forward to getting up and going to work each morning. You always know what you are going to do. You ride through the same pens of cattle day after day."[22] Jim Steiert, a farm and ranch writer, echoed these sentiments: "Riding the range in a modern feedlot just can't be thought of in the same context as cowboying."[23] Apparently caring for cattle is not the principal attraction of being a cowboy.

If the ranch hand is considered superior to the feedlot cowboy, it is in great measure because others have made him so. "People don't want to relate to the pickup or feedlot cowboy," maintains Bank Langmore, a modern day Erwin Smith who has made a life's work of depicting cowboy life only in its most primitive and traditional forms.[24] It is, perhaps, only natural that the public is infatuated with a cowboy figure whose manner and style of life differentiate him from city dwellers. The decline of traditional tasks and skills with which cowboys have always been identified has, however, made the affair difficult to maintain. Even the uniform that once distinguished the cowpuncher from other human beings is no longer a sure clue to his occupation.

The popularity of western clothing has blurred the superficial boundaries between real cowboys and people who are participating in what historian William Savage calls the myth of being a cowboy. High-priced boots made of exotic leathers, fancy shirts of satin and fringe, and feathered hatbands have had a broad appeal. One western wear dealer in Amarillo, a city surrounded by some of the West's most famous ranches and the home of the world's largest cattle auction, estimated in 1980 that only about a quarter of her customers had anything to do with livestock.[25]

Cowboys express amusement, befuddlement, and occasionally even a bit of resentment toward the often ostentatious mutations of apparel originally developed in response to environmental conditions and occupational requirements. Yet they have not been insulated from the latest western dress phenomenon. The demand for western-cut clothing has considerably expanded the variety, quantity, and quality of merchandise available. Today's patterns, colors, and synthetic blends in clothing are a dramatic contrast to a time when cotton or wool was the rule and a starched white shirt was, to a cowboy, synonymous with formal attire. Unfortunately, an appetite for fashion may not be easily satisfied on cowboy wages. Prices have risen with demand and soar higher with inflation.

Historically the waddies of western Texas have been conservative dressers, even by cowboy standards. Their work clothes remain so chiefly because the nature of the job still demands durability, protection, and ease of movement above style. As is the case in other occupations, the quality and style of cowboy clothing and gear are intended to convey an air of professionalism, especially to peers and employers. Clothes, however, do not make a cowboy. Dressing well is no virtue when being bucked off a horse or missing loops at a branding fire. The sarcastic needling from coworkers that inevitably follows such incidents is still very humbling.

From head to toe the basic elements of working cowboy attire are the same as they were for the first punchers on the plains. Broad-brimmed hats still afford protection from the elements though baseball caps have been introduced in some quarters. Most hands have at least two hats, one of which is inevitably well-seasoned by sweat and years of wear in all types of weather. Winter felts, which cost between $60 and $120, are replaced in the summer with lighter, cooler, and less expensive straw hats. Older cowboys are partial to low crowns and more traditional creases. Their young protégés, however, favor modern styles, some of them popularized by professional rodeo cowboys.

A pair of hand-crafted boots is still a desirable part of any self-respecting cowboy's wardrobe. Well over a million pairs are manufactured each year, ranging in style from plain to fancy and in price from seventy to nearly a thousand dollars. Boots with high tops, tall underslung heels, and rounded toes, popular in the 1930s and before, have returned to replace the pointed-toe varieties dominant since World War II.

As fashions change, the most recent siege of cowboy mania must surely pass away, but this is not true of the subject of its ardor. The reality of the American cowboy remains intact, just as resilient and a great deal more malleable than the heroic image that often obscures it. Though their course is yet uncharted, cowboys seem destined to continue to evolve rather than to disappear.

The demand for cowboys on the plains of western Texas appears to be stable, and it may even grow slightly in the future. Agricultural experts have noted a tendency since the early 1960s toward fewer but larger cattle-raising operations. This trend is principally the result of the consolidation of small stock farms rather than the growth of already sizable enterprises. The decline of irrigated farming in the region and the conversion of crop acreage to grazing land have hastened the process as have tax incentives and the comparatively lenient requirements for investments in labor and machinery for ranching.

Modernizing forces are also expected to revise further the methods and the tools with which cowboys do their jobs. By the year 1990, for example, it is predicted that the branding iron will have finally given way either to implanted transponders with individual codes that will allow rapid and accurate transmission of information about stock or to a satisfactory hair dye that can be easily and permanently applied. Likewise, the castrating knife may soon be taken from the cowboy's hand to be replaced by a syringe filled with calcium chloride or some other sterilizing agent that will be injected into the testicles of bull calves. Even if branding and castrating do not fall victim to science, there is the ever-present possibility that they, along with roping and other practices that can be construed as the rough handling of livestock, may be prohibited by the legal maneuverings of humane groups.

The full impact of scientific developments and of the social implications of urbanization are unclear at best. There is already evidence that the demand for cowboy labor is greater than the supply. Town lots and feedlots have become formidable competitors to the ranch house and the range. As long as profit margins on beef remain dollar-bill thin and wages and benefits for hands just as slim, most ranchers must continue to rely heavily on friends, neighbors, and "custom cowboys" to accomplish their cow work. It seems unlikely, however, that cowboys will be completely absorbed either physically or mentally by the urban society that constantly woos their attention.

There is reason for optimism as long as boys are attracted to nature, to horses and cattle, and to a style of life that is perceived as being simple, peaceful, and free. It is as difficult to imagine ranching without cowboys as it is to envision an army without infantry. Contemporary cowboys and those who follow them should not look to antiquated nineteenth-century definitions for their identity, however, nor should they measure themselves against a mythological cowboy hero. They will only be disappointed in their stature. The modern cowboy and his descendants, like the old-time cowpunchers of yesteryear, are and will be unique to their own time.

22. Bergen, "Mike Hobbs: A Proud Way to Live," p. 55.
23. Jim Steiert, "Old School Cowboy Still Rides in the Feedlot," *Texas Farmer-Stockman* 93 (May 1980):11.
24. As quoted in Kurt Markus, "Bank Langmore: Shooting the American Cowboy," *Western Horseman* 42 (August 1977):40.
25. Beth Duke, "Fashions Have Western Flair," *Amarillo* (Texas) *Sunday News-Globe*, October 12, 1980, p. E-2.

CHANGES IN RANCHING

Fences, windmills, and winter feeding were vital parts of the reorganization that the range cattle industry underwent after the collapse of the cattle boom in 1886. During the first forty years of the twentieth century, further changes occurred. The automobile made it possible to transport horses by trailer into remote areas, making distant line camps a thing of the past on most ranches. The automobile also brought summer visitors to the northwestern ranges and made the employment of part-time "dude" labor possible. Improved breeds of cattle were introduced into the West, and ranchers began to experiment with selective breeding to produce hardier and heavier cattle. At the same time, ranchers began to practice modern veterinary medicine, dipping and inoculating cattle to ensure healthy herds. Feed pens, where cattle were fattened for market, became as common as big pastures. In spite of these changes, the cowboy's basic tools remained the horse and the rope; and his stock-in-trade was still judgment, skill, and cow sense.

Farm Security Administration photographers Arthur Rothstein, Russell Lee, and John Vachon recorded many of these changes when they photographed ranch life on the northwestern ranges between 1936 and 1942.

Windmill on a Rapidly Drying Waterhole
North Dakota Range
Arthur Rothstein (b. 1915)
Photograph, 1936
Farm Security Administration File
Prints and Photographs Division
Library of Congress

**Setting Up Camp for the Roundup
Quarter Circle U Brewster-Arnold Ranch
near Birney, Montana**
Arthur Rothstein (b. 1915)
Photograph, 1939
Farm Security Administration File
Prints and Photographs Division
Library of Congress

**Feeding Hay to Cattle in Wintertime
Park County, Montana**
John Vachon (1914–1975)
Photograph, 1942
Farm Security Administration File
Prints and Photographs Division
Library of Congress

Cattle in Dehorning Chute
Jenson's Ranch, Big Hole Basin
Beaverhead County, Montana
John Vachon (1914–1975)
Photograph, 1942
Farm Security Administration File
Prints and Photographs Division
Library of Congress

Hereford Cattle in Corral
Big Hole Basin, Beaverhead County, Montana
Russell Lee (b. 1903)
Photograph, 1942
Farm Security Administration File
Prints and Photographs Division
Library of Congress

**A Cowboy Fills Syringe with Blackleg Serum
Quarter Circle U Brewster-Arnold Ranch
near Birney, Montana**
Arthur Rothstein (b. 1915)
Photograph, 1939
Farm Security Administration File
Prints and Photographs Division
Library of Congress

**Cattle with Hoofrot Are Driven through Pens
Containing a Solution of Blue Vitriol
Cruzen Ranch, Valley County, Idaho**
Russell Lee (b. 1903)
Photograph, 1942
Farm Security Administration File
Prints and Photographs Division
Library of Congress

Cattle in Feedpens at Stockyard
Scottsbluff, Nebraska
Arthur Rothstein (b. 1915)
Photograph, 1939
Farm Security Administration File
Prints and Photographs Division
Library of Congress

Throwing a Calf for Branding during Roundup
Quarter Circle U Brewster-Arnold Ranch
near Birney, Montana
Arthur Rothstein (b. 1915)
Photograph, 1939
Farm Security Administration File
Prints and Photographs Division
Library of Congress

Cowboy at Three-Circle Ranch Roundup
Custer National Forest
Powder River County, Montana
Arthur Rothstein (b. 1915)
Photograph, 1939
Farm Security Administration File
Prints and Photographs Division
Library of Congress

Summer Visitor Working during Roundup
Quarter Circle U Brewster-Arnold Ranch
near Birney, Montana
Arthur Rothstein (b. 1915)
Photograph, 1939
Farm Security Administration File
Prints and Photographs Division
Library of Congress

Roping a Calf during Roundup
Quarter Circle U Brewster-Arnold Ranch
near Birney, Montana
Arthur Rothstein (b. 1915)
Photograph, 1939
Farm Security Administration File
Prints and Photographs Division
Library of Congress

CONTEMPORARY RANCHING

In 1978 the American Folklife Center conducted a study of contemporary ranching in Paradise Valley, Humboldt County, Nevada, a region with a mixed population of Anglo-American, German, Italian, Basque, and Paiute Indian ranchers and cowboys. Folklorists, anthropologists, historians, and photographers documented the everyday life of ranchers and cowboys—or buckaroos, as they are called in Nevada—and their families. The researchers concluded that, although there have been continual improvements in technology, the basic rhythm of the range cattle industry in the Great Basin is much the same as it was in the late 1930s. There still are roundups and brandings. Short trail drives still take cattle from summer range to winter pasture. And cattle are still worked on horseback. As the final report says, the main object of attention is still the cow.

Roping
Carl Fleischhauer (b. 1940)
Photograph, June 1978
    Dan Martinez and Bob Humphrey rope calves at spring branding at the Circle A, Quinn River, Nevada.
American Folklife Center
Library of Congress

Branding
Linda Gastañaga (b. 1951)
Photograph, June 1978
   Rene Martinez, Bruno McErquiaga,
and Dennis Brown work at
a propane branding fire during
the Circle A branding.
American Folklife Center
Library of Congress

Spring Branding
Carl Fleischhauer (b. 1940)
Photograph, June 1978
   Dave Jones helps hold a calf and readies
a can of spray antiseptic, while Alfonso
Marcuerquiaga inoculates the calf and
foreman Dennis Brown cuts an
identifying wattle.
American Folklife Center
Library of Congress

Branding

Carl Fleischhauer (b. 1940)

Photograph, June 1978

    Bob Humphrey and foreman Dennis Brown have lunch by the horse trailer. Humphrey is a retired sheriff who volunteered to help out at the branding.

American Folklife Center
Library of Congress

Branding

Carl Fleischhauer (b. 1940)

Photograph, June 1978

    Rene Martinez hands Dave Jones the day's lunch on a paper plate.

American Folklife Center
Library of Congress

Branding

Carl Fleischhauer (b. 1940)

Photograph, May 1978

    Heifers are being branded as they are held in the squeeze chute on the corral of the Loui Cerri Ranch.

American Folklife Center
Library of Congress

Within the yearly ranch round, the changes wrought in Paradise Valley by improved technology are striking. Not only has the ubiquitous truck put almost every corner of the ranch within a few hours of headquarters, but it also serves as a blacksmith shop, chuck wagon, branding camp, and mobile feeding station. Ranch hands still wear chinks—knee-length chaps—but they also wear billed polyester caps and nylon jackets. They work cattle with nylon ropes and sometimes use squeeze chutes and propane branding fires. They spend almost as much time raising hay and repairing machinery as they do working cattle. The most significant change, however, has been in the status of the buckaroo. Improved technology means that there are fewer hired ranch hands now than there were fifty years ago. Much of the actual cow work on Paradise Valley ranches is done by ranchers and their families, with the help of some hired men and a few weekend volunteers. Many of the hired buckaroos are family men who go home to wives and children at night, instead of going to a bunkhouse. A few single buckaroos still live on ranches and, for short periods of time, in line camps. Married or single, modern Nevada buckaroos share with past generations of cowboys a sense of being part of a unique working tradition.

At Day's End
Carl Fleischhauer (b. 1940)
Photograph, October 1979
   Rancher Fred Miller sets out to go home
after having helped with the branding of
calves on the neighboring 96 Ranch.
American Folklife Center
Library of Congress

Feeding
William H. Smock (b. 1944)
Photograph, March 1980
    Paiute Indian buckaroos Tex Northrup
and Myron Smart feed hay on the 96 Ranch.
American Folklife Center
Library of Congress

Feeding
Richard E. Ahlborn (b. 1933)
Photograph, July 1978
    Rancher Loui Cerri examines hay.
American Folklife Center
Library of Congress

Relaxing after Work
Carl Fleischhauer (b. 1940)
Photograph, October 1979
    From left to right: buckaroo Rusty
McCorkell, an unidentified ranch hand,
trapper Tim Iveson (wearing suspenders),
and rancher Loui Cerri socialize in the
Paradise Valley bar after a day's work.
American Folklife Center
Library of Congress

96 Ranch Crew
Carl Fleischhauer (b. 1940)
Photograph, October 1979
    The October 1979 trail drive crew gathers
at the Hartscrabble line camp cabin. *From
left to right*: Paiute Indian buckaroos Tex
Northrup, Myron Smart, and Theodore
Brown; Mel Winslow, a friend who is helping
with the drive; rancher Leslie J. Stewart and
his son Fred; and the neighboring rancher
Henry Taylor and his son Clay.
American Folklife Center
Library of Congress

Setting Out to Brand Cattle
Howard W. Marshall (b. 1944)
Photograph, July 1978
  Chuck Wheelock leads his horse past buckaroo quarters on the 96 Ranch.
American Folklife Center
Library of Congress

Overleaf:
Cowboy Copter Pilot
Skeeter Hagler (b. 1947)
Photograph, 1980
From the Pulitzer Prize-winning series "The Texas Cowboy"
  Cowboy copter pilot Frank Menix hovers over the historic Pitchfork Ranch near Lubbock, Texas, as he herds cattle from the air.
Skeeter Hagler
Dallas, Texas

A Dialectical Inquiry into the Recurring Fantasy of the Equestrian Herdsman (Singing Variety)

by Dave Hickey

Author's Note: When I was asked to contribute to this catalog on
the American cowboy, I decided to let my two friends Virgil
Childress and Bubba Burkette speak for me. The three of us have
a great deal in common and I can vouch for the authenticity of
their experiences, if not for the veracity of their opinions. At
present the two of them, having survived College in the Sixties
and Marriage in the Seventies are sharing a condominium in the
Oak Lawn section of North Dallas and trying to come to terms
with being Forty in the Eighties. Bubba is a sportswriter covering
professional football (high school through NFL) for a local daily,
and Virgil is a professional musician (electric guitar) and pop-song
writer of moderate success. Although they are totally unaware of
it, they are closely related in my mind to those two mannered
young gentlemen who discuss matters aesthetic and cultural in
Oscar Wilde's *Intentions*, and not unrelated to those two eternal
undergraduates Rozencrantz and Guildenstern as resurrected by
Tom Stoppard, which, I hope, in no way undermines their status
as Good Old Boys, because they are just that, and I am not.

Overleaf:
Lucchese Boots
Joseph Biggert (b. 1952)
Pencil drawing, 1978
McCreedy & Schreiber, Inc.
New York, New York

VIRGIL: Hey, Bubba!

BUBBA: Virgil, dammit, come in and shut the door.

VIRGIL: Sure. . . . Hey, that *is* your pickup out front, isn't it? Blue Chevy? Balloon tires? Gun-rack?

BUBBA: Yeah. Did you run into it?

VIRGIL: No, but I hate to tell you this: somebody done *stole* your "Honk if You Love Willie Nelson" bumper sticker.

BUBBA: I took it off.

VIRGIL: *You took it off!* After all the girls! That damn bumper sticker on a pickup beats a dago-raked Mercedes, and *you took it off!* Have you forgotten? Marilyn and Bambi? *Nude Bumper Pool!*

BUBBA: Naw, I remember . . . .

VIRGIL: You took *off* our Willie-sticker, and you left *on* ' See Ruby Falls?''

BUBBA: Guess from now on we'll just have to be the *honk-ers* rather than the *honk-ees.*

VIRGIL: Cute. Very cute . . . uh . . . hey, Bubba?

BUBBA: Yes, Virgil?

VIRGIL: What is all this stuff? Are you moving out, or do you have twenty nekkid cowboys locked in the bedroom?

BUBBA: Just what 'n the hell do you mean by that?

VIRGIL: What I *mean*, fella, is that I just got home from a hard night at the rock-and-roll factory, and there is this *cowboy crap* all over the floor. What if I'd decided to bring home . . .

BUBBA: It's not cowboy crap, peckerwood, it's my western wardrobe, which I'm putting into storage—all except the boots, which I have to wear on account of my feet, which have never worn anything but boots and consequently hurt like hell in your "mondo-condo" *Adidas* and *Guccis.*

VIRGIL: You're *storing* all this, right? I mean . . . *Denim After Shave? Chaps Cologne for Men?*

BUBBA: I'm throwing that stuff away.

VIRGIL: One peacock feather hatband?

BUBBA: *All right!* Gimme 'at here! Willie give it to me himself at the very first "Fourth of July Picnic." It come off one of his personal peacocks.

VIRGIL: Well, *far* be it from me to touch the feathers off one of Willie-Goddam-Nelson's *personal* peacocks! . . . Jeez, would you lookit all this junk! I swear, Bubba, looks like a whole rodeo just run right outta here to go skinny-dippin'.

BUBBA: Could I remind you, without even raising my voice, that I have been able to whip your tail since the sixth grade.

VIRGIL: Yeah, yeah. Well, just *you* don't forget who helps you read the hard words in those Dallas Cowboy press releases.

BUBBA: Virgil, dammit . . . .

VIRGIL: Okay. Then, could I have your armadillo belt buckle?

BUBBA: Virgil, I'm not gonna say this again . . . .

VIRGIL: Wait! Don't tell me! You've gone Disco!

BUBBA: Virgil . . .

VIRGIL: No! *Punk!*

"That's right, folks, in a move that parallels the retirement of the great Ed ''Too Tall'' Jones from the Dallas Cowboys to pursue a career in boxing, we find out tonight that the byline Bubba Earl Burkette, a name that has become synonymous with mediocrity in sportswriting, will be seen no more, that Burkette has traded in the Crimson Tide for the New Wave! That as of tonight, Bubba Earl Burkette becomes Bubba Texas

of *Bubba Texas and the Nekkid Cowboy Traitors!* And, you heard it first on 'Monday Night Football!' Now back to Dandy Don Meredith up in the booth.''

BUBBA:

VIRGIL: Uh, Bubba? You okay?

BUBBA: Yeah.

VIRGIL: Then say something.

BUBBA: I am waitin' for you to *let me up!*

VIRGIL: Hey, ya big Palooka, I was just kidding. You know how much fun I have at others' expense. Do you want this folded stuff in here?

BUBBA: Sure

VIRGIL: What in the hell are you gonna wear, anyway?

BUBBA: I dunno; my golf stuff, I guess.

VIRGIL: Come on, Bubba, honest injun, what's goin' on?

BUBBA: Uh, nothing really.

VIRGIL: Great! I give him Howard Cosell. He gives me my ex-wife! I come in the door to silence and say: "Hey, baby, what's botherin' you?" She says: "Oh nothing!" This is exactly the kind of thing I need.

BUBBA: It *is* nothing. I just decided to scrap my cowboy disguise for a while. This whole cowboy thing is getting out of hand, and it's making me feel weird.

VIRGIL: In the words of Dandy Don (himself an ex-Cowboy), "Things ain't like they used to be, but then again, they never were.''

BUBBA: Oh come on, Virgil, you got to admit it's getting *very* strange out. I mean first it was just Outlaw Country Music and Redneck Rock: Waylon Jennings, and Willie Nelson, Honky-Tonk Heroes, and Willie's Picnics. Then all of a sudden it's the Hollywood Turquoise Set hanging around: Peter Fonda, Dennis Hopper, and David Carradine, plus all their buddies from *Sports Illustrated.* Well, okay, I can live with that. Jocks don't bother me as long as they don't want to arm wrestle. But then all of a sudden it's John Travolta in "Urban Cowboy," and it's Kenny Rodgers and "Vegas-Folkie Cowboys," and Fonda and Redford in "Electric Cowboys," and Glen Campbell with "Rhinestone Cowboys," not to mention Kinky Friedman and "Ride-Em Jewboys." Then it's Gloria Vanderbilt and Bobby Short selling blue jeans, then it's Calvin Klein! And then it's "Dallas!" On the TV: If I wanted Dallas, which I don't, I'd go outside, and who's the hero? A composite of every asshole in my fraternity at SMU who ever drilled a slant' hole!

VIRGIL: The ghost of Lyndon Johnson walks these streets and smiles!

BUBBA: I mean, really, Virgil, where is that comin' from?

VIRGIL: The Dark Heart of America.

BUBBA: Great! Now that is what I needed to hear. I mean, really, Virgil. You're a songwriter, you ride the waves of pop culture with your electric guitar. You even write a cowboy song from time to time.

VIRGIL: I write songs about everyday people. Sometimes they just happen to be cowboys.

BUBBA: Well, let me put it like this. Every cowboy song you wrote in the last five years has gotten recorded.

VIRGIL: That's true.

BUBBA: Well?

VIRGIL: Well, I think you've got to regard it as a seasonal epidemic. Like the flu. About every twenty years or so, ever since the Civil War, America has this Cowboy Epidemic, then they gradually develop an immunity,

207

and here comes a whole, brand new strain of Galloping Cowboy Influenza. A different strain of the same old virus. First your Cowboy Swine Flu, then your Cowboy Asian Flu . . .

BUBBA: David Carradine in "Kung Fu!"

VIRGIL: Bubba, you amaze me! And then naturally your Cowboy Boogie-Woogie Flu. Seriously, though, I think to understand it you have to assume that the cowboy part is just decoration—a poetic convention.

BUBBA: It's something stranger than that.

VIRGIL: Yeah, it probably is. It *is* pretty amazing that after the sixties with its hippies and revolutionaries and spies, and the seventies with its gays and punks and counterrevolutionaries, we'd get cowboys again. Imagine that. Cowboys again. You're right, Bubba. There is strange afoot in the land. Still I think it's understandable.

BUBBA: Oh yeah.

VIRGIL: Not that I understand it.

BUBBA: Right.

VIRGIL: Anyway, the first thing you have to remember is that conventional dramatic forms like westerns, and private-eye stories, and police and courtroom stories don't really tell you anything about the West, or private eyes, or police, or courtrooms. They really tell you about the guys that wrote them and the world they live in. If people like the story, what they are *liking* is something in the attitude of the writer. That holds true for songwriting too. The song can be about heroin or rodeos, the slave trade or gunfighters; the attitude of the guy that wrote it is what people like or don't like.

Everybody writes about himself, and what he knows. The only difference in being a poet or a novelist, and being a songwriter or a screenwriter, is the *way* you write about yourself. The poet is going to write about himself as an individual, separate from everybody else, the songwriter is going to write about himself as a *citizen*. He's going to write about those things that he thinks or hopes that he shares with everybody else. If he's right, and what he's written is well-crafted, *and* (big "if" here) it gets exposure, it will probably be popular. If it's not, it's *nothing*. You see, a poem, even if nobody likes it, is still a poem; a song or a screenplay, if nobody likes it, if it's not popular, is *nothing*. Popular artists can only hope they share a dream.

BUBBA: And that they get good distribution.

VIRGIL: And that they get good distribution. You can't hide your Beatles under a bushel.

BUBBA: No points for shy.

VIRGIL: No points for anything. Never take points. Take the cash and let the credit go.

Anyway, that's why, when I see a western movie, I'm not really looking at the West. I'm looking at a Hollywood screenwriter's personal psychodrama in cowboy drag. That's why the basic western plot is about this young idealistic cowboy who comes to town and has something that he values (his little spread, his girl friend, his old mentor) stolen or destroyed by the corrupt power structure of this little town. So that, to even the score, even though he is a peaceable fella, he has to become a killer in order to survive and see justice done in "hard land." *Then*, you have my favorite scene: the young cowpoke shooting bottles off the fence, teaching himself gunfighting, getting ready for the showdown.

BUBBA: What does that have to do with screenwriting?

VIRGIL: Well, that's the writer's version of how he made it in films: Sensitive writer comes to Hollywood. Corrupt moguls steal his scripts and ideas, try to run him out of town. Sensitive writer guts it up, and, in order to survive as a "creative person," he becomes a "killer"—a poet and gunman—and bests the moguls at their own game.

BUBBA: Uh, Virg', that don't sound like the plot to "Dallas."

VIRGIL: Naw, that's your *basic* western plot, from back in the thirties when screenwriters were innocent. In those films, the young cowboy-screenwriter kills the baddie, then hangs up his guns and reverts to ranching or poetry. By the forties and fifties the screenwriter-cowboy has started wondering if learning to be a killer is really good for his "creative life," so he writes these so-called Freudian westerns. Monty Clift and Bob Mitchum are forever finding out that the price of winning is "compromise" and "guilt." Even Hank Fonda feels somehow corrupted by killing off the corrupt boss—sometimes he even replaces him. These are really Darwinian westerns.

BUBBA: Like World War II. The hero finds that he has sacrificed his innocence to make the world safe for innocents.

VIRGIL: Or, like the *Magnificent Seven*, a Korean War, police-action western. Where even though the heroes are assholes and killers, they still sacrifice themselves for the peasants on the altar of their lost innocence.

BUBBA: And now we got twelve-year-old hookers in designer jeans, *The Best Little Whorehouse in Texas*, and J. R. Ewing.

VIRGIL: So it would seem. "The Year of the Pimp." No more good guys and bad guys, no more sensitive guys and brutes, no more poets versus accountants. There's only winners and losers; the only space in between them is reserved for hairdressers, courtiers, minstrels, coke-dealers, and pimps who pander to the whims of the winners. So your screenwriter-cowboy has moved from "avenging angel," to "jaded samurai," to "hedonistic masochist." Now, he takes the money and lovingly celebrates the triumph of evil. But in Hollywood. "Dallas" is in Hollywood, Bubba, not in Dallas. J. R. Ewing may talk like the guys in Kappa Sig, but he acts more like the guys in Cosa Nostra.

BUBBA: You may be right there, Virg'. I don't know diddly about Hollywood, but I was thinking the other night that the difference between the people in Dallas and the people on "Dallas," is that the people on the TV talk too much. They communicate their feelings. Hell, they *have* feelings. Anybody, like me, who has to cover Dallas Cowboy press conferences and hear Tom Landry twice a week knows better than that. Everything's much too *personal*, you know, and *emotional*, on TV. If they put the *real* Dallas on TV it would be six alcoholics having a silent dinner on the top floor of a glass building. All the plates and silverware would have the corporate logo on them designed by Mary Wells. When they sit down, somebody would punch a button that would play Billy Graham, prerecorded on video cassette, saying grace. There wouldn't be any time to talk because everybody would be reviewing contracts. You couldn't get it on TV. They wouldn't even be tasting their food.

VIRGIL: Maybe that's why it's popular here. I mean, because

it lets people think they actually have passions.
Like *The Godfather*. It's an Italian western!

BUBBA: "The Good, the Bad, and the Stewardess."

VIRGIL: "A Fistful of Neiman's."

BUBBA: "Welcome Back, Urban Cowboy."

VIRGIL: Maybe you got it, Bubba. 'Cause in my experience most westerners, including your beloved grampa, are mean, abstract bastards. They got drives, and goals, and ambitions, and dreams, but no passion.

BUBBA: Also, they like "equipment." Hell, the hero of that *Urban Cowboy* movie is a *mechanical bull*! So is the hero of "Dallas," for that matter.

VIRGIL: Well, whatever it is, if it's popular, you can be sure of one thing: *It's telling people something they want to hear.* Maybe in the thirties people wanted to hear that you could clean up the town and not get dirty? Maybe people in the forties and fifties wanted to hear that it was perfectly natural to feel a little guilty after you won a war? Maybe now they get some comfort from knowing that *nobody* can ride the mechanical bull?

BUBBA: So take another Quaalude and head for the hot tub!

VIRGIL: Hell, Bubba, I don't know. The only good I can see comin' out of the whole thing is that Waylon Jennings and Willie Nelson are getting paid more or less what they're worth.

BUBBA: Yeah, but, you see, that's why all this *other* stuff has got me so befuddled. The music really *meant* something to me, still does. Willie and Waylon, Shaver and Bare and Tompall. They're really important to me. I can *hear* those songs. The first time I heard them, I understood them, and I *know* that those micro-mini-"J.R.'s" in their Mercedes, and all those suburban-disco-mechanical-bullriders aren't hearing the same music. But they're buying the same records and singing right along.

That's why I took that bumper sticker off. I mean, there's *got* to be more to liking Willie and Waylon than picking up girls with well-developed tits and poorly developed self-images.

VIRGIL: Well, that's a big part of it. Nobody ever got up on stage with a guitar to make the girls *hate* him. You just got to remember that pop song ain't *art*—it's not a thing in itself. It's a costume, comes right off the rack, one size fits all. It never looks the same in the mirror. People put it on and see in it, and in themselves, what they *want* to see. The same Beatles record that helped you become the number one seducer of stewardesses in North Dallas helped Charles Manson become a killer-guru.

BUBBA: Jesus, Virgil, you have a twisted mind.

VIRGIL: Naw, Charles Manson has a twisted mind. I got a cynical mind. I just naturally distrust folks with altruistic motives, but then again, I got you for a roomie to remind me that some folks is really good-hearted

BUBBA: I don't know how to take that, but I do know that I hated all the music that came out in 1972 until you called me from New York and told me to go down to the Dripping Springs Reunion, and I heard Willie and Waylon and Shaver.

VIRGIL: Well, I *knew* you'd like it. That's why I called. I figured that especially Waylon and Billy Joe Shaver were making a new kind of music, at least for the times. You know, country music at that time was almost exclusively "southern"—that is, it was about drinkin' and guilt and marriage, and directed towards a female audience.

There's this great Nashville producer named Billy Sherrill. He's sort of the evil genius of Nashville, and at that time he said that the ideal country song was one so dirty in content and so clean in diction that it would turn on a forty-year-old housewife washing dishes at three in the afternoon in Pittsburg, Kansas. He's the one that recorded Charlie Rich singing "Behind Closed Doors," which *was* that song. Of course, Billy is no fool, he'll go with the flow. The last song I saw his name on was called "The Outlaw's Prayer," recorded by Johnny Paycheck. As always he's having it both ways, clean and dirty. Jesse James and Jesus. But at that time Nashville had screwed up their demographics. They didn't think *men* would buy country music, and they wouldn't. Not the kind they were making.

Also, at that time, rock-and-roll was suffering from the breakup of the Beatles, the stupidity of so-called psychedelic rock, Vietnam, and a concentration of sales effort on the northeastern urban market, where most of the kids were. Laid-back country rock was getting more wimpy by the day and its only genius, Gram Parsons, was just marking time until he over-dosed, Duane Allman only had six months to live, and "Southern Rock" was still drawing better in New York and San Francisco than it was in the South and Southwest.

What was *happening* was "glitter rock," which meant David Bowie, Lou Reed, T-Rex, The Rolling Stones' "Exile on Main Street," and the New York Dolls—all of which was real urban, real hard-drugs, real sexually ambiguous, and *real* loud. But, you see, in the Southwest in '72, they still had *hippies*. Especially in Austin, which is sort of a counterculture museum, and in a place like Austin, you could be fairly certain that "glitter" wasn't going to happen: not-mega-volume-super-star-heroin-mascara-and-queers. Austin was leather-clothes, laid-back, macho, and marijuana.

So, when these three guys I knew from Dallas called me in New York and said they were gonna have an outdoor Country & Western Festival, I told 'em to come down more on the Western than the Country and recommended Waylon, Willie, Shaver, and a couple of others. Their music had a good, antisocial, West Texas edge that was missing in most country music. It also had some rock energy so you could dance to it, and a lot of the macho-cool which was distinctly missing from the rock and roll of that moment. For once in my life I was right. The guys screwed up the Dripping Springs festival, so the Austin thing didn't happen for another year. But I was right, wasn't I?"

BUBBA: You were right, Virgil.

VIRGIL: Okay, I just want it on record.

BUBBA: I don't think it was that cold-blooded though, Mister Media Master. I think you really felt it. I know there wasn't any music for me from about 1969 till I went down to Dripping Springs, and those guys gave me a new sound track for my life, and that was great! It made all the stuff I used to like sound antique, dated. All that late sixties stuff.

VIRGIL: Yeah, I felt it; but I *knew* it too. It was a natural development of the music that I liked in the sixties, which as a decade I *hated*. All I liked about the sixties was Chuck Berry, Buddy Holly, The Rolling Stones, and The Velvet Underground. Survivors' music. Now, the music *you* liked was mostly Beatles-San Francisco-Optimistic-Psychedelic-Revolutionary stuff—which is a credit to your good heart, if not your taste, 'cause let's face it: all that music was supposed to be a curtain raiser for a future that just didn't happen. And there ain't nothing as dated as something futuristic designed for the wrong future. I mean, we aren't living in a yellow submarine, and as a result that yellow submarine looks as dated as Jules Verne's *Nautilus* or one of H. G. Wells's Art Deco spaceships.

BUBBA: What you're saying is that Waylon and those guys were ready for the seventies and all of us buckskin hippies weren't?

VIRGIL: Well, you have to admit that the sixties as a political psychedelic love-nest was pretty much a middle-class phenomenon. While you were painting flowers around coed's navels, those guys were out on the road playing skull-orchards where they strung up chicken wire to protect you from flying bottles. You didn't see any hard-ass outlaws at Monterey Pop, so I think that you can assume they missed the Day-Glo, Make-Love-Not-War aspect of the decade. They growed their hair all right, but they didn't put any flowers in it. For them the seventies was just the same as the sixties. It was about survival, so they survived, and in the process managed to pass the age of thirty without feeling guilty about it.

BUBBA: Yeah, that's something. Anyway, it was to me. I was so damned surprised to be thirty "and still wearing jeans," like it says in the song. The whole time I kept thinking I was gonna wake up one morning and be an insurance executive or a narc. It damn sure surprised me when all of a sudden I was thirty and still writing about football and living like a rodeo-hippie.

VIRGIL: See, there. Waylon was not only telling you what you wanted to hear, he was living proof of it. "It's okay, Bubba, looky heah, I'm thirty and I still feel the same, still wear my jeans and stay up for days and days." He was telling me the same thing. "Looky heah, Virgil, I never settled down. I'm doin' okay." For me that's the bottom line—that's what popular music is all about, TV and movies too, for that matter. To somebody out there, hopefully to a lot of somebodies, you're saying: "It's okay, everything's gonna be all right," or "It's okay, I feel that way too," or just "It's all right," the most repeated line in all popular music.

BUBBA: But, Virgil, cain't you see that I felt good 'cause Waylon and I were still wearing jeans, 'cause all my life I've been more or less of a *cowboy*. I thought it was *cool*, that there were some others out there. It was me and those others that made Willie and Waylon famous, 'cause they were like us, and they sang songs that we could understand. *Now* they get to be stars and everybody is trying to be like *them*. So everybody starts dressing like *us*—like *me*. I feel like Dr. Frankenstein, or at least one of his firm. I feel like something secret has been stolen from me. . . . Actually, I feel like a *Mouseketeer*!

VIRGIL: Not a Mouseketeer, Bubba, a "Junior Deputy" in Gene Autry's *Flying A Ranch Posse*!

BUBBA: Oh, shit, Virgil, *The Flying A Ranch Posse*. Yes! Do you remember them damn white hats and that ring that glowed in the dark, where there was a special compartment for secret messages.

VIRGIL: Of course, I do. But did you ever wonder, Bubba—maybe I asked you this before—but didn't it seem *strange* to you that the ring where you hid all your really secret *Flying A Ranch* stuff *glowed* in the dark? It seemed to me, if you were captured and throwed in a basement, that a glowing ring would be a decided disadvantage. I mean, it would call attention to itself, and wouldn't a ring like that be just the kind of thing a bad guy would want to take off you?

BUBBA: I'll tell you the truth, Virgil, I never give the ring issue much thought. But I still remember being *sorely* disappointed in the quality of them white hats. I was expecting something more in the area of grampa's Stetson. Hell, the old boys that run survey for Dad had better hats than that. I kept thinking, if it was true, like dad said, that you could judge an outfit by the quality of its equipment, then, Gene Autry notwithstanding, the *Flying A* was in one peck of trouble.

VIRGIL: Now right there, you demonstrated my point. Why you feel like a Mouseketeer. Cause you *always* thought you had aholt of the *real* cowboy thing, you know, and everybody else, hell, they just bought stuff off the television.

BUBBA: You're probably right, but, damm it, I did! My grampa was a real old-time cowman!

VIRGIL: But that's the difference: Grampa Burkette, he was a cow*man*, not a cow*boy*. He hated cowboys, and you know it, said they were all lunatics. You remember when we joined the Rodeo Club in high school? He nearly had a stroke.

BUBBA: Yeah, he give us a talkin' to, didn't he? "Organized abuse of stock," I remember that, and a "bane on the cattle business." I still don't know what a "bane" is, but the idea was that he'd spent his whole life trying to keep cowboys from doing the things that the Rodeo Club encouraged us to do.

VIRGIL: And do you remember the "working cowboy" lecture?

BUBBA: Naw, what was that?

VIRGIL: You *really* don't remember? You musta blocked it out. It always started "*The cowboy is a laborer—a common, ignorant, ditch-digger-type laborer.*"

BUBBA: I really must *have* blocked it out.

VIRGIL: Well, it made a strong impression on me, I'll tell you. We must have got that lecture at least twice I can remember. Once about the Rodeo Club, and once when we told the old man we'd made us a "handshake deal" on something.

BUBBA: Oh, yeah. I remember that. It was the Plymouth.

VIRGIL: Right, and both times is started out: "*The cowboy is a laborer—a common, ignorant, ditch-digger-type laborer. The only difference between the cowboy and other laborers is that he often must ride a horse out to where he is to do his labor. And many times his boss, having better things to do, allows the cowboy to work unsupervised, which allows him to drink on the job. Now, the fact that he has rode a horse out to where he is working alone, out-of-doors, added to the fact that he is half-drunk, allows this ignorant poltroon . . .*"

BUBBA: Right, *poltroon*! I remember that!

VIRGIL: Don't interrupt, listen to your grampa: "*. . . added to the fact that he is half-drunk, allows this ignorant poltroon to indulge himself in cavalier fantasies of integrity and independence, when, in fact, he is naught but a social misfit, and an insecure one at that.*
"*Without whiskey he is uncomfortable in any kind of society, since by any social standards, he represents the dregs. With whiskey he is only comfortable with his own*

kind, although any white man willing to part with a little flattery and a lot more whiskey will find him trusting beyond any known standards of childlike gullibility!"

This was the part I liked. Even at the time, I knew I was getting the benefit of some shrewd, if heartless, social observation.

BUBBA: What part? I don't remember any of this. I only remember looking at the toes of my boots and hoping nothing come unglued with the Plymouth deal.

VIRGIL: The part on the gullibility of the cowboy. *"He will use high-sounding phrases to justify his willingness to be fleeced."* This is your grampa talking, *"He will refer to 'The Handshake Deal,' 'The Word of a Cowboy,' and 'The Code of the West,' totally unaware that these are but euphemisms invented by furnishing merchants to lure the illiterate drover unawares into the realm of commerce, where he might be relieved of his money at their convenience!"* Right! Of course you're gonna make a fetish out of the handshake deal; if you can't read the contract!

BUBBA: I remember the next part—the part about cowboys always being done in by smart white men, because the only people they instinctively distrust are girls and blacks—

VIRGIL: Please! Not girls and blacks! *". . . Females and Negroes, these being the only two orders of society whose station is as low as that of the working cowboy!"*

BUBBA: Okay, I remember that, but I don't think I understood it. Still, you got to remember that grampa was an old cowman, and they're *supposed* to talk like that about being a cowboy. Even in the movies the old guys talked like that. John Wayne did it all the time, and Walter Brennan. It's like the Marines, you know, you make it sound tough. . . . It never entered my mind that grampa meant what he said.

VIRGIL: It sure made sense to me, especially the part about "ditch-digger-type labor."

BUBBA: I really thought it was just talk to weed out the sissies . . .

VIRGIL: Like me?

BUBBA: *Yeah*, as a matter of fact! It was like a secret brotherhood; you couldn't understand unless you were a *real* cowboy.

VIRGIL: Come on, Bubba, can you honestly tell me you've ever known a *real* cowboy?

BUBBA: What do you mean?

VIRGIL: I mean, have you ever known a cowboy, working, rodeo, or feedlot, who wasn't completely eat-up with the *idea* of being a "cowboy,"—that didn't spend half his available time watching "cowboys" on TV or "cowboys" in the movies, or listening to "cowboys" on the radio, or reading about "cowboys" in a comic book or in some Louis Lamour novel?

Hell, Bubba, you remember old Pete, dontcha? What about the time we come up on him out by Mary's Creek, and there he is, riding old Alice along this fence he's supposed to be checking, only he's just letting Alice graze along the fence-line while he's sitting up there with his spectacles on reading *Six Gun Vengeance* or some such document. And Pete was sixty years old and been a cowboy all his life.

BUBBA: It makes you wonder all right. I mean, I know they had dime novels and Wild West shows almost as soon as they had cowboys and a Wild West. In fact, most of the guys marketing the West were real Wild West types.

Like Buffalo Bill Cody, and Bret Harte, and Pat Garrett. Can you imagine what it would have been like to be Frank and Jesse James and on the run all the time reading these dime novels about how romantic and what Robin Hoods you were?

VIRGIL: I imagine it's just about like being Willie Nelson and reading about yourself in *People* magazine. The thing of it is, first generation literates have a real hard time not taking anything in print as Gospel. It's hard for any pop musician today to keep from believing his own press. Can you imagine how hard it was for those old-timers? Probably right after the Civil War, though, before the media-mill got cranked up, there were some real cowboys.

BUBBA: I wouldn't bet on it, Virg', not from what grampa said. According to him, cowboying from the first was a Southern thing, and most of the cowboys were Confederates that hadn't *quite* finished the Civil War. As he put it . . . they was poor but proud of their heritage as Southern gentlemen and ex-cavalry officers. Grampa used to say that you only had to take a sharecropper from North Carolina across the Red River into Texas and all of a sudden he was a colonel of the cavalry that had lost a plantation in Virginia.

VIRGIL: And probably, to judge by today's standards, it was the people in the North that found these so-called ex-colonels, now drifting cowboys, the most romantic. I mean, look at it like this: America went into the Civil War as an agrarian democracy, and came out of it as an industrial democracy. The industrial North had destroyed the agrarian South, but how long had the North been industrial? What I mean is that the North destroyed its own past as well as the South's.

Think about it, Bubba, the cowboys, and the Plains Indians, and the cavalry were the "last horsemen"—I mean, really the *last* in the history of the *world*, a romance that went back to Alexander the Great. Now, that's some high energy romance for some kid from North Carolina who was a Confederate corporal to carry around from the wilds of south Texas up to Montana.

BUBBA: There is something about being up on a horse, though. It really does change you. I don't know what, but there's some magic there.

VIRGIL: A Harley-Davidson will change you too. So will an electric guitar with a stack of Marshall cabinets. It's the direct application of power. You nudge a horse, or a Harley, or a cranked up Stratocaster, and *ka-vooom! Power.* Mostly it changes illiterate dorks into macho-sociopaths.

BUBBA No, horses are different. It's more of an earth thing!

VIRGIL *Earth thing!* You sound like an acid casualty!

BUBBA Not really. A Harley or a Strat, they can get you off, but finally, they're just machines. They tie you to the human world. You can make a lot of noise with a Strat but you can't leave your power supply. And you can leave town on a Harley, but you can only go till you run out of gas. Besides, a Harley is a man-made thing. You can leave, go off by yourself on a bike, but you're still a human being with a human machine between you and the world. You leave town on a horse. *That's* something different. Being alone on a horse tends to de-emphasize the human part of you. You and the horse are both animals moving through the natural world.

The horse is a domesticated animal; he's your bridge to the natural way of things. It's really different, and it's hard not to get romantic about it.

VIRGIL: Not unless you come down heavy on the survival and power aspect of life. I tend to agree with Grampa Burkette. The guys back then that weren't eaten up with the *idea* of being a *cowboy* were trying to accomplish something, and if I was a cowman, I'd be the last one to disabuse my cowboys of their silly notions. I'd pay 'em forty bucks a month, work their butts off, and let 'em go right on thinking they were Knights of the Plains.

BUBBA: You wouldn't let them raise their "class consciousness."

VIRGIL: Never! *Cowboys is the opium of the masses.*

BUBBA: Yeah, but you're trying to imply that the West was divided into crazy romantic cowboys, and sensible, pragmatic cowmen. Personally, I think you were right when you said that the guys like my grampa were mean, abstract bastards. They might not romanticize nature, or horses, or even themselves, but they damn sure can romanticize their pretty ambitions into dreams of some kind of cultural destiny. I'll have to take you to a Dallas Cowboy press conference sometime.

You know, there's a quote of Archibald MacLeish's somewhere that says "the West is a country in the mind, and so eternal." Well, he told it better than he knew. 'Cause there may be a lot of cowboy types who want to go with the flow and fit in with their idea of nature, but there are a lot more people in the West who think, just because it's empty, it should embody whatever *idea* they have. Go to L.A. and look at the buildings shaped like brown derbies and phonograph records. Drive through the hills and look at the Dutch windmills, the Bavarian castles, the Swiss chalets. Fly back to Dallas. Look down at the cities from the air, man: cool symmetry. Fly over the Panhandle, where the Commanches used to chase buffalo. What do you see? Geometry, the geometry of the agribusiness. Drive in from the DFW airport down Stemmons Freeway and just *look* at those buildings. They're all *mirrors*! They don't even have *substance*; they're just the reflections of the space around them, on the *idea* of a building. Go to the Cowboy locker room after a game and look at all the bruises and contusions and pain that happens when you try to fit human beings into patterns of *X*'s and *O*'s. Talk about lunacy!

VIRGIL: Yeah, well, *sure*. If you put it like that! I can see how the cowboy thing might become more attractive compared to the Puritans' dance of abstraction. . . Hey, where's my *Seven Pillars*?

BUBBA: In there on the bed, I guess, but I swear I never seen more than three the whole time you been living here, so . . .

VIRGIL: *Seven Pillars of Wisdom*, dummy! It's a *book*. You know, like they keep in libraries. It's a lot like a press release, only real long with lots of words and—

BUBBA: All right! You mean the one with the Arabs? It's over there under that halter . . .

VIRGIL: Jesus, rough symbolism—

BUBBA: You could die, you know? There's nothing says you could survive having your butt kicked from here to Plano!

VIRGIL: Yeah, yeah, here it is! This is Lawrence about the Bedouin, but it's also Grampa Burkette and Tom Landry et al. "*They were incorrigibly children of the idea,*

feckless and color-blind, for whom body and spirit were inevitably opposed . . . a people of starts for whom the abstract was the strongest motive."

BUBBA: That's them all right. But, not just Tom Landry, in your football area. It's every NFL coach I know, except for Bum Phillips. That's what people *like*! Seeing all these crazy red-necks and niggers dominated by a computer. That's why football is the national sport and not rodeo. It's real sad but you cain't get a Brahma to do the same thing twice. I always thought Cowboys was a real dumb name for a football team. Ain't nothin' as "un-cowboy" as professional football.

VIRGIL: Nor nothing as "cowboy" as some of the players I know.

BUBBA: I guess that goes to show grampa was right. You can flatter the poor fools into anything. . . .

VIRGIL: Did you know, by the by, that *cowboy* or rather, *to cowboy* is a verb, now? They use it in the oil business and in the army. It means "to improvise," with negative connotations, as in: "*Well Captain, we can't get a procedural time-frame on this operation, so take in a lot of fire-power and cowboy it.*"

BUBBA: I like that.

VIRGIL: It has its charm, but you see what it is? It's a minority joke, like "nigger-rigging," or "red-neck engineering." To call somebody a cowboy is to call him a flake, a Polish astronaut, an Irish gourmet . . .

BUBBA: All right, what's an Irish gourmet?

VIRGIL: He knows which wine goes with beer.

BUBBA: Cute. But I understand. Cowboys *do* feel like a minority. That's what makes all that majority fashion-mongering so offensive.

VIRGIL: America lives off the eccentricities of its cultural minorities. It's just a part of the rich tapestry of American culture.

BUBBA: Bull.

VIRGIL: Now, you know what spades feel like when stockbrokers want to slap hands and call everything "superfly."

BUBBA: Yeah, but cowboys are . . . well . . . I don't mean to say, cowboys are *white*—

VIRGIL: That's good, 'cause a lot of 'em ain't. . . .

BUBBA: But the cowboy "thing"—you know, the "cowboy fantasy"—that's a white fantasy, a majority fantasy.

VIRGIL: That's what I am telling you, Bubba, *not any more*. Just look around you. What do you see? Black Power! Chicano Power! Disco! Punk Rock! Gay Lib! Women's Lib! Computer Football! Born-Again Christians! Mafia Chic! Native American Associations! What we're talking about, son, is the "White Boy's Last Stand!" Here's all these white guys and they *feel like they're disappearing*! Everybody else got a costume. Everybody else got a *song*. Now white boys got Gilly's and Willie Nelson and Waylon Jennings: singing cowboys again!

BUBBA: It's really just the same, you know?

VIRGIL: What's just the same?

BUBBA: Well, not exactly the same, but when we were kids, you know, we had Gene Autry and Roy Rogers and Tex Ritter, singing cowboys. They were our heroes, when we were boys. I mean, being a kid is like being in a minority, isn't it?

VIRGIL: Incredible, Bubba, that's really it! Or part of it. I mean we grew up and all of a sudden were in a minority again. So who do we get to say, "Hey what about us white boys?" Singing cowboys again. I mean, and those guys, the singers: The singing cowboys were *their* heroes too!

BUBBA: Tex Ritter was the bridge.

VIRGIL: You're right, and you know, he was the only singing cowboy, in his movies, you know, who wouldn't just pull a guitar out from behind a cactus in the middle of the desert and start singing, "I got spurs that jingle jangle jingle." He'd always put the songs into his movies where it would be natural for a cowboy to sing, like around the campfire, or at a barn dance.

BUBBA: And he'd sing *real* cowboys' songs too, Virgil. I remember he sang "Green Grow the Lilacs."

VIRGIL: And "Froggy Went a Courtin'!" I remember talking about that with Bobby Bare, who is a real Tex Ritter fan . . .

BUBBA: He went in the right way too, I mean, for an old cowboy. Didn't he have a heart attack while he was visiting one of his band members in jail? You know what?

VIRGIL: What, Bubba?

BUBBA: It really *is* the same. You know "Luckenbach, Texas?"

VIRGIL: The song? Sure, big hit for Waylon—?

> Let's go to Luckenbach, Texas
> With Willie and Waylon and the boys;
> This successful life we're living's
> Got us feuding like the Hatfields and McCoys.

BUBBA: Virgil, what's the difference between *Luckenbach, Texas* and the *Flying A Ranch*?

VIRGIL: Why, not a damn thing, Bubba. Thirty years, maybe, different passwords, peacock-feather hatbands instead of decoder rings, but basically not a damn thing. It's still a fantasy place, a hideout where white boys can be cowboys.

BUBBA: Well then answer me this. Willie and Waylon, they're real Texans. They really understand the cowboy thing. So why would they be party to the "Disneyizing" of what they stand for? I mean, it's a long way from really heartfelt songs like "Old Five and Dimers" and "Amanda" to "Luckenbach, Texas."

VIRGIL: Not really, Bubba. Besides, they're just trying to share their dream. We're talking about pop songs, here, not poems. On the whole you'd have to say that Willie and Waylon and Bare have done more than their share of preserving and presenting what's best in their own tradition. I mean, Bobby Bare has found half the major singers and most of the major songwriters in the last twenty years and supported them even when it was to his disadvantage. Waylon and Tompall Glaser and Haggard have between them saved the memory and reputation of Bob Wills and Western Swing from oblivion. You know Waylon's song:

> When you cross that old Red River, hoss,
> That just don't mean a thing,
> I don't care who's up in Nashville,
> Bob Wills is still the king.

BUBBA: Yeah, you're right. Waylon, he does those Buddy Holly songs and takes the Crickets on tour. He sings "The Last Letter" almost every show.

VIRGIL: That's supposed to be the first country song.

BUBBA: And he and Willie and Merle keep on singing the Jimmie Rodgers and Hank Williams tunes.

VIRGIL: Hell, Willie did a whole album with Ray Price, and another one of Lefty Frizzell songs. In fact, Willie Nelson's biggest hit was "Blue Eyes Crying in the Rain," which Fred Rose wrote forty years ago.

BUBBA: You still didn't answer my question, Virgil. How could guys like that sing junk like "Mamas Don't Let Your Babies Grow Up to Be Cowboys?"

VIRGIL: I was *trying* to. It's strange but those guys really do have something to say, something to share. It's just something you learn to live with in popular music. If you want to communicate something, you keep looking for that common denominator, that magic key that opens up somebody else's heart, and usually that common denominator is pretty low. You just assume that you hook 'em with the "mammas" and "babies" and the "nekkid girls," then you give 'em what you consider to be the "real stuff." Hell, look at the old western movie stars. They were more cowboys than any modern country singer. Look at Gene Autry, Bob Steele, Tim McCoy, Ken Maynard, Tom Mix, all those old guys. They could ride and rope and shoot. I mean, they were the real thing, and they wanted to communicate some of the real thing, fought for it, really. All those "B-Western Stars," they wanted to communicate something about the West as they knew it, but they were trapped with, uh . . .

BUBBA: Assembly-line production values.

VIRGIL: They wanted to make their own movies just like Waylon and them wanted to make their own records?

VIRGIL: Exactly, and Nashville recordmaking is as close and equivalent as you can get to B-movie production values. Nashville records are traditionally just like B movies: a product with a finite market. They didn't think that they had more than x number of customers out there. So, rather than trying to make one movie or one record that a million people would like, they tried to make ten cheap records or ten cheap movies that their basic audience of, say, ten thousand would accept.

BUBBA: They were wrong, weren't they?

VIRGIL: Damn right, they were, and Tim McCoy and Ken Maynard and Waylon Jennings and Willie Nelson were right, although McCoy and Maynard never really got a chance to prove it. It took the next generation of actors working with directors like John Ford to prove that a Western movie was interesting to somebody other than kids. Waylon and Willie were lucky—they got the chance to prove that they could take their own vision of the world, enhance it with honest, high quality production values, and, as long as they respected the conventions of popular music, sell it to an audience which wasn't predisposed to like it.

BUBBA: That's great, isn't it? That sometimes somebody wins?

VIRGIL: Yeah, but can't you see what happened? *You* were their basic audience, *you* were gonna buy their records even if they sounded terrible, because *you* were predisposed to identify with it. When they got control of their own production and made good records, you were happy, but so were all those assholes whose fandom you so scorn! *They* are the ones who made Willie and Waylon "*Stars*!" in the rock and roll sense of the term.

BUBBA: I really don't see what you're talking about.

VIRGIL: Look at it like this. Waylon Jennings may be your favorite singer, but to you he's not a *Star*!, like something shining in the sky, to be aspired to, emulated. *You* liked Waylon because he was like you. You *identified* with him. All of those other type fans, the ones who have caused you to stack the living room with "western apparel," as you so quaintly call it, they are attracted to Waylon because they *aren't* like him, but would *like* to be. They aspire toward whatever it is they see in him, or in Willie or whoever, because it is something that they *lack*, not something that they *have*. So to them, these singing cowboys are living their fantasy lives. They're like rock and roll stars, in that sense, like kings used to be, surrogates, chosen ones, through whom the less fortunate or less gifted fulfill their dreams, in whose image they adorn themselves, upon whose . . .

BUBBA: Excuse me, Virgil, could I just admit right here that I understand? I mean, before you totally evanesce into the King James version of pop-psychology?

VIRGIL: Oh, yeah, sure, excuse me. You can get a typescript of tonight's sermon by writing Pop Pulpit, that's P-O-P-P-U-L-P-I-T, Box Z, Del Rio, Mexico.

BUBBA: I guess I ought to tell you what really happened.

VIRGIL: When? I mean, what happened, or why—

BUBBA: You sound like my freshman journalism teacher. I mean, the thing that finally decided me. It was the other night. I was driving back from the District AAA semifinal and as I was coming down Fitzhugh . . . well . . . do you remember that old shopping center? The one with the glass brick and the Austin stone? Where the Piggly Wiggly store used to be? Well, now there is this barroom in the Piggly Wiggly space? It's called *The New Longhorn*, right? And it's got your weathered clapboard, "Old-West-saloon" false front. I'm thinking this is a pretty ritzy part of town for a shitkicker bar, but it looks okay. I mean, I've been to a high school football game, and I've filed my story, and now I want a beer, okay? I'm not looking for a place to take Linda Ronstadt, so what the hell? There are some guys hanging around the door and they look like pretty much your average North Dallas cosmic cowboys.

VIRGIL: Red necks, white collars, and blue-chip securities.

BUBBA: *That* type, right. One guy is leaning against the clapboard with his ankles crossed and his hat down over his eyes, like James Coburn in *The Magnificent Seven*, and there's this other dude slouched out on the sidewalk, talking to him but not looking at him. You know, straw hat, Levi jacket, white western shirt, low-top boots. Got one hip shot out to the left and the other ankle bowed-out and kinda pidgeon-toed—

VIRGIL: Paul Newman in *Hud*.

BUBBA: Right!

VIRGIL: And isn't he sucking on his cigarette with it cupped in his hand like he was standing in a fifty-mile-an-hour gale, with his head down so he can kinda look up at you from under his eyelashes like he was trying to decide whether to gun you down or not?

BUBBA: How'd you know?

VIRGIL: Paul Newman, again. Same movie. They even think *that's* cool in Green Witch Village.

BUBBA: No-goddam-doubt. Anyway, ol' "Hud," he flicked his cigarette out into the parking lot so's it made a little red arc and then went sparkle, sparkle when it hit the pavement. I *should* have known right then. He done it *perfect* and—

VIRGIL: Uh, Bubba?

BUBBA: Yeah?

VIRGIL: I know what you're gonna tell me.

BUBBA: You do?

VIRGIL: I didn't just fall off the cedar truck.

BUBBA: Well, I wish to *hell* you'da told me!

VIRGIL: And broke that mighty heart? Dimmed that smile as bright as a desert morning, as wide as all outdoors? Couldn't bring myself to do it, son.

BUBBA: *Jeez*, Virgil—

VIRGIL: See there! Just the *thought* makes you blue as Bob's dungarees. What happened then?

BUBBA: Hell, I just walked right in, went up to the bar, and got myself a long-necked Pearl. And I'm just standing there, you know, chatting with this guy, and he's a pretty nice guy, you know. Does promo for the Dallas Civic Opera—

VIRGIL: A typical honky-tonk denizen, to say the least.

BUBBA: Hell, this *is* Dallas, after all.

VIRGIL: What's this guy's name?

BUBBA: Eric.

VIRGIL: Ah. And just how long did it take you to figure out where you were?

BUBBA: Hell, after we'd talked a while he asked me if I wanted to go over to his place and listen to some Bob Wills tapes—

VIRGIL: Not too kinky so far!

BUBBA: —and have a quiche! I swear to God, that's what he said, and even then, well, Jesus, half the guys in North Dallas *look* gay. You know, trimmed beard, the sunlamp tan, gold chains, but discreet.

VIRGIL: Bubba!

BUBBA: Well, I *kinda* suspected right off, because some of the girls looked pretty tough, even by skull-orchard standards, and a bunch of them was dancing together, though that don't mean nothing in a honky-tonk. Hell, lots of chicks are married to these bad dudes who are too tough to dance, so the girls dance while señor bad-ass sits in the booth with his back to the wall and his gen-u-ine lizard boots sticking out into the aisle. You know, he just sits in the there and *squints* at people, just *praying*, son, just *praying* that some poor fool is gonna come by and trip over them boots . . .

VIRGIL: Bubba, would you please cut to the chase?

BUBBA: Huh?

VIRGIL: Cut to chase! Cut to the chase! "*As you remember, boys and girls, at the conclusion of Episode XVII of BUBBA TEXAS OF RODEO RANCH, we left our hero bellied up to the bar in the New Longhorn Saloon, totally unaware that this establishment was now in the clutches of The Phantom Empire! Eric of the Opera has just cajoled, 'Aw, come on, ya big lug, let's split for my pad and spin some western platters and have a quiche.' And then we left him, kids, in an ecstasy of indecision. Does he know that Eric is an agent of the Phantom Empire? Does he care? Can he envision a bright future beckoning to him, filled with Eric and quiche and western swing? And what of his little buddies back at 'Rodeo Ranch?' Goose, and Hutch, and little Pancho in his iron lung? What of his best girl Trixie, whom the Phantom Empire has compromised by recording her evening with the Olympic Equestrian Team in a sequence of steamy Polaroids?*" What? What?

BUBBA: What what?

VIRGIL: What *happened*, dummy?

BUBBA: Nothing, really. I guess I was sort of an asshole. I mean, I been a sports reporter too long to get too up-in-arms about macho homosexuals, but, you know, it was like I'd been flashed into another dimension. I was *in* this place, and in my western clothes. It was like I was in drag. It was like a bad dream. I couldn't be cool, oh no! I couldn't just tell this guy I was tired, or had a headache or something else to do. Oh, no! I had to make *him* feel bad and make *me* look like I just come from a party at the Playboy Mansion for Anita Bryant. *First* I told him that me and Willie was good pals, and *then* I told him about how girls in Dallas just went crazy over cowboys, so that's why I wore my duds in town, which I usually only wore when I was riding and roping. How my grampa used to tell me about wearing my hat in the house . . .

VIRGIL: Bum Phillips would have been proud!

BUBBA: He would have laughed his ass off! *Then*, forgive me, Lord, I told him how my "Honk If You Love Willie Nelson" bumper sticker helped you chase women!

VIRGIL: You didn't?

BUBBA: I did. Marilyn and Bambi even!

VIRGIL: *Nude bumper pool*?

BUBBA: *Nude bumper pool*, even. And he just stood there with his mouth open and *stared* at me! Like I was a Martian! And I just kept talking, babbling on. I couldn't *stop*, dammit! Finally, I had to take a sip of my beer. By the time I had my bottle back on the bar, Eric had disappeared. I don't even remember walking out of there. Dammit, Virgil, why should the idea of gay caballeros be so revolting? We got gay linebackers. And the idea, you know, of cowboy life is obviously going to appeal to someone who finds other guys appealing. If it's so obvious, why should it be so unsettling?

VIRGIL: I think, maybe, at least to me, it's because cowboy life is a "separate peace"—the fantasy is. It's all about having noncompetitive peers, like when you're a boy. You got a job to do and everybody works together. The boss is somewhere else with his arbitrary authority; the girls are somewhere else with their ability to create status and territorial competition. You introduce sex between the cowboys and you've brought all those elements of dominance and submission back into the world. The life of musicians on the road is exactly that kind of life, with day-to-day specific duties and goals. Introduce a couple of girls onto a tour bus over a period of time and you've got trouble. Hire an aggressive gay guy in an all-straight band and you've got the same thing.

BUBBA: If there weren't industrial culture, then, and places like Dallas and New York, there wouldn't be any need for cowboys, would there?

VIRGIL: Not really. It's one of those compromised alternatives American life has thrown off. Even the Plains Indians would have had no culture if we hadn't introduced the horse. So as long as there was a Plains Indian culture, it was dying: damned by the horse, which was also their salvation. The Indians were condemned the day they were set free. The white man who brought the horse would eventually render both the horse and the Indian obsolete. Cowboy life was damned in the same way. His life was almost immediately perceived as an alternative to life in the industrial cities, but his job was feeding those cities. Basically, he was involved in the mass production of beef to feed the urban Northeast, and the market could only grow and eventually somebody was going to find a better way to raise cattle, or at least a more businesslike program—say, one that didn't involve a bunch of aging adolescents chasing a bunch of undernourished cattle around an unfenced ocean of grass. Anyone with eyes to see could have foreseen it.

BUBBA: Well, I didn't hear anyone bemoaning the tragic demise of the fry cook and the car-wash chamois jockey. Anyway, we're not just talking about adolescent fantasies here. We're talking about an equestrian herdsman, basically, and somehow he represents something heroic to a lot of people out there. You know how you call TV drama and journalism and popular literature "group dreaming?" Well, I think we can safely assume that the cowboy is pretty much of a consensus fantasy, along with the cop and the doctor and the lawyer and the detective.

VIRGIL: He represents something admirable and unique to a hell of a lot of people. That is interesting, I mean all the other heroes are involved in the day-to-day maintenance and upkeep of our society.

BUBBA: They may work for society, all right, but they are also the guys for whom society works!

VIRGIL: So what does that tell us that we want to know? First, the dramas on TV about doctors, lawyers, cops, and so on tell us that the old U.S.A. still offers men, at least brave ones, the possibility of heroism and dignity.

BUBBA: Is that what we want to hear?

VIRGIL: Sure. It means we have choices, at least to the extent of a gerbil in a Skinner box. That's what we want to hear, I think: to know that as things get larger and more complicated, fortune still favors the bold, that self respect is available at risk. If this is so, things aren't as bad as they might be.

BUBBA: Ah, but *risk* is right. If you believe television drama and commercials, the only way to be a "man" is in jobs where you can get killed.

VIRGIL: That's the fail-safe society provides to keep us at punch presses, drop hammers, and other dull but remunerative jobs we might choose. If those ostensibly fulfilling jobs were not dangerous, who would fill in warranty cards, punch tickets, sell antifreeze, and work at the drive-in bank window?

BUBBA: Anarchy would be at hand.

VIRGIL: Ann who?

BUBBA: Arky. She and her sister Miss Management keep reminding me, whispering in my ear: YOU COULD HAVE BEEN A HERO, YOU KNOW, IF YOU'D TAKEN SOME CHANCES. IT WAS YOUR DECISION. BUT WHAT THE HELL IF YOU'RE NOT A HERO? WE AREN'T EITHER. IT'S ALL RIGHT TO BE A REGULAR JOE. I MEAN, WHO WANTS TO GET KILLED. LET'S DANCE AND THEN TAKE A SHOWER, HUH. I'LL TELL YOU ONE THING. IF YOU DO DECIDE TO GO FOR THE GUSTO AND BE A BIG HERO, DON'T COME CRYING TO US WHEN YOU GET YOUR SELF-SATISFIED MACHO ASS SHOT OFF BY A BUNCH OF CATTLE-THIEVING, COKE-DEALING, REAL BLACK PIMPS.

VIRGIL: That's the HEMINGWAY HOBSON'S CHOICE: Either you hide out and spend your life safe and impotent, leave it soft, as it were, or you work up your courage and take your mighty sword out into the street where some dude is gonna shoot it off.

BUBBA: In other words, popular culture, even though it celebrates heroes, discourages heroism!

VIRGIL: Not really. It just emphasizes the value of the safe, harried, cowardly life that most of us lead. That's why it's selling us, 'cause that's what we need to hear. We need to know that you can still be honest and a hero in our society; in fact, that there are so many honest heroes out there serving the public good, that we might as well go bowling. You *do* have choices, if you want to take the risk; if you don't, hey, you're the salt of the earth.

BUBBA: You may be right. I mean your heroes of popular culture are presented to us in the media as *surrogates* rather than role models. "Hey, Mr. Average Joe, don't feel bad about being a sniveling chickenshit, take some Afrin for the runny nose!"

VIRGIL: Now you got me worried about cowboys. What are they a surrogate for? They really don't have a role in society, or *do* anything in a social sense?

BUBBA: You know, that reminds me. I was thinking a little while ago about that song "My Heroes Have Always Been Cowboys," and I had to admit that in my case that was a fact, but right off the bat I couldn't for the life of me think of what I worshipped about those old assholes I used to follow around. They didn't do much, or say much, or think much, you know. Then I realized that what I liked about them was that they didn't change, not over the space of a day, or a week, or a year. My mom and dad did nothing *but* change. I didn't have parents, I had a whole PTA—a personality parade. But those old cowpokes were "constant." They went in a straight line, worked at the same job, looked at me straight. Their images were so solid, so dependable, that even when they died they were still with me in their singularity. You know, they lived their life like it was a dance, a slow deliberate one that had been choreographed at birth, with time out for whiskey. I really loved them.

VIRGIL: Kids love anything dependable. It reinforces their expectations.

BUBBA: Sportswriters like dependable things too. I mean these guys didn't chase nothing nor change nothing.

VIRGIL: Not even their clothes, as I remember. Did you ever think that some of them might have been a little bit, uh, "special?"

BUBBA: Brain-damaged? Yeah, looking back some of them were a few bricks shy of a load, but until I discovered women I preferred a reliable vegetable to an unreliable animal. Hey, I got it. Now tell me, what it is about TV heroes that exasperates you the most?

VIRGIL: Discounting their conventional good luck with women, I guess what I resent most is their freedom from the world of cheating tradesmen, lost laundry, drive-in banking, plastic plumbing, planned obsolescence, and unresponsive vending machines. If I were spared these petty defeats I could be a hero, too.

BUBBA: That's it! Our heroes have lives and lifestyles. We just have existence and survival tips. I mean, our heroes are chasing tomorrow, but, you know, *America* is moving too.

VIRGIL: We *are* a technological liberal democracy, Bubba. We believe in progress and thus do we progress . . .

BUBBA: Not *we*. We aren't progressing Virgil, or chasing tomorrow. We're running as fast as we can just to keep up with *today*. If we stop to rest or have the flu or an affair, the world just runs away from us. And we trot along after it.

VIRGIL: Even if we don't *like* where we're going.

BUBBA: Even if we spend our lives in longing for where we been. Don't you see, Virgil. Cowboys *don't change*. They are the best of where we've been.

VIRGIL: You got it, Bubba. Wearing cowboy clothes. It's like a priest's collar or a monk's habit. It tells everybody that you respect certain virtues, have a certain morality.

BUBBA: It says you're dragging your feet on your way into the future.

VIRGIL: Discos, Mega-Sex, Multi-Grope, Ruffled Shirts! We say, fuck it! We'll stand with Johnny Paycheck and Marilyn and Bambi.

BUBBA: No sex with boys! Only girls and domestic animals without prosthetic devices!

VIRGIL: You're pure, Bubba, sure pure. It's like the *Phantom Empire*, you know, with the—

BUBBA: What!

VIRGIL: *Phantom Empire*! Didn't we watch it here one night . . . Gene Autry?

BUBBA: I'd remember if it was Gene.

VIRGIL: It's just what we're talking about, Bubba, really. It was this lame serial that came out in 1934. I can't believe you didn't see it. It's the seminal work in Urban Cowboy Cinema.

BUBBA: All right!

VIRGIL: Oh, well, you see, Gene Autry is a singing disc jockey in this little western town which could only exist in Autry land. They had trail drives and roadsters and all the guys carried side arms even to Gene's little radio station, which has a pump and a trough out front. And a saloon with faro.

BUBBA: Sticklers for detail.

VIRGIL: Hey! You know Gene. Well it gets better! Somehow by accident of radio equipment or something, Gene discovers that right under this western town is an entire futuristic *Empire*!

BUBBA: You're kidding, Virgil, under the—

VIRGIL: Right out of Flash Gordon! It's this techno-regimented dictatorship. The Main Baddie is a ringer for Ming the Merciless; maybe it really was Ming.

BUBBA: Ming? and cowboys? and radio?

VIRGIL: Gene just stopped wherever he was, pulled his guitar out from behind a cactus or an atomic reactor, and lifted his *voice* in song.

BUBBA: I can't believe I *missed* this.

VIRGIL: I couldn't believe I was seeing it. I just sat there with my mouth open.

BUBBA: H. G. Wells meets Louis Lamour it just don't seem. It always seemed to me that people who liked sci-fi and people who liked westerns were, uh . . .

VIRGIL: Different.

BUBBA: Right. From one another. I mean Gene versus . . . uh . . .

VIRGIL: Muranians. You know, satanic beards, capes, leotards. Standard now among costume kinkies and little-theater heavies, but very far out at the time. Also the Muranians had these robot soldiers . . .

BUBBA: Who looked like . . .

VIRGIL: Hot-water heaters, maybe, with hints of aerosol shaving foam cans in certain aspects. They guarded the Muranian women who were in custody because they had the hots for Gene and his songs. If there were any more like him at home, the girls were splitsville with Murania, where they were forced to wear these industrial four-snap bras which made them look like Buicks with cellulite.

BUBBA: I got it. The futuristic set was on the sound stage next door, so to fill in the schedule they assigned Gene's production company some of the downtime on the future set, soooo . . .

VIRGIL: That's what I figured, too—a quick excursion to futureland to expedite the budget. Wrap a few Future-Carhops up in cellophane and pop them in the Atomic Toaster, and the Muranians are on dangerous ground, 'cause know it or not, folks who disintegrate folks in these parts are cruising for bruising. Gene just don't cotton to the brand of Euro-Pervo . . .

BUBBA: Euro?

VIRGIL: Oh yeah. I think Gene was under the impression Murania was a health spa for Rumanians or some race devoted to Spandex . . .

BUBBA: You saw all the chapters?

VIRGIL: Educational TV showed all twelve and didn't cut away once for a report on the Cowboy game . . .

BUBBA: And . . . ?

VIRGIL: It worked! I really couldn't figure out how, though, or why. But it got to me somehow; at some level I just couldn't figure out, it was telling me what I wanted to hear. First I figured out that western fans love the past and sci-fi fans are afraid of the future, and hey the same writers write them, the same actors act them, why *not* put them together? They all feed the same fantasy conglomerate! I mean 1934, right? Depression. Factories empty, farms abandoned, theaters full. What were those folks seeing in the *Phantom Empire*?

BUBBA: Bookends!

VIRGIL: Bubba! Hey, first try.

BUBBA: I got depression roots, man.

VIRGIL: I mean here were all these people who were citizens of this badly damaged progressive democracy which has gone high-tech. They look back and what do they see?

BUBBA: The green, green grass of home. Pastoral repose. Medieval serenity.

VIRGIL: And cowboys and the endless prairie. Constant—

BUBBA: Cowboys don't change!

VIRGIL: Bucolic.

BUBBA: Lost forever, even though it never existed.

VIRGIL: Fading into the twilight and what's up ahead?

BUBBA: Murania! 1984!

VIRGIL: Future Fascists! Atomic Storm Troopers!

BUBBA: Leotards and leatherette. Squirrel cage coolers, blimps, and oppression by a technological elite who have hoarded all the radium.

VIRGIL: No wonder Gene was moved to song.

BUBBA: It's not gonna happen here, Virg'—not if this kid can stop it.

VIRGIL: I believe you, Bubba. Merle can go Third World, Waylon can play the Poconos, Billy Bobs can go disco, but as long as there's one cowboy out there—

BUBBA: Riding Old Paint—

VIRGIL: Keeping the faith—

BUBBA: Drinking whiskey and abusing barmaids—

VIRGIL: Throwing up on his lizard boots—

BUBBA: Singing them damned old songs of the prairie and a man up on a horse—I'm all choked up.

VIRGIL: That's okay, big fella. You got a big heart and big feelings—

BUBBA: Don't *touch* me! You silly savage!

EXHIBITION ITEMS NOT ILLUSTRATED

THE REAL LIVE COWBOY

Progress II
Luis Jimenez (b. 1940)
Fiberglass, 1976–81
Courtesy of the artist

Wm. Perryman's Ranche
Henry Worrall (1825–1902)
Facsimile of a woodcut from *Historic Sketches
of the Cattle Trade* by J. G. McCoy
Kansas City, Missouri: Ramsey, Millet &
Hudson, 1874
SF196.U5M3
Rare Book and Special Collections Division
Library of Congress

Drunken Cow-Boy on the War Path
Henry Worrall (1825–1902)
Facsimile of a woodcut from *Historic Sketches
of the Cattle Trade* (1874)

Five-Year Profit Table
Facsimile from *The Beef Bonanza; or, How to
Get Rich on the Plains* by James S. Brisbin
Philadelphia: J. B. Lippincott & Co., 1881
SF51.B86
Rare Book and Special Collections Division
Library of Congress

Holding the Horse Herd
Andrew Alexander Forbes (1862–1921)
Photograph, Texas–Oklahoma panhandle
area, ca. 1885
Western History Collections
University of Oklahoma Library
Norman, Oklahoma

"W" from "DW" Branding Iron
Registered in 1883 in Scurry County by
D. W. Wallace
Dallas Historical Society
Dallas, Texas

Pair of Stirrups
Wood, date unknown
Panhandle-Plains Historical Museum
Canyon, Texas

THE COWBOY HERO

Lasso
Staffordshire, transfer-printed
Manufactured by W. Bourne, England,
ca. 1855
Collection of Petra Williams
Jeffersontown, Kentucky

Toro
Staffordshire, transfer-printed
Manufactured by Charles Allerton and Sons,
England, 1854
Collection of Petra Williams
Jeffersontown, Kentucky

"Hurricane Bill"
Beadle's Dime Novels, No. 316
New York: Beadle and Adams, 1874
Dime Novel Collection
Rare Book and Special Collections Division
Library of Congress

Cowboy Life–Riding a Yearling
Woodcut after a photograph by Charles D.
Kirkland (1851–1926)
In *Frank Leslie's Illustrated Newspaper*
(New York), vol. 66 (May 1888)
American Folklife Center
Library of Congress

**Frank I. Frayne
as Si Slocum**
Lithograph, Metropolitan Litho Studio
Copyright 1879
Poster Collection
Prints and Photographs Division
Library of Congress

**Walnut St. Theatre
Buffalo Bill Combination
Buffalo Bill's New Drama "20 Days"**
Lithograph printed in colors, 1882
A. Hoen & Co., Baltimore, Md.
Staples & Charles, Ltd.
Washington, D.C.

Miller 101 Cowgirl
(unidentified)
Photographer unknown, ca. 1914
Western History Collections
University of Oklahoma Library
Norman, Oklahoma

**Miller 101 Cowboy Performing Tricks on
Rearing Horse**
Emil W. Lenders (d. 1934)
Photograph, ca. 1930
Western History Collections
University of Oklahoma Library
Norman, Oklahoma

**Miller 101 Cowboy Picking Object Off Ground
While Riding Horse**
Emil W. Lenders (d. 1934)
Photograph, ca. 1930
Western History Collections
University of Oklahoma Library
Norman, Oklahoma

Miller 101 Cowboy Riding Four Horses
Emil W. Lenders (d. 1934)
Photograph, ca. 1930
Western History Collections
University of Oklahoma Library
Norman, Oklahoma

Miller 101 Cowboy Roping Longhorns
Emil W. Lenders (d. 1934)
Photograph, ca. 1930
Western History Collections
University of Oklahoma Library
Norman, Oklahoma

Among the Cow-Boys—Breaking Camp
Woodcut after drawing by W. A. Rogers
(1854–1931)
In *Harper's Weekly*, October 2, 1880
American Folklife Center
Library of Congress

"Post Office in Cow Country"
Frederic Remington (1861–1909)
Oil on canvas, 1901
Gertrude Vanderbilt Whitney Gallery
Buffalo Bill Historical Center
Cody, Wyoming

Frederic Remington to Owen Wister
Manuscript, April 1900
(Concerning *A Bunch of Buckskins*)
Owen Wister Papers
Manuscript Division
Library of Congress

"Old Ramon"
In *A Bunch of Buckskins*
Frederic Remington (1861–1909)
Lithograph printed in colors, 1901, after a
drawing in pastel
Copyright by Robert Howard Russell, 1901
Popular and Applied Graphic Art Collections
Prints and Photographs Division
Library of Congress

"Bronc to Breakfast"
Charles M. Russell (1864–1926)
Watercolor on paper, 1908
Montana Historical Society
Helena, Montana

"Life on the Plains"
Charles M. Russell (1864–1926)
Photogravure, copyright 1887
Copyright deposit copy
Chicago Photogravure Company
Popular and Applied Graphic Art Collections
Prints and Photographs Division
Library of Congress

Page of a Sketchbook
Erwin E. Smith (1886–1947)
Photograph of pencil sketches, ca. 1907
The Nita Stewart Haley Memorial Library
Midland, Texas

"Rhymes from a Roundup Camp"
By Wallace D. Coburn (dates unknown)
Great Falls, Montana: W. T. Ridgeley Press,
1899
First edition
PS3505.C15 R5
General Collections
Library of Congress

"Ranch Verses"
By William Lawrence Chittenden
(1855–1928)
New York: G. P. Putnam's Sons, 1914
PS1294.C3 R3
General Collections
Library of Congress

"The Cattle Queen of Montana"
By Elizabeth M. Collins (dates unknown)
St. James, Minn.: C. W. Foote, Publisher,
1894
F595.C7
General Collections
Library of Congress

**"Twenty-Four Years a Cowboy and
Ranchman"**
By William Hale Stone (dates unknown)
Hedrick, O. T.: W. H. Stone, 1905
F391.S88
Rare Book and Special Collections Division
Library of Congress

Frederic Remington to Owen Wister
Manuscript, undated
(Concerning collaboration on *The Evolution
of the Cowpuncher*)
Owen Wister Papers
Manuscript Division
Library of Congress

"The Evolution of the Cowpuncher"
By Owen Wister (1860–1938)
In *Harper's New Monthly Magazine*,
September 1895
AP2.H3
General Collections
Library of Congress

"The Virginian"
By Owen Wister (1860–1938)
Braille book, 1911
Vol. 1 of 4 vols.
Louisville, Ky.: printed for the Library of
Congress at the American Printing House for
the Blind, 1971
MSN-C.1 BR-1625
*National Library Service for the Blind and
Physically Handicapped*
Library of Congress

"Ranching, Sport, and Travel"
By Thomas Carson (dates unknown)
London: T. Fisher Unwin, 1912
F786.C32
General Collections
Library of Congress

"Chip, of the Flying U"
By B. M. Bower (1871–1940)
Illustrations by Charles M. Russell
New York: G. W. Dillingham Company, 1906
Jeff Dykes
College Park, Maryland

"Western Stories"
By B. M. Bower (1871–1940)
New York: Grosset & Dunlap, Publishers,
1933
PZ3.S6149Bi
General Collections
Library of Congress

"Rivals of the Range"
By Robert J. Horton (dates unknown)
Western Story Magazine, August 25, 1928
B. Byron Price
Canyon, Texas

**Cherry Wilson, Max Brand, Dane Coolidge,
and Others**
Western Story Magazine, July 12, 1930
B. Byron Price
Canyon, Texas

"Prairie's End"
By Robert J. Horton (dates unknown)
Western Story Magazine, June 6, 1931
B. Byron Price
Canyon, Texas

Two Boxes of Research Cards
Marked "Cattle and Cattle Trails," etc.
Belonging to Clarence Mulford (1883–1956)
Clarence Mulford Papers
Manuscript Division
Library of Congress

Hopalong Takes Command
Frank Schoonover (1877–1972)
Oil on canvas, 1905
Delaware Art Museum
Wilmington, Delaware

"Arizona"
America's Greatest Play
Augustus Thomas (dates unknown)
Lithograph
Russell-Morgan Print
Copyright U.S. Lithograph Co., 1907
Poster Collection
Prints and Photographs Division
Library of Congress

Theodore Roberts as Canby in "Arizona"
(Production opened September 10, 1900)
Photograph by Fowler, Evanston, Ill.,
ca. 1900
Theatre Collection
Museum of the City of New York

An Arizona Cowboy
Lithograph
Russell-Morgan Print, Cincinnati and
New York
Copyright U.S. Lithograph Co., 1907
Poster Collection
Prints and Photographs Division
Library of Congress

**Edison Home Phonograph and Horn
Special Home and Traveling Outfit
(The Suitcase Model)**
Thomas A. Edison at Orange, N.J., U.S.A.
Patented May 1888–May 1898
National Museum of American History
Smithsonian Institution
Washington, D.C.

Wax Cylinder and Case
Edison blank, Form No. 639
Copyright by the National Phonograph Co.,
Orange, N.J., 1900
Federal Cylinder Project
American Folklife Center
Library of Congress

"The Buffalo Skinners"
Poem, author and date unknown
Newspaper clipping (mounted on paper) with
manuscript annotations by John A. Lomax,
ca. 1910
Eugene C. Barker Texas History Center
University of Texas at Austin
Austin, Texas

"Cowboy Songs and Other Frontier Ballads"
Collected by John A. Lomax (1867–1948)
New York: Sturgis & Walton Co., 1910
PS595.C6 L6
General Collections
Library of Congress

**Listening Station with Lomax Field
Recordings**

**Chaps Worn by Theodore Roosevelt
(1858–1919) During His Ranching Days in
Dakota**
Leather, ca. 1885
National Museum of American History
Smithsonian Institution
Washington, D.C.

**Log Cabin on the Chimney-Butte Ranch Near
Medora, North Dakota**
Home of Theodore Roosevelt, 1883–84
Photograph by J. Kithin(?), Walhalla, N.D.,
1904
Presidential File
Prints and Photographs Division
Library of Congress

Rough Riders Bandanna
Neckerchief, Uniform of Cuban Campaign
Cotton, 1898
Rough Riders Memorial and City Museum
Las Vegas, New Mexico

Col. Theodore Roosevelt of the Rough Riders
Strohmeyer & Wyman, Publishers, 1898
Sold by Underwood & Underwood
Stereography—Presidents
Prints and Photographs Division
Library of Congress

**Roosevelt, the Great American of Today, in
Roughing Costume Ready for the Trail, West
Divide, Colorado**
H. C. White Co., Bennington, Vt., 1903
Stereography—Presidents
Prints and Photographs Division
Library of Congress

**President Roosevelt Speaks on Irrigation and
Public Schools to Wide-Awake Audience,
Wallula, Washington**
Underwood & Underwood, 1903
Stereography—Presidents
Prints and Photographs Division
Library of Congress

**Cowboys Following Train and Cheering
President Roosevelt, Hugo, Colorado**
Underwood & Underwood, 1903
Stereography—Presidents
Prints and Photographs Division
Library of Congress

Indians Racing with President Roosevelt's Train, Idaho Mountains Near Pocatello
Underwood & Underwood, 1903
Stereography—Presidents
Prints and Photographs Division
Library of Congress

At Home in the Saddle—President Roosevelt on a 60-Mile Ride, Laramie to Cheyenne, Wyoming
Underwood & Underwood, 1903
Stereography—Presidents
Prints and Photographs Division
Library of Congress

"Pot Luck" with the "Boys"—President Roosevelt's Cowboy Breakfast, Hugo, Colorado
Underwood & Underwood, 1903
Stereography—Presidents
Prints and Photographs Division
Library of Congress

Abernathy Holding Wolf by Jaw
Alexander Lambert, 1905
Stereography—Presidents
Prints and Photographs Division
Library of Congress

President Roosevelt's Choicest Recreation, Amid Nature's Rugged Grandeur on Glacier Point, Yosemite
Underwood & Underwood, 1903
Stereography—Presidents
Prints and Photographs Division
Library of Congress

William S. Hart in "Square Deal Sanderson"
Still photograph
Paramount-Artcraft, 1919
William S. Hart Collection
Prints and Photographs Division
Library of Congress

Viewing and Listening Station: Monologue by William S. Hart
Reel 1, 286 ft. = 8 min., *Tumbleweeds*
Reissued by Astor, 1939

The Cowboy and the Lady
Four still photographs
Copyright 1938, The Samuel Goldwyn Company
Rerelease, 1954, The Samuel Goldwyn Company
Motion Picture, Broadcasting, and Recorded Sound Division
Library of Congress

Dark Command (John Wayne)
Rerelease, 1952, Copyright National Telefilm Associates, Inc., Los Angeles, California
Motion Picture, Broadcasting, and Recorded Sound Division
Library of Congress

"Red River"
(John Wayne and Joanne Dru)
Still photograph
Copyright 1952, United Artists Corporation
Motion Picture, Broadcasting, and Recorded Sound Division
Library of Congress

Ken Maynard in "Smoking Guns"
Lithograph
Copyright 1934, Universal Pictures Corporation
Private Collection

"The Phantom of the West"
Chapter 1
"The Ghost Riders"
Lithograph
Morgan Lithography Co., Cleveland, Ohio
Copyright 1931
Poster Collection
Prints and Photographs Division
Library of Congress

"The Phantom of the West"
Chapter 10
"Rogue's Roundup"
Lithograph
Morgan Lithography Co., Cleveland, Ohio
Copyright 1931
Poster Collection
Prints and Photographs Division
Library of Congress

On Top of Old Smoky
(Gene Autry and Champion)
Offset
Columbia Pictures Corporation
Copyright 1952
American Folklife Center
Library of Congress

Gene Autry Rodeo Saddle
Made by Ed Gillmore, Hollywood, Calif.
Tooled leather, ca. 1947
National Cowboy Hall of Fame and Western Heritage Center
Oklahoma City, Oklahoma

King of the Cowboys
(Roy Rogers and Lloyd Corrigan)
Still photograph, 1943
Copyright, National Telefilm Associates, Inc., Los Angeles, Calif.
Motion Picture, Broadcasting, and Recorded Sound Division
Library of Congress

The Arizona Kid
(with Roy Rogers)
Color offset, 1939
Morgan Litho. Corp., Cleveland, Ohio
Stephen Sally
New York, New York

"Curtains of Sorrow"
Arbie Gibson and Rex Allen
Sheet music, copyright 1946, Preview Music Co.
M1630.2A
Music Division
Library of Congress

"Just a While"
Music by Eddie Dean, words by Hal Blair
Sheet music, copyright 1942, American Academy of Music, Inc.
M1630.2D
Music Division
Library of Congress

"Long Time Gone"
Tex Ritter and Frank Harford
Sheet music, copyright 1944 and 1946, Capitol Songs, Inc.
M1630.2R
Music Division
Library of Congress

"San Antonio Rose"
Words and music by Bob Wills
Sheet music, copyright 1940, Irving Berlin, Inc.
M1630.2.W
Music Division
Library of Congress

"Home in San Jose"
Words and music by Dick Charles, Eddie White, and Larry Markes
Sheet music, copyright 1947, Bob Miller, Inc.
M1630.2.M
Music Division
Library of Congress

Listening Station with a Selection of Cowboy and Western Songs
Diner booth and wall-mounted jukebox

Roy Rogers Bedspread, Lamp, Mug;
Roy Rogers and Trigger Dell Comic Book;
Color Lithograph of Roy Rogers; and
Roy Rogers Trick Lasso
Hake's Americana & Collectibles
P.O. Box 1444
York, Pennsylvania 17405

Roy Rogers' Trigger and Bullet Coloring Book
Drawings by John Ushler
(authorized edition)
Racine, Wisconsin; Whitman Publishing Co.
Copyright 1956, Frontiers Inc.
Victoria Westover
Baltimore, Maryland

Bucking Belt
Worn by bronc busters while breaking horses
Leather, ca. 1920
Panhandle–Plains Historical Museum
Canyon, Texas

Bull Rider
Lawrence Mad Plume (b. 1936), Blackfeet
Polychrome wood, 1969
Museum of the Plains Indian
United States Department of the Interior
Browning, Montana

"The Diary of a Dude Wrangler"
By Struthers Burt (1882–1954)
New York: Charles Scribner's Sons, 1938
Private Collection

Will Rogers's Lariat
Cotton cord with brass honda, date unknown
Will Rogers Memorial
Claremore, Oklahoma

Will Rogers's Boots
Leather, ca. 1920
Will Rogers Memorial
Claremore, Oklahoma

Will Rogers's Hat
Stetson, Clear Beaver, ca. 1930
Will Rogers Memorial
Claremore, Oklahoma

Bronco Export Beer
Lithograph printed in colors, 1907
Popular and Applied Graphic Art Collections
Prints and Photographs Division
Library of Congress

Bronco Brand
Packed by Redland Foothill Groves
Lithograph printed in colors, date unknown
Western Litho. Co., Los Angeles, Calif.
American Folklife Center
Library of Congress

Somewhere West of Laramie
Produced by Edward S. "Ned" Jordan
(1882–1959)
Lithograph, 1923
National Automotive History Collection
Detroit Public Library
Detroit, Michigan

Here Comes Wrangler
Photograph by Richard Noble (b. 1943)
Copyright 1981, Blue Bell Inc.
Blue Bell, Inc.
Greensboro, North Carolina

O. J. Dingo
Kurt Haiman (b. 1935)
Art Director, Grey Advertising Inc., New
York, New York
Four-color proof, mechanical, and artwork,
1980
Acme Boot Company, Inc.
Clarksville, Tennessee

Acme—The Real West
Kurt Haiman (b. 1935)
Art Director, Grey Advertising Inc., New
York, New York
Four-color proof, 1981
Acme Boot Company, Inc.
Clarksville, Tennessee

Nutcracker in Cowboy Dress
Red River
Wood, paint, plastic, fabric, and string, 1981
Neiman-Marcus
Washington, D.C.

"Eldorado Dude" Coffeepot
Jeanne Otis (b. 1940)
Porcelain, salt glaze with lusters and decals,
1977
Elaine Horwitch Gallery
Scottsdale, Arizona

"Ole Scottsdale Dude" Coffeepot
Jeanne Otis (b. 1940)
Porcelain, salt glaze with lusters and decals,
1977
Elaine Horwitch Gallery
Scottsdale, Arizona

Cowboy Hat
Paul White (b. 1953)
Tinted glass and feathers
American Folklife Center
Library of Congress

Bronco Buster
Julie McNair (b. 1953)
Bronze, 1979
Julie McNair
Mississippi State, Mississippi

Ode to the Bronze Boot
Julie McNair (b. 1953)
Bronze, 1980
Julie McNair
Mississippi State, Mississippi

"Don't Try to Drink and Draw" Goblet
Jim Cotter (b. 1944)
Bronze, 1973
Jim Cotter
Vail, Colorado

MEANWHILE, BACK AT THE RANCH

Rope
Nylon, Dacron, 1982
Bill Price's Western Shop
Lubbock, Texas

Vest
Nylon, down-filled, 1982
Bill Price's Western Shop
Lubbock, Texas

Bandanna
"Wild rag"
Silk, 1982
Bill Price's Western Shop
Lubbock, Texas

Pair of Silver Mounted Spurs with Straps
Steel, silver, leather, 1976
Bill Price's Western Shop
Lubbock, Texas

Contemporary Bridle with Headstaff, Reins, and Bit
Steel, silver, leather, 1976
Bit: *Billy Klapper, Pampa, Texas*
Headstaff and reins: *Bill Price's Western Shop, Lubbock, Texas*

Vaccinating Gun
Franklin Syrum Co., Fort Worth, Texas
Metal
Bill Price's Western Shop
Lubbock, Texas

Earmark Set
Franklin Syrum Co., Fort Worth, Texas
Metal
Bill Price's Western Shop
Lubbock, Texas

Electric Cattle Prod
Hot-Shot Products Co., Savage, Minnesota
Plastic, metal, 1982
Bill Price's Western Shop
Lubbock, Texas

**Contemporary Western Stock Saddle, Roping
Tree, and Navajo Saddle Blanket**
Wilford Lewis, saddlemaker
Leather, wool, wood, wild rose stamp
pattern, 1982
Bill Price's Western Shop
Lubbock, Texas

Contemporary Saddle Tree
(Chuck Sheppard style)
Lewis Brothers Saddle Tree Co., Fort Worth,
Texas
Laminated pine, rawhide cover, 1982
Bill Price's Western Shop
Lubbock, Texas

Branding at the Loui Cerri Ranch
Carl Fleischhauer (b. 1940)
Photograph, June 1978
American Folklife Center
Library of Congress

Squeeze Chute
Carl Fleischhauer (b. 1940)
Photograph, May 1978
American Folklife Center
Library of Congress

Baling Hay
Richard E. Ahlborn (b. 1933)
Photograph, July 1978
American Folklife Center
Library of Congress

A Cowboy's Shrine
Carl Fleischhauer (b. 1940)
Photograph, April 1980
American Folklife Center
Library of Congress

Breakfast in Ranch Quarters
William H. Smock (b. 1944)
Photograph, October 1979
American Folklife Center
Library of Congress

Viewing and Listening Station:
Autumn Work at the 96 Ranch, Paradise
Valley, Nevada

Selected Reading

This list of books and articles is not intended to be a bibliography of the cowboy and his myth or even of the works consulted in preparing this book. The former can be found in the Dobie and Adams bibliographies listed below; the latter, where they are obscure or where they support a controversial statement, are cited in footnotes. This guide to further reading is simply a selection of works that may lead the interested reader to a deeper understanding of the life and work of the historical cowboy or of the development of the cowboy myth. Where titles have not been completely self-explanatory, an amplificatory note has been appended to them. Much of the research on the cowboy myth has been published as articles in scholarly journals, rather than in books; it is hoped that the general reader will take the trouble to search these out, and that he will find them as rewarding as the authors of this book have.

The Reality

Abbott, E. C., and Helena H. Smith. *We Pointed Them North: Recollections of a Cowpuncher*. New York: Farrar and Rinehart, 1939. "Teddy Blue" Abbott was an Englishman who worked on the northwestern ranges; this is a frank and entertaining account of his life.

Adams, Andy. *The Log of a Cowboy*. Boston: Houghton Mifflin Company, 1903. A fictional account of a trail drive that is better than the work of many historians.

Adams, Ramon F. *The Rampaging Herd*. Norman: University of Oklahoma Press, 1959. The standard bibliography of ranching and cowboy life.

Clay, John. *My Life on the Range*. New York: Antiquarian Press, 1961. First published privately in 1924 by the author, who came from Scotland to manage some of the largest British-owned ranches in the West.

Cleaveland, Agnes Moreley. *No Life for a Lady*. Boston: Houghton Mifflin Company, 1941. A witty and humane woman's account of ranch life in New Mexico.

Cleland, Robert G. *The Cattle on a Thousand Hills*. San Marino, Calif.: Huntington Library, 1941. A scholarly study of Spanish-Mexican ranching in California.

Dale, Edward Everett. *The Range Cattle Industry*. Norman: University of Oklahoma Press, 1960.

Dary, David. *Cowboy Culture: A Saga of Five Centuries*. New York: Alfred A. Knopf, 1981.

Dobie, J. Frank. *A Vaquero of the Brush Country*. Dallas: Southwest Press, 1929. Dobie's "re-telling" of the life of John Young, who worked cattle in south Texas in the 1870s.

———. *Cow People*. Boston: Little, Brown and Company, 1964. Pithy portraits, some of them drawn from life, of ranchers and trail drivers.

———. *Guide to the Life and Literature of the Southwest*. Dallas: Southern Methodist University Press, 1952.

Dykstra, Robert R. *The Cattle Towns: A Social History of the Kansas Cattle Trading Centers*. New York: Alfred A. Knopf, 1968.

Emmett, Chris. *Shanghai Pierce: A Fair Likeness*. Norman: University of Oklahoma Press, 1953. How a penniless boy from New England built a Texas cattle empire. Pierce was the model for the popular conception of the cattle baron.

Haley, J. Evetts. *Charles Goodnight, Cowman and Plainsman*. Boston: Houghton Mifflin Company, 1936. Very possibly the best range biography ever written. Goodnight was a pioneer rancher in west Texas and was actively involved in ranching for sixty-five years.

Hendrix, John. *If I Can Do It Horseback*. Austin: University of Texas Press, 1964. Reminiscences of cowboy work in the early years of this century.

Hunter, J. Marvin, ed. *The Trail Drivers of Texas*. 2 vols. San Antonio: Jackson Printing Company, 1920–23. The best firsthand look available at the everyday life of the nineteenth-century cowboy. Hunter asked hundreds of former cowboys to write up their experiences; they are given here in their authors' own words.

James, Will S. *Cow-Boy Life in Texas, or 27 Years a Maverick*. Chicago: Donohue, Henneberry and Company, 1893. Memoirs of an open-range cowboy who became a well-known preacher.

Jordan, Terry G. *Trails to Texas: Southern Roots of Western Cattle Ranching*. Lincoln: University of Nebraska Press, 1981.

Kramer, Jane. *The Last Cowboy*. New York: Harper & Row, 1977. The poignant biography of a contemporary cowboy who cannot make the reality of his life fit the cowboy myth.

Lea, Tom. *The King Ranch*. 2 vols. Boston: Little, Brown and Company, 1957.

Mora, Jo. *Trail Dust and Saddle Leather*. New York: Charles Scribner's Sons, 1946. Much material on California vaqueros, with illustrations by the author.

Osgood, Ernest Staples. *The Day of the Cattleman*. Minneapolis: University of Minnesota Press, 1929. The classic history of the northwestern ranges.

Patterson, Paul. *Pecos Tales*. Austin: Texas Folklore Society, 1967. The most enjoyable compilation of cowboy humor there is.

Pearce, William M. *The Matador Land and Cattle Company*. Norman: University of Oklahoma Press, 1964. A business history of a Scottish company that owned ranches from Texas to North Dakota.

Rollins, Philip A. *The Cowboy*. New York: Charles Scribner's Sons, 1922. An attempt to realistically describe the life of the working cowboy to easterners who had been subjected to four decades of Wild West shows, rodeos, and Tom Mix movies. This may still be the best single book written on cowboy work and life.

Siringo, Charles A. *A Texas Cowboy, or, Fifteen Years on the Hurricane Deck of a Spanish Pony*. Chicago: Umbdenstock and Company, 1885. The granddaddy of all cowboy memoirs.

Skaggs, Jimmy M. *The Cattle-Trailing Industry*. Lawrence: University of Kansas Press, 1973.

Sonnichsen, C. L. *Cowboys and Cattle Kings: Life on the Range Today*. Norman: University of Oklahoma Press, 1950.

Webb, Walter Prescott. *The Great Plains*. New York: Ginn and Company, 1931. Describes the cultural and geographic setting within which the range cattle industry developed.

The Myth

Adams, Ramon, and Homer Britzman. *Charles M. Russell, the Cowboy Artist: A Biography*. Pasadena, Calif.: Trail's End Publishing Company, 1948.

Alter, Judith MacBain. "Rufus Zogbaum and the Frontier West," *Montana* 23, no. 4 (1973):42–53.

Amaral, Anthony. *Will James, the Gilt Edged Cowboy*. Los Angeles: Westernlore Press, 1967. A sympathetic account of the tragic and schizophrenic life of Ernest Dufault, who renounced his family and his French-Canadian heritage to fit the cowboy myth when he became Will James, cowboy artist and writer.

Bluestone, George. "The Changing Cowboy: From Dime Novel to Dollar Film," *Western Humanities Review* 14 (1960):331–37.

Branch, E. Douglas. *The Cowboy and His Interpreters*. New York: D. Appleton and Company, 1926. The first serious critique of western fiction.

Brownlow, Kevin. *The War, the West, and the Wilderness*. New York: Alfred A. Knopf, 1979. A substantial portion of Brownlow's book describes how the earliest westerns were filmed.

Carson, William G. B. "The Theatre of the American Frontier: A Bibliographical Essay," *Theatre Research* 2 (1960):163–74.

Clancy, Frederick "Foghorn." *My Fifty Years in Rodeo*. San Antonio: Naylor Company, 1952.

Collings, Ellsworth. *101 Ranch*. Norman: University of Oklahoma Press, 1938. History of the Miller 101 Ranch and the Wild West show that grew out of it.

Easton, Robert. *Max Brand: The Big Westerner*. Norman: University of Oklahoma Press, 1970. Biography of the most prolific pulp western writer of all time.

Etulain, Richard W. "Changing Images: The Cowboy in Western Films," *Colorado Heritage* 1 (1981):37–55.

Etulain, Richard W., and Michael T. Marsden. *The Popular Western: Essays Toward a Definition*. Bowling Green, Ohio: Bowling Green University Popular Press, 1974.

Fenin, George N., and William K. Everson. *The Western: From Silents to the Seventies*. New York: Grossman, 1973.

Green, Archie. "Midnight and Other Cowboys," *JEMF Quarterly* 11 (1975):137–52. Looks at counterculture cowboys of the late 1960s and early 1970s.

Frantz, Joe B., and Julian E. Choate, Jr. *The American Cowboy: The Myth and the Reality*. Norman: University of Oklahoma Press, 1955. Still the most comprehensive treatment of the subject.

Hagedorn, Hermann. *Roosevelt in the Bad Lands*. Boston: Houghton Mifflin Company, 1921. Examines the origins of TR's enthusiasm for the cowboy.

Harris, Charles W., and Buck Rainey. *The Cowboy: Six Shooters, Songs, and Sex*. Norman: University of Oklahoma Press, 1976.

Kahn, Gordon. "Lay That Pistol Down," *Atlantic* 173 (April 1944):105–8. Advances a theory for the popularity of the singing cowboy.

Lomax, John A., and Alan Lomax. *Cowboy Songs and Other Frontier Ballads*. New York: Macmillan Company, 1941. The collected prefaces in this third edition make clear both John Lomax's romantic attitudes toward cowboys and the book's subsequent influence on the public's perception of them.

Malone, Bill C. *Country Music, U.S.A.: A Fifty-Year History*. Austin: American Folklore Society, 1968. One chapter is entitled "The Cowboy Image."

Marowitz, Sanford. "Romance or Realism? Western Periodical Literature, 1893–1902," *Western American Literature* 10 (1975):45–58.

Mix, Paul. *The Life and Legend of Tom Mix*. New York: A. S. Barnes, 1972. Shows in great detail how Mix's public relations agents created a fictional cowboy background for him.

Munden, Kenneth J. "A Contribution to the Psychological Understanding of the Origin of the Cowboy and His Myth," *American Image* 15 (1958):103–48.

Pomeroy, Earl. *In Search of the Golden West: The Tourist in Western America*. New York: Alfred A. Knopf, 1957.

R. W. Norton Art Gallery. *Frederic Remington: Paintings, Drawings and Sculpture*. Shreveport, La.: R. W. Norton Art Gallery, 1979. Brian Dippie's introduction to this exhibit catalog is an especially perceptive account of Remington's life and motives.

Rodnitzky, Jerome. "Recapturing the American West: The Dude Ranch in American Life," *Arizona and the West* 10 (1968):111–26.

Rothel, David. *The Singing Cowboys*. New York: A. S. Barnes, 1978.

Roundy, Charles G. "The Origins and Early Development of Dude Ranching in Wyoming," *Annals of Wyoming* 45 (1973):5–26.

Russell, Don. *The Lives and Legends of Buffalo Bill*. Norman: University of Oklahoma Press, 1960.

―――. *The Wild West: A History of the Wild West Shows*. Fort Worth: Amon Carter Museum, 1970.

Savage, William. *The Cowboy Hero: His Image in American History and Culture*. Norman: University of Oklahoma Press, 1979. A thoughtful supplement to Frantz and Choate's *The American Cowboy*; the two should be read together.

Smith, Henry Nash. *Virgin Land: The American West as Symbol and Myth*. Cambridge: Harvard University Press, 1950. Places the mythical cowboy in his larger mythical setting.

Taft, Robert. *Artists and Illustrators of the Old West, 1850–1900*. New York: Charles Scribner's Sons, 1953.

Tuska, Jon. *The Filming of the West*. Garden City: Doubleday and Company, 1976.

Vorpahl, Ben Merchant. *"My Dear Wister": The Frederic Remington-Owen Wister Letters*. Palo Alto, Calif.: American West, 1972.

Walker, Don D. "History and Imagination: The Prose and Poetry of the Cattle Industry, 1895–1905," *Pacific Historical Review* 45 (1976):379–98.

Weissman, Dick. "Cowboy Songs: From the Open Range to the Radio," *Colorado Heritage* 1 (1981):57–67.

Westermeier, Clifford P. *Man, Beast, Dust: The Story of Rodeo*. Denver: World Press, 1947.

White, G. Edward. *The Eastern Establishment and the Western Experience*. Examines the roles of Remington, Wister, and Roosevelt in shaping the eastern view of the West.

INDEX